REITS: THE FIRST DECADE

A Collection of Writings

REITS: THE FIRST DECADE

A Collection of Writings

Edited by
John T. Hall
Editor, REIT REVIEW

Published under the direction of
Patricia Hare
Special Publications Editor, REIT REVIEW

Published by:

John T. Hall, Inc.
12340 North Granville Road
Mequon, Wisconsin 53092

CONTENTS

v

FOREWORD

During the decade of the sixties, real estate investment trusts grew to become an established financial institution. From its birth in 1960 until 1973 the REIT industry has matured to an asset strength of over $16 billion. As with any investment method, the REIT is not the "perfect" investment vehicle. Problems related to rapid growth, management, intricate legislative controls, investor education, and other areas have periodically placed obstacles in the path of growth and development. Nonetheless, the real estate investment trust as an investment vehicle stands as a sound, viable option to the investor.

This compilation, presented from a historical vantage point, provides some of the knowledge necessary for appreciation of the industry. The collection is intended to be helpful both to the expert and to the novice. However, each trust is operated under a specific charter and deserves special scrutiny by the interested investor.

Real estate investment can be lucrative when under the guidance of experienced professionals. The REIT provides the means by which the small investor can share in this opportunity. It is up to the investor to select that particular trust whose management philosophy matches his own. Inherent in any investment are risks and rewards. Conceptually, the REIT can minimize the many risks involved in real estate investment while providing a sufficient return to the investor. Overall, I believe they are doing just that.

REALTY INVESTMENT TRUSTS POISED FOR LAUNCHING

By John C. Williamson,

*Director, Department of Governmental
Relations, National Association of Real Estate
Boards, Washington, D.C.: Counsel to the
Realtors' Washington Committee*

The newest investment medium, the tax-exempt real estate trust, is defined and described, and compared with the real estate syndicate and mutual funds. Mr. Williamson recounts the six-year fight to extend the "conduit theory" of taxation which since 1936 was the exclusive property of regulated investment companies. He reviews the applicability of SEC registration, the Trust Indenture Act of 1939 and the Investment Act of 1940 requirements; the taxation differentials for realty trust with various permitted holdings; and the leverage restrictions. The writer warns on the need for expert tax counsel, and he comments on the recent establishment of a trade association to serve this challenging segment of the real estate industry.

On Sept. 14 when President Eisenhower affixed his signature to Public Law 86-779, he brought to culmination six years of effort by the National Association of Real Estate Boards, through the Realtors' Washington Committee, to extend to real estate investment trusts the "conduit theory" of taxation which since 1936 has been applicable only to regulated investment companies holding stocks and bonds.

The six-year period witnessed the inception and phenomenal growth of the real estate syndicate, a less direct and sometimes perilous (tax wise) method of accomplishing some of the objectives envisioned by the tax-exempt real estate investment trust. It was a period which experienced a Presidential veto of a similar bill in 1956 and a subsequent personal plea by Past NAREB President James M. Udall to President Eisenhower at the White House in February 1959 that the Treasury re-evaluate and reconsider its objections to the measure. It was also a period of study and effort by

1

many persons in the tax field directed at removing this inequity in the Federal Tax Code and thereby "remove taxation to the extent possible as a factor in determining the relative size of investments in stocks and securities on one hand, and real estate equities and mortgages on the other." (House Report 2020, 86th Congress). An outstanding contribution to a better understanding of this measure during the six-year effort was made by a former Chairman of the Tax Section of the American Bar Association.*

Let us now examine the new law.

Organization of the Trust

Generally speaking, the real estate investment trust is simply the means by which small investors may pool their savings to buy or develop a piece of property or originate and service mortgages because of their proven or potential high rate of return. Thus a real estate investment trust provides an opportunity for the small investor, by taking advantage of centralized management and diversification of investment, to reap the benefit of the high rate of return which is the essence of real estate investment.

Under the Act, real estate investment trusts are defined as *unincorporated trusts or associations* which—

(1) are managed by one or more trustees

(2) have transferable shares of beneficial interest

(3) are a type of organization which would be taxed as an ordinary domestic corporation in the absence of the new law. This means that the trust or association must have the indicia of the corporation i.e., continuity of life, limitation of personal liability, transferability of shares, etc.

*See statement of H. Cecil Kilpatrick, Esq., before the House Ways and Means Committee, published by that Committee in "Tax Revision Compendium" (1959) Vol. 3, pp. 1697-1705.

2

To emphasize the objective of the bill to encourage the pooling of small savings, the Congress provided that the beneficial ownership be held by 100 or more persons, and that no five persons may directly or indirectly own more than 50% of the trust. The trustees or managers of the trust must elect to be taxed as a real estate investment trust and the trust may not hold any property *primarily for sale to customers in the ordinary course of its trade or business.* That is to say that the trust may not engage in the "business" of buying and selling properties, although provisions are made for the disposition and acquisition of properties in the normal course of exercising the fiduciary relationship of the trustees and the beneficiaries.

A realtor who organizes a trust could arrange for one or more of the principal investors (three would be preferable) to be the trustees, and these should be individuals with experience in real estate investments and in the handling of trust estates.

State law governing trusts should be examined closely before venturing into this area. For example, the "rule against perpetuities" may apply, which means that the trust may have a limit on its life; i.e., the life or lives of persons living and referred to in the trust instrument plus 21 years. In such cases it would be desirable to mention the names of young children of trustees in the trust instrument in order to achieve substantial continuity of life. This will be no problem should Congress amend the Act to permit corporations to qualify, an amendment certainly not beyond the realm of probability.

SEC Registration

Generally, a trust will be organized with a specific income-producing property in mind, although such trusts will be so organized as to permit for the subsequent accumulation of trust properties and issuance of new shares. If the certificates of beneficial ownership are to be offered to the public in interstate commerce (there is a presumption or "rule of thumb" that an offering to more than 25 persons is an offering to the public in interstate commerce), then a prospectus must be filed with the Securities and Exchange Commission pursuant

3

to the Securities Act of 1933. Because the Act provides for a minimum of 100 shareholders, registration under the Securities Act of 1933 should be contemplated. The prospectus reveals pertinent details regarding the trust, identity of the trustees, details concerning the properties acquired, etc.

These real estate investment trusts will probably not be subject to the more rigid requirements of the Trust Indenture Act of 1939 and the Investment Act of 1940 unless the trusts deal substantially in the shares of other trusts.

For obvious reasons the Realtor who contemplates managing the trust properties, and earning commissions on properties sold to and by the trust, will not be a trustee. Within certain limitations set forth subsequently in this article, he may acquire shares in the trust.

Profusion of Rules Warns of Pitfalls

Let us assume that there has been compliance with the Securities and Exchange Commission requirements, and that 100 or more shareholders have been acquired. We then turn our attention to the rules with which Congress expressed its intention that the real estate investment trust is not to be a device for the tax exemption of active real estate operations. The rules are a series of percentage rules which, to the trade, will ultimately be referred to as the "90% and 75% tests," "the 30% rule," "the 75% and 25% tests," "the 35% rule," and "the 10% rule." Obviously, the lego-tax technicians of the Treasury left their mark on this legislation — another monument to the complexities of the Internal Revenue Code.

The 90% and 75% tests. The law provides that 90% or more of a trust's *gross income* must be derived from dividends; interest; rents from real property; gains from the sale of stock, securities, and real property; and abatements and refunds of taxes on real property. This conforms to the income test for regulated investment companies. However, in addition the Congress superimposed on the 90% test a 75% test which provides that at least 75% of the trust's gross income must, in one way or another, be derived from real property; i.e., rents from real property, interest on mortgages, gains from the sale of real property, dividends and other distributions from qualifying real estate investment trusts, and abatements and refunds of taxes on real property. The interaction of these tests, therefore, permits 15% of the gross income to be derived from nonreal estate sources such as dividends or gain from stocks or bonds (listed above under 90% rule), and 10% of gross income to come from any source.

The 30% rule relates to *short-term gains* from the sale of property. The trust, in order to qualify for tax exemption, must limit its short-term gains (sales of securities held for less than six months and real property held for less than four years) to less than 30% of its *gross income*. The four-year holding period is rather harsh but it reflects the determination that the trust hold properties for investment purposes and not for trading. The three-year rule applicable to the collapsible corporation provisions of the Code may have been more appropriate.

The 75% and 25% tests relate to investment requirements. At least 75% of the *value* of the trust's assets must be in real estate assets, cash and cash items and government securities. The 25% test is designed to provide diversification of the trust investments *other than real estate*. Thus *not more than 25% of the value of the trust's assets* may be represented by the securities (other than government securities) of any one issuer; and these must not be greater in value than 5% of the trust's total assets and should not represent more than 10% of the voting securities of the issuer.

There are savings clauses to prevent disqualification because of changes in values of properties after acquisition. In such cases disqualification may be overcome within 30 days after the close of the calendar quarter in question.

Management of the Trust by Realtor

The 35% rule relates to management and the application of this rule should be studied closely by the realtor. The rule stems from the desire of the Congress that the trusts be passive in nature. The Act provides that the trust *may not directly* furnish or render services to the tenants, and the trust *may not* manage or operate the property. This is where the realtor, who has been the organizing force behind the trust, moves a step further into the picture. The Act permits the trust to engage an independent contractor to manage or operate the properties. The realtor who proposes being the manager must not own more than 35% interest in the trust. Also, not more than 35% of the stock (or voting power) or interest in the realtor's management organization can be held by a person holding a 35% or greater interest in the trust.

It is at this point that the realtor and his tax counsel must be wary of Section 318 of the Code and the "attribution rules" of the Internal Revenue Service. Unless care is exercised the realtor might find that the ownership of stock by a corporation in which he owns stock might be "attributed" to him, resulting in a violation of the 35% rule.

The 10% rule is designed to foreclose the opportunity of any substantial relationship between the trust and the business of any tenant. Under the rule there would be excluded from the definition of rents received, any amounts received from any person if the trust has an interest of 10% or more in the assets of profits of that person. Furthermore, the rental income may not include amounts dependent in whole or in part on the income or profits of the tenant, although leases based on a *fixed percentage of sales receipts* are permitted.

Taxation of Trust's Income

Now as to the taxation of the trust's income. The Act provides that the trust will be exempt from the corporate tax if 90% or more of its otherwise ordinary taxable income is distributed annually to its beneficiaries who will pay ordinary income tax on such distribution. The 90% distribution rule does not include long-term and short-term capital gains which may be retained by the trust for reinvestment in other properties. Also, any "ordinary taxable income" retained by the trust, in excess of the 90% distribution, is subject to the regular corporate income tax.

Any capital gains derived by the trust from the sale of any of its properties will be taxable to the beneficiaries as capital gains rather than as ordinary income to the extent that such gains are distributed to the beneficiaries. The trust will pay the capital gains tax to the extent that such gains are not distributed.

Will the Trust Permit High Leverage?

The 90% distribution requirement has some real estate investors concerned that this may prevent heavily mortgaged property and thereby preclude the high leverage in real estate investment which ofttimes finds one dollar of investment doing the work of several.

The Act requires that distribution be made of at least 90% of *the income that would be taxable if it were not for the Act.* This means that the depreciation deduction taken by the trust must provide the means for payment of high mortgage principal. Otherwise, a high mortgage principal payment (which is non-deductible) is likely to prevent 90% distribution.

For example, assume a real estate investment trust which owns a shopping center which is encumbered by a 20-year mortgage at 6½%. During the first year the amortization payments on the $1 million project, with a mortgage of $650,000, is $58,154.76 with $16,387.25 allocable to principal. Assume $200,000 allocable to land and $800,000 to improvements. Straight line depreciation would permit a deduction of $20,000 (at 2½%) which is more than sufficient to pay on the mortgage principal. In this example the trust would have no difficulty making the 90% distribution of taxable income.

If the declining balance depreciation formula is used, then a larger principal payment could be permitted along with increased yield to the beneficiaries. However, as depreciation deductions decrease and mortgage principal payments increase, the situation changes but this should be no problem to tax-wise real estate investors (is there any other kind?).

Because the trusts eligible for the benefits of this act must be trusts which would be taxable as a corporation they cannot allocate depreciation to the beneficiaries. This is an advantage because without the tax shelter over the trust income, the trust would not be able to obtain the desired leverage which comes from mortgaging the trust properties.

7

Trusts Dealing Exclusively in Mortgages
Have Less Restrictions

We have been discussing real estate investment trusts which hold income-producing properties such as apartment houses, shopping centers, office buildings, etc. However, the Act permits the trust to hold real estate mortgages exclusively and still be subject to the tax exemption provisions.

In considering a real estate investment trust which holds mortgages exclusively, we find that certain restrictions applicable to trusts which receive rents *do not apply* to trusts receiving "interest on obligations secured by mortgages on real property or on interests in real property." For example, a trust receiving rents from real property must engage an independent contractor, who is subject to the 35% and 10% rules, to manage the properties. However, the real estate investment trust holding mortgages would be able to *originate, process and service them* without regard to these percentage rules and the "independent contractor" requirement. The potentialities here for pooling savings for mortgage investment are impresssive.

A New Industry—Ergo, a New Trade Association

It must be obvious by this time to the reader that the intricacies of the legislation and the tax risk to the unwary require consultation with tax counsel during the trust organization process. So important are the "do's and don'ts" set forth in the Act that the interest of mutual assistance and exchange of ideas dictated the early organization of a national trade association to serve the interests of this new and challenging segment of the real estate industry. Indeed such a trade association, *The National Association of Real Estate Investment Funds,* was recently incorporated and has opened offices at 1300 Connecticut Avenue in Washington, D.C. We have been advised that Realtors are playing an important part in the organization of the association. Presumably the new trade group will apply to the Securities and Exchange Commission for official recognition as a self-policing association under the Securities Act of 1934 — a highly desirable objective in view of the abuses which might flow from the sale to the public of certificates of beneficial interest in a real estate investment trust by individuals lacking the essential experience in real estate.

Reprinted by special permission of publisher, *Commercial and Financial Chronicle*, 110 Wall Street, New York, N.Y. 10005, Vol. 192 (October 6, 1960).

COMING BOOM IN REAL ESTATE TRUSTS

**Change in tax law paves way for flood
of offerings of new type of investment shares
backed by real estate.
Here's what to watch for**

Investment in real estate — once restricted by its nature to the wealthy few — is increasingly opening up as an opportunity available to the small investor.

Two financial structures are being used to allow the investor of moderate means to participate in transactions involving huge sums. One is the syndicate in which a real estate operator sells participations in a property in the form of limited partnerships. The other is the real estate trust.

The second vehicle was given great impetus recently when the President signed the Real Estate Investment Trust Act. This complicated piece of federal law provides that a real estate trust which, among other things, distributes at least 90% of its net income to shareholders, is exempt from federal income taxes. The act also requires that the trust have at least 100 shareholders and that no five persons can own more than 50% of its shares. Furthermore, to qualify under the act at least 75 % of the trust's assets and income must consist of real estate; an additional 15% of income must come from dividends and interest rather than from such things as management fees.

Eliminates Double Taxes

The stated intent of Congress in passing the law was to permit small investors to share in real estate transactions without their being subject to the double taxation involved in corporate ownership. This is expected to bring more capital into the real estate market and thus expand such needed activities as urban renewal.

One of the unforeseen results of the law has been the alacrity with which hotel chain operators have seized upon it as a means of improving their financial structures. First to approach this problem was the Sheraton Corporation, which operates 50 hotels in the United States — 48 of which it owns — and three office buildings — two of which it owns. Ernest Henderson, Sheraton president, says that plans are being studied to convert some of the corporation's hotels into a real estate investment trust. He has said that should these plans qualify under the new law "it is conceivable we could double our earnings and pay $1.20 a share on our common stock instead of the current rate of 60 cents a share annually."

It is possible, Mr. Henderson explains, that hotel properties now reporting a loss because of large depreciation allowances but throwing off cash, could be sold to a publicly owned trust and then leased back by Sheraton. Such an arrangement would free considerable cash for profitable investment by the company. It would also remove the large depreciation figures from Sheraton's profit and loss statement and thereby practically double its reported earnings.

Others in the hotel industry have the idea that what is good for Sheraton might suit them as well. The value of trust arrangements under the new law to currently operating corporations will be in direct relation to the extent to which they own the real property they operate.

Tax officials in Washington state that the Congressional debate on this legislation made no mention of relief for large corporations operating in this field. They stress the idea that the law was intended to encourage the small investor. They have also hinted that should the law work to cause a serious loss of revenue to the Treasury, Congress will be asked to plug the loophole.

On this point, hotelman Henderson says that in order to participate in the benefits of the law, real estate companies will have to pay out nearly all their earnings — instead of the roughly 50% they now pay — plus what they save on taxes. This in some instances means dividend distributions could as much as quadruple. Taxes that individuals would pay on these increased dividends would in many cases exceed those now collected from existing real estate corporations and their shareholders.

Public Interest Guarded

Some questions have been raised about the new law aside from its purely tax considerations. There is the possibility that unscrupulous operators will dress up broken-down realty and try to unload it on the public at fancy valuations via the trust share route. The public, however, is not without protection. Offerings of trust shares will come under the Securities Acts and therefore must comply with Securities and Exchange Commission rules. In addition, the real estate fraternity has set up the National Association of Real Estate Investment Funds through which it hopes to police its own industry.

Aside from the problems that arise under the law, there are investor opportunities on one side and prospects for general economic growth on the other. By providing a vast new pool of capital, the legislation should encourage increased construction throughout the country.

Heretofore, small shareholders could participate in real estate income through holdings in large real estate corporations and were subject to double taxation — the corporation paid income taxes on its earnings and the stockholder paid income tax again on the earnings he received in the form of dividends. Large investors, who can swing big real estate deals as individuals, have been enjoying as much as 11% and more in cash flow on income real estate. Now the small investor will have a similar opportunity through the real estate trust.

The net effect of this wider public participation in the real estate market may be a reduction in these returns. The situation does open up, nevertheless, a new avenue for the investor. But like all investments, ventures into real estate should be carefully investigated before commitments are made. Laws, commissions, and associations can work to protect the public, but in the last analysis the investor is his own best protector. If he insists on having the facts and on learning all he can about the management of the trust, the investor can make prudent decisions.

While there are possibilities for abuses in the Real Estate Investment Trust Act, the over-all result should be beneficial to the country at large and to many small individual investors as well.

Reprinted by special permission of publisher, *Financial World*, Vol. 114 (October 12, 1960).

NEGATIVE ASPECTS OF REALTY INVESTMENT TRUST LAW

By Marvin Kratter.*

President and Chairman of the Board
of Kratter Corporation

Real estate investment trusts face many barriers to getting off to the quick start which its enthusiasts may not know about. Mr. Kratter's analysis of the Act designed to have real estate investment trusts treated the same as regulated investment companies deals with a number of unfavorable and potentially troublesome aspects affecting the organization and operation of this new real estate vehicle. Until these negative factors are corrected, Mr. Kratter predicts this valuable method of real estate financing will not be too hasty in selling securities to the public.

No other event in the real estate field in recent years has had as much publicity and created as much interest and enthusiasm as has enactment of the new real estate investment trust law. However, now that the initial burst of unrestrained acclaim appears to have waned somewhat, a more critical appraisal of the new Act has become both feasible and desirable.

Enthusiasm for the new Act derives from the fact that it amends the Internal Revenue Code of 1954 to provide substantially the same treatment for real estate investment trusts as present law provides for regulated investment companies. Under present laws, regulated investment companies that distribute 90% or more of their ordinary income are taxed only on their retained corporate earnings and thus the distributed portion of earnings are taxable only to the shareholders. This same general type of tax treatment is now to be accorded to real estate investment trusts, effective with respect to taxable years beginning after Dec. 31, 1960.

---

*An address by Mr. Kratter before the General Meetings Committee of the Real Estate Board of New York, Inc., New York City.

Unfavorable Aspects

Unfortunately, there are also a number of unfavorable and potentially troublesome aspects to the Act that must be faced by persons intending to organize and operate real estate investment trusts. These may be classified, as follows: (1) uncertainties with respect to explanatory regulations under the Act issuable by the U.S. Treasury Department; (2) restrictive and ambiguous provisions contained in the Act; (3) uncertainties and restrictions in the various State laws potentially affecting and restricting operations; (4) problems in connection with underwriting and sale of securities of real estate investment trusts; and (5) Federal and State securities laws and regulations.

In the time allotted, only brief reference can be made to each of these items.

It will probably be some time before the Treasury issues its explanatory regulations. The regulations possibly could severely restrict flexibility under the Act and make tax benefits available only to companies operating within strict limits. In setting up regulations, consideration, undoubtedly, will be given to the reports of the Senate Committees on Finance and Ways and Means, which clearly expressed, for example, the intention that this tax treatment be restricted "to what are clearly passive real estate investments, as contrasted to the active operations of businesses involving real estate." Regulations reflecting this intention very possibly could nullify intentions expressed by managements of various types of operating and hotel companies to use real estate investment trusts as a means of reducing taxation now paid by these operating companies.

Example of Ambiguity

To cite an example of a restrictive and ambiguous provision of the Act, there is a provision that "the term 'rents from real property' excludes rents from interests in real property, if the determination of such amount depends in whole or in part on the income or profits derived by any person from such property (except that any amount so received or accrued shall not be excluded . . . solely by reason of being based on a fixed percentage or percentages of receipts or sales." Inasmuch as the inclusion of income-sharing and profit-sharing clauses has become an important feature in real estate operations, restrictive interpretation of this one ambiguous provision by Treasury regulations could negate many of the anticipated benefits expected to be gained from enactment of the new bill, by virtue of removal of important anti-inflation protection.

Among the uncertainties are the uncertainties of operation of the trusts under the various state laws. Under some state laws, for example, it would seem probably that ownership of the trust's assets would be vested in the various shareholders of the trust. It should be apparent that operation of a trust under such condition from a legal real estate *title* point of view would be forbidding, if not impossible.

Compared With Mutual Funds

Probably the most important reason for great enthusiasm by many observers is the comparison with sales of mutual fund shares that naturally immediately comes to mind. If billions of dollars of shares of securities investment companies are sold each year, why should not large sums of shares of real estate investment trusts also be sold? But, investment company shares are sold by well-organized organizations formed and developed for the purpose. For an organization currently very successful in selling *securities* investment company shares to shift is a very important step, and to do so for an uncertain product is somewhat hazardous. We are informed that at least one would-be underwriter of a real estate investment trust is encountering serious difficulties in lining up selling organizations.

With reference to Federal and state securities laws and regulations, these can be very troublesome and time-consuming. For example, the concept of variable annuities, also hailed as a wonderful new innovation about five years ago, has been largely tied up by technicalities in connection with Federal and State laws and regulations.

It should be noted that even the tax advantages granted by the new Act are of less significance to real estate operations than they would be to almost any other type of activity, inasmuch as most purchases of real properties generate sufficient legal depreciation deductions to enable large proportions, and sometimes all, of the net cash flow to be "tax free" with the tax impact (on a capital gains basis) deferred until the properties are sold. Also, the new real estate investment trusts still may be subject to most, or all, corporation taxes.

On balance, the new Act would appear very likely to prove one day to be a valuable vehicle for public real estate financing. However, the negative aspects surrounding this new law would appear to limit at least its near-term potential, as well as to preclude hasty action in the sale of securities to the public.

Reprinted by permission of *Commercial and Financial Chronicle*, 110 Wall Street, New York, N.Y. 10005, Vol. 192 (December 15, 1960).

REALTY INVESTMENT TRUSTS AND THE POTENTIAL INVESTOR

By Richard H. Swesnik,*

President, Swesnik and Blum, Inc. and
of Swesnik and Blum Securities
Corp., Washington, D.C.

Assessment of real estate investment vehicles ranges from limited partnerships, so popular in the 1950's, to the currently burgeoning real estate investment trusts. Mr. Swesnik is dismayed by the lack of knowledge of, and the failure to make known, the dangers said to be inherent in real estate corporate ownership. The real estate syndication expert contends limited partners of real estate syndicates with patience could have merged into an investment trust which would have wiped out syndication's disadvantages and eliminated the corporate tax as well. In selecting a trust, he recommends most of the weighting be given to management as against quality and location of property.

Because of a new law signed on Sept. 14, 1960 known as Public Law 86-779, billions of dollars of investment capital may find its way into the real estate markets of America. The new Real Estate Investment Trust Law went into effect Jan. 1, 1961. Prior to this effective date, the financial columns of the major newspapers were filled with news items about the plans of various companies to enter the new field.

To understand the impact of the new law upon the industry and the general public, it is important to consider why Congress felt new legislation was needed in this area. Immediately after World War II, under the impetus of new construction and plenteous capital which had been accruing during the war years, real estate syndicates began to mushroom, principally in the larger Eastern cities.

---

*Based on a talk by Mr. Swesnik before the American Conference on Real Estate Funds.

In order to lessen the impact of the corporate tax many of these syndicates were formed as "thin" corporations whereby the investor would invest as little as 20% of his money as capital, the other 80% of his total investment would be accounted for by his receiving bonds or debentures as evidence of the corporation's debt.

Bonds Retired as Fast as Possible

As the property owned by the corporation developed income, the principal method of returning income to the investor was to retire the bonds as fast as possible. Very little of the investor's income then was subject to Federal tax inasmuch as the major portion of his income was return of his capital through the liquidation of a portion of the bond or debenture. The corporation that owned the property, however, despite all the intricate debenture arrangements, nonetheless paid income taxes. And unless the method of selling the property at a later date was carefully handled, this, too, often resulted in the paying of a corporate tax. Inasmuch as the major consideration for an investor is stability of the property and the size of his return, most organizers of syndicates are constantly studying ways to improve the ownership position with special emphasis on the avoidance of paying the corporate tax.

Because of these studies, the decade of the 1950's saw the limited partnership method of owning real estate burgeon into use and become the principal method of owning income-producing property. The typical limited partnership, and again, emphasizing the tax aspects, is able to generate "tax free" income because this method allows the depreciation to flow directly to the partners. The obvious advantages to investors who are receiving income, much of which is "tax free," has de-emphasized the disadvantages inherent to limited partnerships.

Taxation of Limited Partnership

In October, 1960, the Internal Revenue Service issued regulation No. 301,7701-2 governing the taxation of limited partnerships. In effect, the following criteria are the main factors evaluated by Internal Revenue to determine if a "partnership" is to pay corporate taxes. These criteria are continuity of life; transferability of interests; unlimited liability, and centralized management. If the partnership has continuity of life, if there is no liability to any of the partners, if the ownership interests are freely transferable and if there is centralized management, you may call it what you like, but you pay corporate taxes.

If, however, "on balance" three of the four criteria aforementioned do not exist then the partnership would pay no taxes, and the partners would each pay taxes on their prorata share of the partnership profits.

To favorably meet the criteria established by the Internal Revenue Service, the limited partnership should have no continuity of life. If the general partners die, the partnership ends. It is possible to form a new partnership, of course, but as a practical matter it presents some accounting and legal problems. Additionally, minors should not be parties to the limited partnership agreements. It is difficult for investors seeking to provide their children with incomes to use an investment in a limited partnership as the correct vehicle for accomplishing their purposes. Also, borrowing becomes "sticky" because the general partners have unlimited liability for partnership obligations even for nominal amounts.

Substitute for Original Partner Is Time Consuming

Further, the transfer of a limited partnership interest is necessarily restricted by requiring the unanimous consent of the general partners, in order to avoid the free transferability of interest test. The admitting of substitute limited partners, when the original limited partner wishes to sell his interest, is a time consuming, paper shulling process requiring the signing of four or five different legal documents. Also, the operation of a limited partnership usually prohibits the dividing of a limited partnership unit of interest into smaller units than one.

For example, if a limited partnership interest originally cost the investor $5,000 he is, of course, not as liquid as if he owned 100 units for which he paid $50 each. Additionally, because of the foregoing restrictions, formal markets such as are found on the major stock exchanges and less formal markets such as are found in over-the-counter trading do not exist. It is unusual, other than in a syndicator's office, to find a formal market for the trading of limited partnership interests.

Another point to consider is that limited partnerships are "one-shot" transactions, i.e., the money is raised to purchase a single income property and the partnership itself, rarely, if ever, requires another property. The complexity of re-arranging partnership interests and the possibility of being taxed as an active real estate corporation are two major reasons why partnerships remain tied to one purchase. In order to achieve diversification an investor must acquire an interest in a shopping center, an interest in an apartment house and another interest in an office building.

Because of the minimum unit size of the investment, his invested capital to obtain diversification may be as little as $10,000, but more probably, $20,000.

While these disadvantages are very real, even the least sophisticated investors love to receive "tax free" income. The advantages of owning real estate with allowable depreciation that generates such "tax free" income has heretofore been so favorable that the investor has tended to overlook the aforementioned disadvantages of limited partnerships.

Three Groups at Work

Of course, Utopia to the syndicator would be a situation which would retain the tax advantages of the limited partnership and would eliminate the disadvantages which have been outlined. While many syndicators were dreaming of such Utopia, three different groups of people were busily working on plans to have things changed in their favor.

The first group were trustees of the real estate investment trusts already in operation which were being taxed as corporations but nonetheless were operating properties, many of which had managed to survive the foreclosures during the

21

"Great Depression" of the early '30's. This group was unashamedly lobbying for a Federal act which would eliminate the corporate tax and permit the operation of their investment trusts in much the same way as regulated mutual funds.

A second group were syndicate managers who were seeking ways and means of eliminating the disadvantages of the limited partnerships while at the same time retaining favorable tax treatment. And the syndicate managers, some of whom were Realtors, joined with the first group to help obtain favorable Federal tax legislation.

At the same time they also were active in helping to obtain clarification from the Internal Revenue Service of their regulations governing limited partnerships. Such new regulations have now been published and they eliminate much of the "fuzzy gray area" which existed prior to the promulgation of these regulations.

A third group of syndicators energized by heavy emphasis on the disadvantages of the limited partnerships and de-emphasizing the tax advantages of limited partnerships have sold their investors on the idea of merging all the limited partnerships into large publicly owned corporations. In other words, they reversed the cycle, and were at apparent odds with the thinking of real estate investment trust groups and syndicators still favoring more liberalized treatment of limited partnerships and other legal vehicles which would allow the "tax free" treatment.

Some Dangers Not Well Known

Some of the dangers inherent in the corporate ownership of real estate are not too well known, nor have they been too widely publicized or properly evaluated by the investing public and the stock market professionals. While the corporate organization is almost a necessity in the development of new land into finished income-producing buildings, it appears to have very limited advantages as an owning vehicle.

The promoters of an investing real estate corporation, in most cases, have absolute control over the disbursing of funds to the corporate investors, and because of this reason, and the usual control of the Board of Directors, can make future acquisitions virtually at will. Through the device of corporate borrowing, coupled with the retention of funds, the controlling promoters leave the investor with little or no control of future purchases. Thus, the corporate heads of such "public" corporations who were tired of going back to the public for new funds and the public's approval may now happily make real estate acquisitions without public review.

Consequently, they have closed the tax advantage door on their investors, if not now, certainly within a few years when their allowable depreciation is considerably below present levels. Think how difficult their position may be when their investors discover that by merely exercising patience, these former syndicators, now corporate moguls, could have retained their earlier tax advantages when the properties were held individually in limited partnerships.

They could have merged these limited partnerships into real estate investment trusts! The Real Estate Investment Trust Law eliminates the corporation tax from properly organized real investment trusts and, in addition, virtually eliminates in one fell swoop all of the seven or eight disadvantages of limited partnerships.

May Be Organized to Guarantee Perpetuity

Initially, the trust may be organized in such a way as to virtually guarantee its perpetuity, as trustees may name their own successors therefore eliminating the ending of trust business in the event of a trustee's death. Minors could receive gifts of the trust's certificates as it is not necessary for them to become parties to an agreement as in the case of partnerships.

Parents could set up income plans for their children using trust certificates as the source of such income. Unlike the general partners in limited partnerships, the trustees could borrow monies from time to time to meet emergencies, and such borrowings would not become their personal responsibilities, the lenders looking at only the physical assets of the trust and not the trustees.

The transfer and mobility of the certificates would be easily handled through transfer agents, just as readily as stock and bonds. It is entirely probable that shares in trusts with desirable income-producing properties and with large numbers of investors could be traded. Of course, this would depend upon the total cash worth of the trust and the number of certificate holders. Some of the larger trusts eventually could probably be traded on the New York Stock Exchange, some on the American Exchange while others would be quoted in the less formal over-the-counter markets.

If the trust held a number of diversified properties such as shopping centers, apartment houses, and office buildings, the certificates would represent this diversification and its owners need have very little cash invested. In fact, for as little as $25, they could achieve the diversification or "mix" that could cost as much as $20,000, in a series of purchases in limited partnerships.

Would Generate Tax Free Income

Tax wise, the trust would do the same things for the investor that limited partnerships now do, that is, to avoid the corporate tax and generate some "tax free" income. We are still a long way from Utopia, however, as the new Real Estate Investment Trust Law has some disadvantages, too. It is not possible, for example, to own property in trust form and create a tax loss. The best that could be done would be to pay a return to the investor that is entirely "tax free." This tax loss (in excess of actual cost returns) rarely happens however in properties that are well capitalized and that are fairly new. This event usually occurs where extremely rapid depreciation is taken on older buildings which have shorter economic life. It can also occur in situations where the cash down payments on buildings are small and the repayment of the mortgage is on an interest-only basis or the mortgage requires little repayment of its principal. This slight disadvantage is specious inasmuch as the majority of the leaders in the industry are not particularly charmed with ultra rapid depreciation of older properties because of the speed with which such depreciation forces them to dispose of the property.

The speedy depreciation ultimately causes taxable income on dollars the investors are not receiving, which is the opposite situation from that which most investors desire. Further, if conventional methods of financing are used and sensible ratios of land to improvements are followed, such losses as may be developed through last depreciation usually occur only at the outset, and usually last for only a year or two.

Additionally, while a speedy tax depreciation may be desirable for a particular property when this property is mixed with the other properties held by the trust, it is highly improbable that a tax loss in excess of actual cash distributions could be developed.

Disadvantages in Cases of Small Holdings

A trust would be disadvantageous in the event only one or two properties were the only principal assets. For this reason many astute leaders in the multiple ownership field are convinced that the most successful real estate investment trusts will be those which are either mergers of existing limited partnerships or those with large number of properties which were held in corporate form prior to the new law. The new trust appears to have limited use for those syndicators or promoters whose "stock-in-trade" has been to acquire older properties to develop tax losses for high-income bracket individuals.

When Congress enacted the Real Estate Investment Trust Law one of the first provisions was that it have a minimum of 100 or more persons holding the shares or certificates of the trust. Therefore, the trust would lose its tax benefits if it had less than 100 shareholders. In addition, no five beneficiaries of the trust can, directly or indirectly, own more than 50% of the trust. Quite a few syndications using the limited partnership technique could not have been accomplished using a real estate investment trust because of this provision.

Trust May Not Render Services to Tenants

Another provision of the law is that the trust may not furnish or render services to the tenants of the property it owns, nor may it directly manage the property. It must be

25

managed through an independent contractor. And the test of whether the contractor is independent or not is that the trust may not own, directly or indirectly, a 35% interest in the assets or profits of the independent contractor. The law further provides that the contractor may not be classified as "independent" if he or it owns, directly or indirectly, 35% of the shares of the real estate trust.

Another restriction which prevents the trust from setting up an "active trader business" is that the trust may not receive rent from real property where the trust has an interest of 10% or more in the stock, assets, or net profit of the lessee. Of course none of the foregoing restrictions would apply to the organization of limited partnerships, so that it is apparent that the real estate investment trust vehicle will not always be chosen as the proper method of organizing a real estate syndicate.

In addition, the entire theory behind the enactment of the new law was that the income received by the investment trust would be "passive." Therefore, the trust could not be in the business of selling or developing of land as this income does not qualify. There are various technical restrictions in the trust; the first set of restrictions governing the trust assets; the second set of restrictions governing the trust income. Briefly, at least 75% of the value of the trust assets must be represented by real estate, cash or government securities. This 75% test guarantees that the trust investments are substantially in real estate. There are several other minor investment requirements with respect to the trust assets, which are clearly stated in the law itself.

The major income requirement of the trust is that 90% or more of such income must be from rents, dividends, interest, gains from the sale of stock, securities, or real properties and abatements or refunds of taxes on the property, and within this 90% income rule is another rule which requires that 75% of this income be from rents, mortgage interests, real properties and abatements or refunds of taxes on the property.

Provision Governs Distribution of Income

A major requirement regarding income stops all corporate nonsense, with respect to future acquisitions, with one magnificent Congressional provision. This provision governs the distribution of the trust's dollars. A minimum of 90% of the trust's income *must* be distributed to the shareholders. Thus the trust has no way of accumulating cash for syndicators who are reluctant to go to the public for each acquisition.

The trustees or trust promoters *must* go back to their investors prior to any acquisition, for that all important commodity, the money with which to make the acquisition. Therefore, unless the public realty corporations now in existence have a history of careful and conservative management, the tax disadvantages along with the facts herein indicated, may serve as a warning bell to the investors who in their anxiety to receive good income have bid the price of these shares to fantastically new highs.

There are several other minor restrictions governing the trust income but these are all expressly pointed out in the law.

In summation, it appears that in order to take advantage of the new Real Estate Investment Trust Law, a trust must hold income-producing property managed by an independent contractor and it must be large enough both in its capital structure and variety of ownership to produce benefits for the investor which the Congress intended as well as having over 100 shareholders.

Like any other business the real estate investment trust business must be organized and operated by men who are technically competent and ethically tuned to their responsibilities as organizers and managers. Many persons, aware that the new law will attract fresh capital, will seek to take advantage of the investing public. There is no substitute for quality and location in real estate; and there is no such thing as a real estate bargain.

An investor seeking advice may very well weight his decision 25% as to quality and location of the property and

75% as to the men who must select and operate the property. If this formula appears lopsided and needs correction, let us do it now. Make it 10%-90%. In other words, invest in persons, not things . . . "things" never make money.

Reprinted by special permission of publisher, *Commercial and Financial Chronicle,* 110 Wall Street, New York, N.Y. 10005, Vol. 193 (April 6, 1961).

THE REAL ESTATE INVESTMENT TRUST
—New Federal Income Tax Aspects

By David C. Anchin, CPA, LL.M.*

The need and desirability of increasing investor participation in our Nation's economy has, as was inevitable, brought about a liberalization of the federal tax rules governing real estate investment trusts. However, the liberality is tempered with rigid conditions and harsh requirements. This article describes the conditions to be taken into account and the lurking hazards, before one embarks on the organization or qualification of a trust.

In 1960 Congress created a new form of tax free conduit known as the Real Estate Investment Trust. The new tax entity is described in Part II of Subchapter M of the Internal Revenue Code and is herein referred to as an "M2 Trust." Final regulations have not yet been promulgated, thus this discussion is based on the proposed regulations.

The purpose of the M2 Trust is to allow investors to own real estate in a corporate-like entity without incurring a corporate income tax. If all the rigid requirements discussed below are satisfied, the corporate income tax is avoided on *distributed* income. Some authorities anticipate that M2 Trusts will become as popular with investors as mutual funds.

Prior to the days of corporate income taxes, large scale real estate investments were often financed through use of investment trusts. The imposition of the corporate tax attributed to the decline of the real estate investment trust. However, the new tax incentives may bring the trust entity form back into favor since it can adopt more of the desired corporate-like qualities than is possible with the partnership form.

---
*DAVID C. ANCHIN, CPA, LL.M., is a former Chairman of our Society's Committee on Cooperation with Bankers and is presently serving as a member of the Society's Board of Directors. Mr. Anchin is a partner in the firm of Anchin, Block & Anchin, CPAs.

The M2 Trust is a new vehicle for real estate "syndication." Syndicators have found the partnership form of entity attractive in recent years because the avoidance of corporate income tax results in a higher rate of return to investors. The M2 Trust has been referred to as a real estate mutual fund. Actually there are many differences. The mutual fund is usually a corporation that invests its funds in marketable securities. The M2 Trust cannot be a corporation and most of its investments must be in real estate. Mutual funds generally follow the practice of redeeming their shares based on daily asset values because their securities can be valued daily, and the per share value of the mutual fund is readily determinable. Real estate, however, can hardly be valued daily. Furthermore, since real estate equities are not traded on an exchange, the M2 Trust will not be as flexible in its investment position as the mutual fund.

General Description of An M2 Trust

M2 Trust status is achieved by an election filed with the first tax return for which it is desired to qualify for this treatment, provided that the many technical requirements discussed below are met. The election, which is irrevocable, is first available for taxable years beginning after 1960. The election is made by computing taxable income as an M2 Trust.

The M2 Trust is an unincorporated trust or association managed by trustees. It cannot be a corporation, but it must so resemble a corporation that it would be taxed as a corporation if it didn't elect to be treated as an M2 Trust. The trustees must hold legal title to the assets.

There must be 100 or more shareholders owning transferable shares on at least 335 days of a 12 month year or on a proportionate number of days in a short tax year. No five individuals may directly or indirectly own over 50% of the value of the outstanding shares at any time during the last half of the taxable year. This 50% stock ownership test is the same as prescribed for the Personal Holding Company test, and the broad Personal Holding Company constructive ownership rules of Internal Revenue Code Section 544 apply. There is no requirement that the M2 company shares have voting rights, thus the trustees may be a self-perpetuating group.

At least 90% of the annual net income, other than net long-term capital gains, must be distributed. The M2 Trust is taxed as a corporation on *undistributed* income. Unless capital gains are currently paid out they are taxed to the M2 Trust. Later distribution would be ordinary income to the shareholder. The *excess* of net long-term capital gains over net short-term capital losses is taxed to the M2 Trust at capital gain rates, unless distributed.

Dividend distributions, including capital gain dividends, can be made within 12 months after the fiscal year end, provided the dividend is declared before the tax return is filed, and provided it is paid not later than the date of the first regular dividend payment made after such declaration. The election to treat such a later dividend paid as a distribution applicable to the fiscal year in which earned is made by claiming the deduction for the dividend payment in the tax return for that year.

Within 30 days after the fiscal year end the shareholders must be advised of the amount of capital gain dividends paid during the fiscal year. All or part of any dividend payment with respect to the fiscal year can be characterized as a capital gain. In January, 1963, for example, a dividend paid by an M2 Trust during its fiscal year ended December 31, 1962 with respect to 1962 earnings could be characterized as capital gain. If in 1962 a capital gain dividend was paid with respect to 1961 income, the shareholders must also be advised of the amount of such dividend.

Federal Taxation of Investor Income

Except for capital gain dividends, all dividends are taxable to M2 shareholders as ordinary income in the year received. Corporate shareholders do not receive the 85% dividends received deduction. Individual shareholders do not receive the 4% dividends received credit or the $50 dividend exclusion. Capital gain dividends are taxed as long-term capital gains to both individual and corporate shareholders.

Distributions which are not out of current or accumulated earnings represent a return of capital, reducing the basis of the shareholder's investment. However, current year earnings and profits of an M2 company are not reduced by any amount not allowable as a deduction. For example, a net capital loss would not reduce current year earnings. If an M2 company with no prior accumulated earnings had a current year net capital loss of $200,000 and other current year earnings of $100,000, distributions of up to $100,000 would represent ordinary income dividends to the shareholders. If less than $90,000 were paid out as dividends, the M2 company would be taxed on all its income. If over $90,000 but less than $100,000 was paid out only the undistributed income would be subject to corporate income tax. The excess of distributions over accumulated earnings would be treated as a reduction of paid in capital.

The ordinary rules for determining capital gain and loss on the sale or exchange of securities by investors apply to the sale or exchange of M2 company shares. However, in order to prevent conversion of short-term capital gain, on another transaction, to a long-term capital gain, by buying Real Estate Investment Trust shares immediately before the payment of a capital gain dividend and selling the shares immediately after the dividend, a loss on the sale of shares held for less than 31 days, during which period the shareholder receives a capital gain dividend, is treated as a long-term capital loss. A taxpayer could, however, receive a dividend at the end of his tax year and take his loss on sale in the following year.

Restrictions on Investments

1. *75% rule*. As of the end of each quarter of the taxable year, at least 75% of the value of its total assets must be represented by real estate assets, cash, receivables arising from operations and Government securities. Real estate assets include real property, interests in real property, mortgages, and shares of other M2 companies but do not include mineral, oil, or gas royalty interests.

2. *25% rule*. As of the end of each quarter of the tax year, no more than 25% of the value of the total assets may be

represented by securities other than allowed in the 75% rule above, and for the purpose of this limitation:

10% rule. No more than 10% of the outstanding voting securities of the issuer company may be owned by the M2 company as of the end of each quarter of the taxable year.

5% rule. No more than 5% of the total assets of the M2 company may be invested in securities of any one issuer.

3. *Relief Provision.* Percentage requirements not satisfied at the end of a quarter because of an acquisition during the quarter can be satisfied by eliminating the discrepancy within 30 days after the close of the quarter. A failure to satisfy these percentage requirements at the end of a quarter, which is caused by a change in values rather than an acquisition during the quarter, does not cause disqualification.

The trustees determine the values of assets where market quotations are not available.

Restrictions on Trust Income

a. 75% of the gross income must be from:

Rents from real property

Interest from real estate mortgages

Net gain from sale of real estate or mortgages on real estate

Distributions from, and net gain from the sale of shares of, other qualifying Real Estate Investment Trusts

b. 90% of the gross income must be from the sources specified in the 75% rule, or the following additional sources:

Other dividends

Other interest

Net gain from the sale of stock and securities

c. Less than 30% of the gross income must be from the sale of:

Stock or securities held for less than six months

Real property held for less than four years

33

For the purpose of the 30% limitation, losses are not netted with gains in determining the numerator for the computation, though the loss is reflected in gross income for the purpose of the denominator in this computation. An election to report gain in installments might avoid disqualification.

Restrictions on Rental Income

Rental income will not qualify as such if it is based on a percentage of a tenant's profit. Rents may, however, be based on a percentage of the tenant's receipts.

If the M2 Trust owns, directly or indirectly, 10% or more of the voting stock or of the total shares of stock, or an interest of 10% or more in the assets or net profits of a tenant, income received from such tenant will not be considered rental income. The proposed regulations require that the income tax return contain a schedule setting forth the details of such "tainted" rent receipts. The rules of constructive ownership in Internal Revenue Code Section 318 apply, and, insofar as the rules of constructive ownership apply to corporations and stockholders, instead of the attribution applying where there is a 50% stockholder, they apply where there is a 10% stockholder.

Great caution will have to be exercised to avoid M2 disqualification because of the attribution rules. If, by application of the attribution rules, an M2 shareholder who owns 10% of the shares of the M2 Trust, is also a 10% stockholder of a tenant corporation, the rent from this tenant will not be treated as rental income to the M2 Trust. Let us suppose for example that A owns 10% of the M2 Trust shares and is a 10% stockholder of a non-tenant corporation X, and that B, another 10% stockholder of X, owns 100% of the stock of corporation Y. If corporation Y is a tenant of the M2 company, the rental income from Y is disqualified, since by the application of the constructive ownership rules, the M2 Trust will be treated as a 10% stockholder of Y corporation. Since only 10% of the M2 Trust's gross income is not restricted as to source, the disqualification of relatively small rental income could result in the imposition of the corporate income tax on the entire M2 Trust income. The proposed regulations indicate that an allocable portion of rent stemming from a subtenant would not qualify as rent, if directly or indirectly the M2 Trust had a 10% interest in the subtenant.

In order to qualify as rental income, the real estate must be managed by an independent contractor from whom the M2 Trust derives no income. If the M2 Trust manages or operates the property, or furnishes or renders services to the tenants of such property, the rental income will not qualify as rent. An independent contractor is one who doesn't own a 35% or more interest, directly or indirectly, in the M2 Trust. Nor may one or more persons, directly or indirectly, own 35% or more of the M2 Trust shares and own more than 35% of the stock, assets, or net profits of the "independent contractor." For the purpose of the 35% tests, the rules of constructive ownership of Internal Revenue Code Section 318, as discussed above, apply.

A trustee of an M2 Trust cannot, per the proposed regulations, be an officer or employee of, or have any direct or indirect proprietary interest in any independent contractor which furnishes or renders services to the tenants of the M2 Trust property or manages or operates such property.

The independent contractor must not be subject to the control of the M2 Trust; he must be adequately compensated; and the relationships must be on an arm's length basis.

The proposed regulations permit trustees to establish rental terms, choose tenants, enter into and renew leases, deal with taxes, interest, and insurance, and make capital expenditures. Maintenance and repairs must, however, be controlled and paid for by an independent contractor. The proposed regulations require that "hotel, motel, warehousing, parking lot, maid, janitor, elevator, telephone, switchboard, guard or similar services" may not be provided by an M2 Trust or its employees but may be rendered by an independent contractor.

Further Income Tax Considerations

The net operating loss deduction is not available to the M2 Trust and losses are not passed through to the shareholders. As a result, M2 qualification in loss years would not be desirable. The capital loss carry forward, however, is available to the M2 Trust.

An entity which qualifies for M2 treatment has committed itself to be taxed as a corporation unless it meets all of the M2 requirements. However, if an M2 company were disqualified for not sufficiently resembling a corporation, the income tax result might not necessarily be adverse since there would be no corporate income tax.

The disallowance of a deduction by the Internal Revenue Service could cause M2 disqualification and mean that the corporate tax would apply to all income. This could happen, for example, if the depreciation deduction was reduced. To minimize this danger, an M2 company could distribute more than 90% of its taxable income, exclusive of net long-term capital gains, or enter into an agreement with the District Director as to the rate and method of depreciation and salvage value. The allocation of values between land and building, and the deductibility of repairs as current expenses, should be carefully considered in this connection.

Practical Considerations

The M2 company trustees will have to watch the cash flow carefully since 90% of the ordinary income must be distributed to the shareholders. If mortgage amortization exceeds the depreciation allowance, cash distribution may be difficult. The amount of leverage desired, the method of depreciation and capital improvement requirements must be carefully studied.

Registration requirements under state securities acts and with the Securities Exchange Commission should be considered by the Trust's attorneys. The state laws should be investigated since this form of entity may be impractical or impossible under the laws of some states. State tax laws will also have to be considered.

An M2 company can invest exclusively in mortgages. The 10% and 35% limitations do not apply to mortgages. The proposed regulations indicate that for the purpose of the gross income percentage limitations, only lawful interest will be included (in the numerator). Where mortgages cover both real and personal property, an allocation must be made for the purpose of the 75% requirement.

Conclusion

The Real Estate Investment Trust will not displace the partnership or corporation form of real estate ownership. In many situations, the latter entities will be preferred. The partnership form actually provides a *fuller conduit tax result* than M2. The regulations regarding associations now offer guidelines enabling a partnership with some corporate-like traits to avoid being taxed as a corporation. M2 offers the opportunity of corporate-like structure without corporate Federal income tax.

The M2 Trust will be a new source of real estate investment capital. By purchase of M2 company shares, a small investment in real estate is possible. Small investors will now be able to invest in real estate and achieve the kind of diversification previously available only to wealthier investors who can own, or share in the ownership of several properties. The M2 Trust investor can share in the ownership of valuable properties and benefit from expert management. The anticipated high income return may be particularly attractive to tax exempt entities. Aided by the new tax provisions, this form of real estate ownership may become very popular, especially if the shares become readily marketable.

The onerous technical requirements will "make life difficult" for the M2 Trust management. An unrestrained free transferability of shares could lead to disqualification, because of the many conditions of ownership and operation that must be observed. Moreover, the M2 Trust will be compelled to secure considerable personal information from its shareholders. Although some of the tax-free reorganization provisions are applicable, the Internal Revenue Service has indicated that it will not issue rulings.

Accountants for such organizations, too, will face problems of responsibility in helping to keep managements from unwittingly losing their status.

Reprinted by permission of *The CPA Journal*, Vol. 31 (July, 1961).

REAL ESTATE INVESTMENT TRUSTS

By Victor R. Wolder

The author is a New York City attorney

The new Real Estate Investment Trust Law which was enacted as part of the Omnibus Tax Law of 1960 will bring about a "new" form of investment set-up which will be as "old as the hills." However, it has once and for all created an investment vehicle which taxpayers will know prevents the possibility of double taxation. Up to the time of the new Real Estate Investment Trust Law, there were several investment formulas used. But no matter what the form, the question always presented was: "Will the set-up be taxed as an 'association,' taxable as a corporation, no matter what form we use or call it." Sometimes it was a limited partnership, sometimes a trust, sometimes a general co-partnership, sometimes a pool or unincorporated association. Sometimes it was merely called a syndication or a joint venture. Yet, no matter what the name, if such items were present as "central management," "continuity of interest," "limited liability," "transferability of interest," etc., one would not be too sure whether the enterprise would have its income taxed first as a corporation, and then have the investors taxed again upon receiving the distributions. The writer would venture to say that a vast number of investors in the large, widely held syndication have never been aware of the problem. Able tax counsel usually gave opinions as to whether the enterprise might be taxed as an association which could result in a double tax. But, as we know, opinions are not final determination. The new Real Estate Investment Trust Law now gives us an answer. The purpose of this article is to review the new law and point out various questions which come to the writer's mind. Some day, of course, there will be some very extensive regulations promulgated by the Treasury Department, which will answer most of the questions. The courts will answer the rest in years to come.

38

IRC Section 856(a) In General

(1) *A real estate investment trust must be either an unincorporated association or an unincorporated trust.* An unincorporated trust would most likely follow the usual pattern of a so-called "Massachusetts" trust, or business trusts. 156 ALR 22. It could probably be any form of express trust. An unincorporated association may be one of many things.

"The term 'association' is not used in the Code in any narrow or technical sense. It includes any organization, created for the transaction of designated affairs or the attainment of some object, which, like a corporation, continues, notwithstanding that its members or participants change, and the affairs of which, like corporate affairs, are conducted by a single individual, a committee, a board, or some other group, acting in a representative capacity. It is immaterial whether such organization is created by an agreement, a declaration of trust, a statute, or otherwise. It includes a voluntary association, a joint-stock association or company, a 'business' trust, a 'Massachusetts' trust, a 'common law' trust, an interinsurance exchange operating through an attorney in fact, a partnership association, and any other type of organization (by whatever name known) which is not, within the meaning of the Code, a trust or an estate, or a partnership. An 'investment' trust of the type commonly known as a management trust is an association, and a trust of the type commonly known as a fixed investment trust is an association if there is power under the trust agreement to vary the investment of the certificate holders. See *Commissioner v. North American Bond Trust*, 122 F. (2d) 545, cert. denied 314 U.S. 701. If the conduct of the affairs of a corporation continues after the expiration of its charter or the termination of its existence, it becomes an association. Certain proprietorships and partnerships can elect to be taxed as corporation. This, however, does not affect unincorporated associations having centralized control and management, etc. Such associations are taxed as corporations."

Query: Would the new law exclude a joint stock association such as is approved under Article 2 of the General Associations Law of the State of New York for the reason

39

that a joint stock company has all the essentials of a corporation except limited liability, and the Internal Revenue Code defines "corporations" to include "associations and joint stock companies." (Code Sec. 7701 (a) (3), *Hibbs v. Brown*, 112 A. 214, affd, 190 N.Y. 167, 82 N.E. 1108.)

(2) *The beneficial ownership of the unincorporated association or trust must be evidenced by transferable shares or by transferable certificates of beneficial interest.* This means that the certificates or shares must be in a form so that they can be transferred by delivery or by assignment. There is nothing to indicate that they can or cannot be in registered form. But it would seem that reasonable requirements on registration would be permitted.

(3) *The unincorporated association or trust must be one which (were it not for the provisions of the new section of the tax law) would be otherwise taxed as a corporation.* However, as it will be noted further on in this article, the taxpayer is given the option to elect whether it will qualify under this section or not. If the trust would ordinarily be treated as a trust and not as a corporation, then it cannot be taxed under this new section of the law. The same would hold true with a partnership. If the unincorporated enterprise would be taxed as a corporation then it would come under new law if it so elects. But if it would be treated as a partnership, it cannot come under this law. It must be remembered that in the final analysis, it is not the local law which determines whether for tax purposes a corporation exists or not. It is the federal tax law that controls.

(4) *The association or trust must not hold any property primarily for sale to customers in the ordinary course of its trade or business.* While this does not seem to present much of a problem in the ordinary case because most of the large real estate investment trusts will deal with a large improved property such as an office building, apartment house, shopping center, hotel, motel, industrial building, yet in some situations, unwittingly, the following could occur. A real estate investment trust could acquire a large tract on which it builds a large motel, office building or the like. Then, having a large

area of land left over, it decides to sell the same. It plots the land and starts to sell off lots. In such a case, beware if there are too many sales.

(5) *The beneficial ownership of the unincorporated association or trust must be held by one hundred or more persons.* Query: Would a share or certificate owned by a partnership which in turn has five partners be considered as being beneficially owned by five persons or just one person? What about a certificate held in the name of a husband and wife in a community property state? Would one certificate owned by ten people either jointly or co-owners representing a quarter of one per cent of the beneficial ownership in the trust be considered as ten persons or one person? These questions await final answering by the Treasury Department regulations. If we take the law literally such a holding would seem to indicate that there are ten persons beneficially interested — not just one.

(6) *The association or trust must not be a personal holding company if all of its gross income constituted personal holding company income.* This means primarily that one has to consider the distribution of the ownership of the shares or certificates of beneficial interest. (See Sec. 542(a)(2).) One of the requirements of a personal holding company is that at some time during the last half of the taxable year more than 50 per cent in value of the outstanding stock is owned directly or indirectly by or for not more than five individuals. There are certain rules as to stock attribution by way of constructive ownership. For example: Stock owned by corporations, partnership, estates, trusts are considered as owned proportionately by its stockholders, partners or beneficiaries. An individual is deemed to own the stock of his brothers, sisters, partners, children, descendants and ancestors. An individual having an option on stock is considered as owning such stock. (See IRC Sec. 544.)

There is nothing in the Code that says the rules of stock attribution are to be considered for any purpose of beneficial ownership in determining whether the number is 100 or more persons beneficially interested in the ownership if a personal holding company is not present.

Of course, there are other provisions which would keep an association from being a personal holding company other than the number of people who own its stock. This section of the law must be carefully reviewed.

(7) *There are other requirements which also must be met or adhered to. These are set forth later on in this article.*

IRC Section 856(b) Determination of Status

In order for a trust or association to qualify as a real estate investment trust, the conditions set forth in subsections (1) (2) (4) inclusive, above, must be met during the entire taxable year. The condition in subsection (5) above must exist during at least 335 days of a taxable year of 12 months or during a proportionate part of a taxable year of less than 12 months. It is to be noted that the code does not say that the 335 days need be consecutive.

IRC Section 856(c) Limitations

Moreover, a trust or association will not be considered a real estate investment trust in any taxable year unless the following conditions are met:

(1) It must file with its tax return for the taxable year an election to be a real estate investment trust; or the trust must have made such election for a prior taxable year which began after December 31, 1960.

(2) At least 90 per cent of its gross income is derived from (a) dividends; (b) interest; (c) rents from real property; (d) gain from the sale or other disposition of stock; securities, real property (including interests in real property and interests in mortgages on real property); and (e) abatements and refunds of taxes on real property.

The term "interests in real property" is hereinafter defined. Care must be taken to distinguish between rents from real property and personal property which is rented at the same time along with real property, such as furnishings, equipment and the like.

(3) At least 75 per cent of its gross income must be derived from (a) rents from real property; (b) interest on obligations secured by mortgages on real property or interests in real property; (c) gain from the sale or other disposition of real property including interests in real property and interests in mortgages on real property; (d) dividends or other distributions on, and gains from the sale or other disposition of transferable shares (or transferable certificates of beneficial interest) and other real estate investment trusts which meet the requirements of this part of the law; and (e) abatements and refunds of taxes on real property.

No particular comment needs to be made concerning this subsection "3" as the various provisions are seemingly clear each and unto themselves.

(4) Less than 30 per cent of its gross income must be derived from the sale or other disposition of (a) stock or securities held less than six months, and (b) real property and interests in real property not compulsorily or involuntarily converted, held for less than four years.

(5) At the close of each quarter of the taxable year (a) at least 75 per cent of the value of its total assets must be represented by real estate assets, cash and cash items (including receivables) and government securities, and (b) not more than 25 per cent of the value of its total assets is required to be represented by securities (limited with respect to any one issuer, not to exceed five per cent of the total asset value of the real estate investment trust nor more than ten per cent of the outstanding voting securities of such issuer).

The term "value" has a special definition in this new section of the tax law, and this definition is referred to later in this article.

Real Estate Investment Trust and Its Qualified Status

A real estate investment trust which meets the requirements at the close of any quarter will not lose its status because of a discrepancy during a subsequent quarter between the value of its various investments and such requirements, unless such discrepancy exists immediately after the acquisition of any security or other property and is wholly or partly the result of such acquisition. This provision seems to mean among other things, that if a discrepancy occurs during a subsequent quarter after acquisition because of increase or decrease of value of assets alone, the real estate investment trust, which has previously qualified, will not lose its qualification. A discrepancy which will cause the real estate investment trust to lose its qualification would seem to be one which arises from the acquisition of the security or other property itself and is wholly or partly a result of such acquisition. It would seem that where a security was acquired in good faith and did not result in a disqualification for the real estate investment trust, which rose very rapidly in value after its acquisition, it would not necessarily cause a real estate investment trust to lose its qualified status.

Opportunity to Correct Errors in Status

A real estate investment trust which does not meet the requirements of this subsection at the close of any quarter by reason of a discrepancy existing immediately after the acquisition of any security or other property which is wholly or partly the result of such acquisition, during such quarter, shall not lose its status for such quarter if such discrepancy is eliminated within 30 days after the close of such quarter. This would mean that there would have to be a constant and prompt evaluation of all assets currently so that within the 30-day period all necessary action would have been taken. This would mean, too, that real estate investment trust which would seek to have constant qualification under this section of the law would have to be careful in its selection of any assets which may cause it trouble. If an asset would be difficult to dispose of; if it would be hard to find a buyer; if it would be difficult to obtain necessary financing with reference to a sale of a troublesome asset, it might unwittingly lead to the real estate investment trust losing its necessary qualification.

As used in this section of the real estate investment trust law, there are certain definitions given for "value," "real estate assets," "interest in real property" and "all other terms."

Definition of Value

"Value" means the following: Market valuations in the case of securities for which there are quotations. As to other securities and assets "fair value" as determined in good faith by the trustees but "fair value" shall not exceed "market value" or "asset value," whichever is higher. This definition of value gives the trustees a lot of leeway. It would be assumed that in the ordinary case the usual standards by which fair value is determined will be used. Perhaps it would have been much easier to have said "fair value" as determined in good faith by the trustees and let it go at that. Of course, fair value in the minds of the trustees could be higher than market value because the trustees could feel that the fair value is higher than an asset would bring in the market at a given time or vice versa. But what does asset value mean to an asset having value independent of its fair value, its market value or its fair market value? Does an asset have a value because it has a nuisance value? There are always a great many factors to be taken into consideration in connection with the valuation of an asset such as appraisals; book values; earnings; offers to buy and offers to sell; quotations in the market place; federal and state tax values; forced or quick sale values; fractional interest value; value affected by imminence of war; restricted sales covenants; anticipated current or subsequent events such as possibility of condemnation proceedings; discount value; anticipated earnings; value based upon a cash sale and value based upon payment of purchase price made on installment or deferred payment method; depreciation factors; and loan value. As generally employed, fair market value means the price at which property would change hands between a willing buyer and a willing seller, neither being under any compulsion to buy or sell. This is the definition used for federal estate tax law purposes and the definition is of judicial origin. Apparently a new body of law on the subject of valuation is going to come into existence all of which will appear to be realistic depending upon whose side you are on.

Definition of Real Estate Assets

"Real estate assets" is defined to mean real property, and interest in real property, and interest in mortgages on real property, and shares and transferable certificates of beneficial interest in other real estate investment trusts. It should be noted in connection with this definition that personal property in and of itself, is not considered within the definition of "real estate assets." However, if personal property is owned by another real estate investment trust and shares or transferable certificates of beneficial interest are owned by the real estate investment trust in question then for the purpose of the real estate investment trust in question, personal property indirectly becomes within the definition of real estate assets.

Moreover, what about an interest in a mortgage which covers both real property and personal property? Would that be deemed a real estate asset or would it be prorated according to the value of the real estate and personal property covered.

Definition of Interests In Real Property

"Interests in real property" is defined to include fee ownership and co-ownership of land and improvements thereon, leaseholds of land and improvements thereon, but does not include mineral, oil, or gas royalty interests.

Definition of Other Terms

"All other terms" are defined to have the same meaning as the Investment Company Act of 1940 as amended. The Investment Company Act can be found in title 15 USCA Section 80a-1 and following. There are a host of definitions found in title 15 USCA Section 80a-2 and 3.

Definition of Section 856(d) Rents from Property

Rents from property as used in this section of the law has a definition of its own. "Rents" includes rents from

46

interests in real property. Since we noted above that interests in real property, as defined in the law, does not include anything specific with respect to personal property leased along with real property, then it would not necessarily include rents from interests in personal property. Just how far the Commissioner of Internal Revenue will go in this connection will have to await the regulations.

Rents include rents based upon a fixed percentage or percentages of gross receipts or sales. However, it does not include any amount directly or indirectly received or accrued if the determination is based in whole or in part on the income or profits derived by any person from such property.

Moreover, as defined in the law, care has to be taken with respect to rent received from any corporation if the trust directly or indirectly was 10 per cent or more of the total combined voting power of all classes of stock of said corporation entitled to vote or 10 per cent or more of the total number of shares of stock of such corporation. The law provides that for the purposes of this section of the law, rents from real property do not include any rent received from any such corporation if the trust directly or indirectly owns 10 per cent or more of the total combined voting power of all classes of stock of the corporation entitled to vote or 10 per cent or more of the total number of shares of stock of such corporation.

In addition to the above, care likewise has to be taken in case any rent is received with respect to any real property if the trust furnishes or renders services to the tenants of such property or manages or operates such property other than as an independent contractor from whom the trust does not derive or receive any income. Specifically, the law says that rents from real property does not include any rent received from any real property if the trust furnishes or renders services to the tenants of such property or manages or operates such property other than as an independent contractor from whom the trust does not derive or receive any income. There is no specific definition as to what the furnishing or rendering of services to tenants includes but in the absence of any regulations, which specifically excludes from the broad coverage from the word "services" then it would be reasonable to suppose that any service to tenants would be included in the definition. Services could embrace such items as the furnishing of gas, heat, water, air conditioning, cleaning, repairs, telephone, maintenance, parking, delivery, as well as a host of others. Management and operating services are of the well known and usual kind.

As to what constitutes an "independent contractor" who furnishes or renders his service or manages or operates the real property, the law had a special definition. An independent contractor is defined to mean (a) a person who does not own directly or indirectly more than 35 per cent of the shares or certificates of beneficial interest in the trust, or (b) a corporation not more than 35 per cent of the total combined voting power of whose stock or 35 per cent of the total shares of all classes of stock, or if not a corporation, not more than 35 per cent of the interest in whose assets or net proceeds directly or indirectly is owned, by one or more persons owning 35 per cent or more of the shares or certificates of the real estate investment trust.

Determination of Ownership

In determining the ownership of stock, assets, or net profits of any person, for purposes of determining whether an "independent contractor exists," Section 318(a) of the Internal Revenue Code applies except that it is necessary to substitute 10 per cent for wherever 50 per cent is set forth in Section 318(a) (2) (C). Thus:

Members of family. — An individual is considered as owning the stock directly or indirectly by or for his spouse (other than a spouse who is legally separated from the individual under a decree of divorce or separate maintenance) and his children, grandchildren and parents. Moreover, a legally adopted child of an individual is treated as a child of such individual by blood.

Partnerships and estates. — Stock owned, directly or indirectly by or for a partnership or estate shall be considered as being owned proportionately by its partners or beneficiaries. Stock owned directly or indirectly by or for a partner or

48

a beneficiary is considered as being owned by the partnership or estate.

Trusts. — Stock owned directly or indirectly by or for a trust shall be considered as being owned by its beneficiaries in proportion to the actuarial interest of such beneficiaries in such trust. Stock owned directly or indirectly by or for a beneficiary of a trust shall be considered as being owned by the trust unless such beneficiaries' interest in the trust is a remote contingent interest. For the purpose of this provision, a contingent interest of a beneficiary in a trust shall be considered remote if, under the maximum exercise of discretion by the trustee in favor of such beneficiary, the value of such interest computed actuarily is five per cent or less of the value of the trust of the property. Stock owned directly by or indirectly by or for any portion of certain trusts of which a person is considered the owner, (that is, relating to grantors and others treated as substantial owners under subpart "E" of part "1" of subchapter "J" of the Code) shall be considered as being owned by such person, and such trust shall be considered as owning the stock owned directly or indirectly by or for that person.

It should be pointed out, however, that with respect to this item of constructive ownership of stock, the law specifically states that it shall not apply with respect to any employees trust described in Section 401 (a) of the Internal Revenue Code which is exempt from tax under Section 501 (a).

Corporations. — If 10 per cent or more in value of the stock in a corporation is owned directly or indirectly by or for any person then (1) such person shall be considered as owning the stock owned directly or indirectly, by or for that corporation, in that proportion which the value of the stock which such person so owns bears to the value of all the stock in such corporation; and (2) such corporation shall be considered as owning the stock owned, directly or indirectly, by or for that person.

Options. — If any person has an option to acquire stock, such option shall be considered as owned by such person. Moreover, an option to acquire such an option, and each one owning series of such options, shall be considered as an option to acquire such stock.

Constructive ownership as actual ownership. — In general, stock constructively owned by a person as above set forth in subparagraphs "1," "2" and "3" is to be treated as actually owned by such person, except, however, that stock constructively owned by an individual by reason of being a member of a family is not to be treated as owned by him in order to make another the constructive owner of such stock. Further, the law goes on to say that if stock may be considered as owned by an individual either by reason of being a member of a family or by reason of having an option, then it is to be considered as being owned by him by reason of having an option.

From all the above it becomes apparent that where individuals will seek to dominate the ownership or control of real estate investment trust and also will seek to dominate management in service companies with respect to the real estate properties in which the real estate investment trust is directly or indirectly interested, many problems are sure to come up.

Taxation of Real Estate Investment Trust and Its Beneficiaries

Now that we have set forth what makes up a real estate investment trust, how it qualifies and what limitations are placed on it, we come to the taxation of the trust and its beneficiaries. Here again, in order for the real estate investment trust and its beneficiaries to receive whatever tax benefits the law provides strict adherence to additional provisions of law are required.

Ninety per cent distribution necessary. — In order to receive the benefits for a particular taxable year the real estate investment trust must obtain a deduction for dividends paid during the taxable year (as defined by Section 561 of the Internal Revenue Code, but without regard to capital gains dividends) of at least 90 per cent of its real estate investment trust taxable income for the taxable year determined without regard to the dividends paid.

Ownership in outstanding shares or certificates must be disclosed. — The real estate investment trust must comply with the regulations of the Secretary of the Treasury for the purposes of ascertaining the actual ownership of the outstanding shares or certificates of beneficial interest of such trust.

Undistributed Income of Trust Subject to Regular Corporate Taxes

The tax on a real estate investment trust is the regular normal and surtax as computed as provided in Section 11 of the Internal Revenue Code. These are the regular taxes applicable to all corporations. However, there is a special definition for what makes up the taxable income of a real estate investment trust. First of all, the Code says that the taxable income and dividend paid deduction (which is to be computed without regard to capital gains dividend) shall be reduced by the deduction provided in Section 242 of the Code relating to partially tax-exempt interest. Further, the real estate investment trust taxable income means taxable income adjusted as follows:

(a) There shall be excluded the excess, if any, of the net long term capital gain over the net short term capital laws.

(b) There shall be allowed the special deductions for corporations provided in Part VIII of subchapter "B" of the Internal Revenue Code, to wit: Section 241 and following sections relating to the allowance of special deductions, with the exception that the deductions of organizational expenditures under Section 248 are to be recognized.

(c) A deduction shall be allowed for dividends paid which shall be computed without regard to capital gains dividends. Dividends will take the well-defined meaning as set forth in Section 561 of the Code.

(d) Taxable income of the real estate investment trusts is to be computed without regard to Section 443(b) of the

Code relating to computation of tax on change of annual accounting period.

(e) Net operating loss deductions as provided in Section 172 of the Code are not to be allowed.

Undistributed Capital Gains Subject to Tax

With respect to capital gains the tax is to be computed as follows:

(a) There is imposed upon the real estate investment trust a tax of 25 per cent of the excess, if any, of net long term capital gain over the sum of (i) the net short term capital loss and (ii) the deduction for dividends paid determined with reference to capital gains dividends only.

(b) A capital gain dividend received by shareholders for beneficial interest holders of a real estate investment trust shall be treated as a gain from the sale or exchange of a capital asset held more than six months.

(c) A capital gains dividend is defined as any dividend or part thereof which is designated by the real estate investment trust as a capital gains dividend in a written notice mailed to its shareholders or holders of beneficial interests at any time before the expiration of 30 days after the close of the taxable year. If the aggregate amount so paid with respect to the 'trusts' taxable year (including Section 858 dividends as hereinafter referred to) is greater than the excess of the net long-term capital gain over the net short-term capital loss of the taxable year, the portion of each distribution which shall be a capital gain dividend shall be only that portion of the amount so designated which such excess of net long-term capital gain over the net short-term capital gain bears to the amount distributed.

Loss on sale or exchange of a share or interest in a trust held less than 31 days shall be treated as loss from sale or exchange of capital asset held for more than six months, if and only to the extent that such taxpayer would have to treat capital-gains dividends by the trust as a gain from a long term capital asset.

For the purposes of this paragraph the rules set forth in Section 246(c)(3) are to be applied in determining whether the holding has been for less than 31 days. This means that the day of disposition but not the day of acquisition shall be taken into account. Moreover, there shall not be taken into account any day which is more than 30 days after the date on which a share becomes ex-dividend.

Restrictions Applicable to Dividends Received from Real Estate Investment Trust

For the purposes of Section 34(a) relating to credits for dividends received by individuals, Section 116, relating to exclusions for dividends received by individuals, and Section 243 relating to deductions for dividends received by corporations, a dividend received from a real estate investment trust which meets the requirements of this new section of the law shall not be considered as a dividend. Of course, the reason for this is obvious. Having eliminated one tax by reason of the new section of the law, the Treasury Department had to reserve its right to have the income taxed at least once.

Earnings and Profits of Real Estate Investment Trust

The earnings and profits of a real estate investment trust for any taxable year (but not its accumulated earnings and profits) shall not be reduced by any amount which is not allowable as a deduction in computing its taxable income for such year. For the purposes of this section of the law a real estate investment trust includes domestic trusts and associations which are unincorporated and which are real estate investment trusts determined without regard to Section 857(a) of the Internal Revenue Code.

Now we see that the Internal Revenue Code injects the thought that there are real estate investment trusts which are determined without meeting the requirements of the new section of the law.

Section 858 Internal Revenue Code Dividends Paid by Real Estate Investment Trust

We see here that under certain circumstances a real estate investment trust can obtain a credit for dividends paid after the close of the trusts' taxable year. This, of course, is only equitable because the trust cannot finally determine its income until its tax year is closed, otherwise how would it know as a certainty whether it has declared 90 percent of its taxable income as dividends. The law says that if the real estate investment trust declares a dividend before the time prescribed by law for the filing of its return for the taxable year, including any extensions granted, and distributes the dividends in the 12 months following the close of the taxable year, but not later than the date of the first regular dividend, payment made after such declaration, then the amount so declared and distributed shall (to the extent the trust elects on such return) be considered as having been paid during the taxable year. There are some exceptions. The first exception is that insofar as the recipient shareholder or beneficial certificate holder is concerned, the dividend is to be treated as received in the taxable year in which the distribution is made. The second exception is that notice must be given to shareholders with respect to which such dividends apply, not later than 30 days after the close of the taxable year in which the distribution is made.

We can therefore see that from these provisions of the law the real estate investment trust is given ample time in which to compute its taxable income for the year in which to make the dividend distributions. Care should be taken that while the period in which to declare the dividend runs up to and including the last date for filing the return for the taxable year, including any extensions granted, yet the time with respect to making the distribution is limited to 12 months following the close of the taxable year and there are no apparent extensions of this even though the time for the filing of the tax return may have been extended.

Reprinted by special permission of author and the publisher of *TAXES, The Tax Magazine,* Vol. 39 (August, 1961).

TAXATION OF REAL ESTATE INVESTMENT TRUSTS AND THEIR SHAREHOLDERS

By H. Cecil Kilpatrick

Kilpatrick, Ballard and Beasley;
Washington, D.C.

THE REAL ESTATE TRUST form of ownership originated in Massachusetts in the early part of the nineteenth century, because of limitations imposed by Massachusetts law on the corporate ownership of real estate. Under the standard form of organization, the shares of the beneficiaries of these trusts were evidenced by transferable certificates and title to the property was vested in the trustees, who were governed by a declaration of trust, which could be amended only by the vote of a substantial majority (normally 75 percent) of the shares. This permitted small, as well as large, investors to pool their funds and get equity interests in real estate with centralized management and the safety of diversification without the personal liability attached to partnership interests. Funds pooled in this way were largely responsible for the development of Boston during its great period of growth in the nineteenth and early twentieth centuries, and of the Middle West and Far West. These trusts were responsible to a large degree for the early development of such cities as Detroit, Chicago, Minneapolis, St. Paul, Kansas City, Omaha, Duluth and Seattle.

The trusts were formed continuously until the depression of the thirties. Upon emerging from that depression, they were faced with the severe income tax treatment discussed below, and since that time, many of them have been liquidated and few, if any, formed until enactment of the tax statute herein discussed.

Along with the real estate investment trusts there later appeared trusts of the same form to invest in securities. Many of the early mutual funds were so organized, in order to provide centralized management, diversification of investment, limited liability for investors and readily transferable shares of beneficial interest.[1]

Income Tax Treatment from 1913 to 1936

The Revenue Act of 1913[2] followed the pattern of taxing corporations on their income and also taxing the shareholders on corporate distributions from earnings, making the corporate tax apply to "every corporation, joint stock company or association." The income of trusts, on the other hand, which was distributable or distributed to beneficiaries was taxed only to the beneficiaries. This pattern, insofar as the present discussion is concerned, was repeated in all subsequent acts. However, none of these statutes defined an "association" which was taxable as a corporation. All of the Commissioner's regulations,[3] prior to 1935, had consistently ruled that "where trustees hold real estate subject to a lease and collect the rents, doing no business other than distributing the income less taxes and similar expenses to the holders of their receipt certificates, who have no control except the right of filling a vacancy among the trustees and of consenting to a modification of the terms of the trust, no association exists and the cestui que trusts are liable to tax as beneficiaries of a trust the income of which is to be distributed periodically, whether or not at regular intervals." This regulation was no doubt the result of the 1919 decision in *Crocker v. Malley*, 1 USTC #24, 249 U.S. 223, where the Supreme Court held that trustees who held title to a mill property, leased to the operating company, and merely collected and distributed the rents, did not constitute an association. The distinction seemed clearly drawn between such a passive type of operation and one where the trustees engaged in other more active types of business.

---

[1]This historical note is based upon a speech by Mr. John H. Gardiner, vice president and trustee of Real Estate Investment Trust of America, before the New England Realtors' Convention, June 28, 1961.

[2] 38 Stat. 172.

[3] See Article 1504 of Regs. 45, 62, and 69, and Article 1314 of Regs. 74 and 77.

Enterprising people, attempting to stretch the trust concept to more active operations, used this type of organization to carry on many kinds of business, which led to attack by the taxing authorities and a substantial amount of litigation. Prior to 1935, the cases had held, with substantial unanimity, that *Crocker v. Malley* had drawn the line at the right place, and that such a Massachusetts trust which went into active business operations, as constrasted with the passive collection and distribution of investment income, would be taxed as an association, and hence as a corporation, but that the passive type would continue to be taxed as a trust.[4]

Morrissey and Related Cases

However, in 1935, four cases[5] involving this issue came to the Supreme Court, which persuaded the Court of the "need for a further examination of the Congressional intent" as to the meaning of "association."[6] In the *Morrissey* case, the trust was formed to engage in the construction and operation of golf courses and club houses and the subdivision and sale of lots. In *Combs* the trust was to engage in oil well drilling and sale of gas and oil produced. The other two cases involved the ownership and operation of apartment houses.

The government's position in these cases was that the distinction between associations and trusts is between "business trusts on the one side" and other trusts "which are engaged merely in collecting the income and conserving the property against the day when it is to be distributed to the beneficiaries" and that Congress intended that all "business trusts" should be taxed as associations.[7]

---

[4] See *Hecht v. Malley, 1 USTC* ¶93, 265 U.S. 144, 159 (1924), and 93, 265 U.S. 144, 159 (1924), and cases there discussed.

[5] *Morrissey v. Commissioner,* 36-1 USTC ¶9020, 296 U.S. 344; *Swanson v. Commissioner,* 36-1 USTC ¶9021, 296 U.S. 362; *Helvering v. Combs,* 36-1 USTC ¶9023, 296 U.S. 365; and *Helvering v. Coleman-Gilbert Associates,* 36-1 USTC ¶9022, 296 U.S. 369.

[6] *Morrissey v. Commissioner,* cited at footnote, 5 at p. 356.

[7] See footnote 6.

The Supreme Court, however, rejected this operational test and on December 6, 1935, without specifically overruling *Crocker v. Malley,* substituted an organizational test. Briefly stated, it was held that if a trust instrument has the following characteristics, which give it a resemblance to corporate form, the trust is taxable as an association: [8]

(1) Title to trust property held by trustees;

(2) Centralized management by trustees, who act in much the same manner as corporate directors;

(3) Continuity of existence in case of death of beneficiary;

(4) Transferable beneficial interests; and

(5) Limited liability of beneficiaries.

Revenue Act of 1936

The decision in the *Morrissey* and related cases caused great consternation on the part of investment trusts — both security and real estate investment trusts — which under the regulations and decisions above noted, had not been subjected to the corporate tax. The trusts which confined their investments to stocks and bonds immediately appeared before the Senate Finance Committee and asked for legislative relief on the ground that these organizations served merely as conduits to permit small investors a means of obtaining an interest in a diversified group of securities.[9] As a result, Section 48 (e) of the Revenue Act of 1936 gave this conduit treatment to a "mutual investment company" which was defined as "any corporation (whether chartered or created as an investment trust or otherwise) . . . if . . . it is organized for the purpose of, and substantially all its business consists of holding, investing or reinvesting in stocks or securities."

---

[8] *Morrissey v. Commissioner,* cited at footnote 5, at pp. 359-361.

[9] Senate Finance Committee hearings on H.R. 12395, 74th Cong., 2nd Sess., pp. 776, and following, and p. 799, and following.

Section 170 (c) of the Revenue Act of 1942 changed "mutual investment company" to "regulated investment company," which was defined as "any domestic corporation (whether chartered or created as an investment trust or otherwise) . . . which at all times during the year is registered under the Investment Company Act of 1940 . . . or which is a common trust fund . . ."

These provisions have remained without substantial change in all subsequent revenue acts and now appear in Sections 851-855 of the Internal Revenue Code of 1954.

1960 Legislation

Section 10 of Public Law 86-779, enacted September 14, 1960, which added Sections 856-858 to the Code, was designed to provide "substantially the same tax treatment for real estate investment trusts as present law provides for regulated investment companies."[10] That section has become popularly known as "the real estate investment trust act of 1960," and will be hereafter referred to as the 1960 Act. Real estate investment trusts will be sometimes called REITs.

Tentative regulations under the 1960 Act were published under notice of rule making in the *Federal Register* of January 20, 1961. Numerous written suggestions and objections to these tentative regulations were filed with the Commissioner and hearings were held thereon on March 8, 1961. At this writing final regulations have not been issued, but some comments will be made herein on the tentative regulations.

As of August 1, 1961, 19 RITTs had filed registration statements since the enactment of the 1960 Act, with public offerings of over $176 million, and seven such statements had become effective.

---

[10] H. Rept. 2020, 86th Cong., 2nd Sess., p. 2. This report related to H.R. 12559 which was passed by the House and thereafter added by the Senate, without change, as Section 10, to the bill which became P.L. 86-779.

General Structure of 1960 Act

While running somewhat parallel to Sections 851-855 of the 1954 Code, relating to the taxation of mutual funds, the new act has a number of variations, some of which are rendered necessary by the difference between the holding of corporate stocks and bonds, on the one hand, and real estate assets, on the other, which may be summarized as follows:

(1) A corporation may not qualify as a REIT. The legislative history discloses no reason for confining this tax treatment to a trust with transferable shares which otherwise would be taxed as an association. One may speculate that the Treasury opposition to broadening the coverage may have caused this restriction. The statute says clearly that a REIT is an "unincorporated trust or an unincorporated association." This implies that an association not in trust form may qualify, but the further requirement that it be managed by one or more "trustees" leaves this in doubt.

(2) While the "mutual fund" (which we shall use as meaning the regulated investment company) is subject to no such limitation, Section 856(a)(4) and 856(b) provides that the REIT may not "hold any property for sale to customers in the ordinary course of its trade or business" at any time during the taxable year. This provision was designed to restrict the beneficial tax treatment to "passive" income, and prevent trusts which are in fact dealers or are engaged in "an active business enterprise" from qualifying.[11]

(3) Section 856(a)(5) requires that the REIT have at least 100 shareholders. This was apparently patterned on some theory of symmetry, on Section 3(c)(1) of the Investment Company Act of 1940,[12] which excludes from the term "investment company" any issuer whose outstanding securities are beneficially owned by not more than 100 shareholders and which does not make a public offering. The logic of including this limitation in the tax provisions is not clear, particularly

---

[11] Source cited at footnote 10, at p. 5.

[12] USCA, Title 15, Sec. 80-a-3(c)(1)

since the stock ownership rules of the personal holding company provisions apply to REITs under Section 856 (a) (6).

(4) *Limitation on capital gains.* — In order to restrict the benefits of the 1960 Act to "passive" income, Section 856 (c) (4) will disqualify the trust for any taxable year in which 30 per cent or more of its gross income is derived from the sale of (a) stock or securities held for less than six months, and (b) real property (including interests in real property,[13] held for less than four years (unless as a result of involuntary conversion). This requirement is somewhat like, but more strict than, that of Section 851 (b) (3), which disqualifies a mutual fund if 30 per cent or more of its gross income is from sales of stock or securities held for less than three months. As in the case of the mutual funds,[14] the tentative regulations under the 1960 Act[15] provide that losses may not be netted with gains in computing the percentage of gross income derived from such sales.

(5) *Profit sharing with tenant.* — Other provisions designed to hold the conduit tax treatment to passive investment income disqualify rents received from a tenant whose rent is measured by his net profits (not gross receipts) [16] or received from a tenant if the trust has a 10 per cent or more interest in the stock, assets or net profits of the tenant.[17]

(6) *Property management and services to tenant.* — Also to restrict the benefits to passive investment income, the trust must turn over to an "independent contractor" (a term hereinafter discussed in more detail) the actual management of rental properties and the supplying of services to tenants.

---

[13] Under Sec. 856 (c) (6), the term "interests in real property" includes fee ownership and co-ownership of land and improvements and of leaseholds, but excludes mineral, gas and oil royalty interests. See, below, as to effect of local law in definition of "real property."

[14] Regs. 1.851-2 (b).

[15] Tentative Regs. Sec. 1.856-2 (c) (2) (iv).

[16] Code Sec. 856 (d) (1).

[17] Code Sec. 856 (d) (2).

This is to insure that income derived from these operational sources will be taxable.

Aside from these variations, the 1960 Act follows substantially the same pattern as Sections 851-855 of the 1954 Code relating to the mutual funds. A REIT which meets the act's requirements and conditions and which distributes 90 per cent or more of its "real estate investment trust taxable income" during the taxable year[18] will be taxed only on the amounts retained. "Real estate investment trust income" is computed by making the same adjustment to taxable income as in the case of the mutual funds, namely:[19]

(1) Capital gains are excluded. If distributed, they are taxed at capital gain rates to the shareholders.[20]

(2) The deduction for dividends received by the trust is now allowable.

(3) The Section 561 deduction for dividends paid is computed without regard to capital gains.

(4) The computation of tax on change of annual accounting period, under Section 443(b) shall not apply.

(5) Net operating loss deductions under Section 172 are not allowable.

The computation of net income and of the percentage distributed requires a most conservative approach by the trust. High mortgages, calling for substantial principal payments, can cause difficulty, since payments on the principal debt are not deductible. Also, depreciation deductions, though determined in the utmost good faith, may be reduced to such an extent on audit (when it is likely to be too late to make

---

[18] Dividends declared before the due date of the return and paid within 12 months after the close of the taxable year have the same tax consequences to the trust as if they had been paid during the taxable year, but are taxable to beneficiaries in the year received by them. Code Sec. 858.

[19] Code Sec. 857(b).

[20] If retained by the trust, its net long term capital gain is taxed at 25 per cent.

further qualifying distributions) that less than 90 per cent will have been paid out. The penalty is a 52 per cent tax. The Treasury has been asked to provide by regulation that a change in depreciation deductions taken in good faith shall not have this disastrous effect. In any event, the trustees should make sure that no doubtful deduction item is of sufficient size to reduce the distributions below the 90 per cent. Another suggestion would be to enter into an advance agreement, under Section 167(d) of the Internal Revenue Code, on depreciation rates.

Other Detailed Provisions

Determination of Status.[21]—The trust must, throughout its taxable year, meet the requirements that:

(a) It be managed by one or more trustees;

(b) It have transferable shares of beneficial interest;

(c) It be an organization which would otherwise be taxed as an association;

(d) It hold no property primarily for sale to customers.[22]

The tentative regulations prohibit any power of control over the management of the trust in the shareholders of the trust, "other than the right to elect trustees."[23] The evident purpose is to limit the application of the statute to those entities which are recognized as trusts rather than as partnerships under the common law tests of certain states.[24] Ironically, some states having jurisdiction over the sale of securities, in promulgating regulations concerning REITs, are requiring an increase in shareholder rights apparently

---

21 Code Sec. 856(d).

22 If the trust has an interest in a partnership which holds property for sale, Section 1.856-3(g) of the tentative regulations treat the trust as owning its allocable part of such property for the same purpose.

23 Tentative Regs. Sec. 856(d)(1).

24 See footnote 46.

beyond that permitted by the tentative Treasury regulations. In California, for example, the regulations of the Commissioner of Corporations, effective May 17, 1961, require annual election of trustees by the shareholders, and provide for termination of the trust at any time by a majority of the shareholders, and prohibit any change in the declaration of trust without the vote or written consent of such majority. It is at least questionable whether such powers in the shareholders will square with the Treasury regulations. However, a California statute[25] defines a real estate investment trust as "an unincorporated trust or association which complies with or intends to comply with" the 1960 Act as presently existing or hereafter amended. Presumably, therefore, if the final Treasury regulations conflict with the May regulations of the California Commissioner of Corporations, the latter will be amended, in view of the July statute, and also since the corporation regulations conclude with a statement that the rules "are subject to exception in any case in which applicant shows that any procedure different from that set forth above . . . is necessary to comply with applicable Treasury Department regulations."

On the other hand, the requirement that the beneficial ownership be held by 100 or more persons need be met only during 335 days (or approximately 11 months) of a 12-month taxable year or during a proportionate part of a shorter taxable year.

The tentative regulations throw no light on the question of what restrictions, if any, may be placed upon the free transferability of shares. The regulations relating to "associations" provide that, while there must be "free transferability of interests," if a shareholder must first offer his shares to other members before transferring it to an outsider, this will be permitted as a "modified form of free transferability."[26] In the case of the REIT, the unrestricted right to transfer shares might seriously affect, if not destroy, the conduit type of tax treatment. Such a transfer might disqualify the trust

---

[25] Assembly Bill 2453, enacted July 20, 1961.

[26] Regs. Secs. 301.7701-2(e).

if it results in the ownership of more than 50 per cent of the shares by five or fewer individuals, under Section 856(a)(6); or it might disqualify rents if the transfer, under the attribution rules, results in the trust having an interest of 10 per cent or more in a tenant, or results in a 35 per cent common ownership of the trust and the building manager. The Treasury has under consideration a proposal that the regulations permit the trust to refuse to recognize a transfer, and to redeem shares actually transferred, if the transfer would have any of these adverse effects.

Election to be taxed as a REIT. — Like the mutual funds, the REIT, under Section 856(c)(1) must file, with its return for the first year in which it so elects, a written election to be taxed in this way. Having so elected, it may not thereafter change. The only permissible method of election is for the REIT to compute its taxable income as such in the return for the first year to which the election is applicable.[27] An existing REIT with net loss carry-overs of sufficient amount would postpone this election until the full benefit of the carry-overs is obtained.

The gross income requirements. — Under Section 856(c), there are two income tests. The first is that at least 75 per cent of the trust's gross income must be derived from what may be considered real estate investment sources, namely:

(a) Rents from real property;[28]

(b) Real estate mortgage interest;

(c) Gains from sale of real property, or interests therein, on real estate mortgages;

(d) Dividends from, and gain on sale of shares in, other qualified REITS; and

(e) Real estate tax abatements and refunds.

---

[27] Tentative Regs. Sec. 1.856-2(b).

[28] Sec. 1.856-3(g) of the tentative regulations provides in substance that if the REIT has an interest in a partnership which has real estate rental income, the REIT's share of such income shall be so treated in its hands.

The second income requirement is that at least 90 per cent of gross income must be from these real estate investment sources and dividends and other interest. As stated by the Ways and Means Committee in its report,[29] this is substantially the same as the present 90 per cent test provided for regulated investment companies by Section 851(b)(2) of the Code, except for the addition of the income from real estate sources. The net result is that at least 75 per cent of gross income must be from real estate sources; and if income from those sources is more than 75 per cent but less than 90 per cent of gross income, the difference must come from the same sources as in the case of the mutual funds, namely, dividends, interest and gains from the sale of securities.

Diversification. — Section 856(c)(5) is obviously intended to parallel the provisions of Sections 851(b)(4) and 851(d). Section 851(b)(4) disqualifies a mutual fund unless, at the close of each quarter of the taxable year, at least 50 per cent of the value of its total assets is represented by (1) cash, cash items, government securities and securities of other mutual funds; and (2) other securities, provided it may not have in this second category more than the value of five per cent of its total assets in the securities of any one issuer nor own 10 per cent or more of the stock of one issuer. In this respect, the rules relating to the REIT are that at least 75 per cent of the value of its total assets must be represented by "real estate assets,"[30] cash, cash items and government securities, and not more than 25 per cent can be represented by other securities, with the same five per cent and 10 per cent limitations.

These diversification requirements, like those of Section 851(b)(3) in the case of mutual funds, must be met at the close of each quarter of the taxable year. However, the 1960 Act parallels Section 851(d) in providing (1) that if a dis-

---

29 See footnote 10.

30 "Real estate assets" means "real property (including interests in real property and interests in mortgages on real property) and shares . . . of other real estate investment trusts which meet the requirements of this part." Sec. 856(c)(6)(B). See below as to effect of local law on definition of "real property."

crepancy between the trust's various investments and these requirements does not result from the acquisition of property during the quarter-year in question, the trust will not lose its status because of such discrepancy; and (2) the trust otherwise will have 30 days after the close of that quarter to cure the discrepancy.

The term "real estate assets," as has been noted, includes shares in other qualified REITs. In dealing with the diversification requirements the tentative regulations state[31] that if Trust Z owns shares of Trust Y, these may be included in Z's real estate assets at the end of any given quarter if, at that time, Y is a qualified REIT, but that if Y ceases to be a qualified REIT "at any time during the taxable year" Z may not include Y's shares as real estate assets (for purposes of the diversification test) "as of the close of any quarter of such taxable year as long as the disqualification exists." Since Y might become disqualified on a number of grounds, without Z's knowledge, wisdom would dictate that Z limit its holdings of Y shares to a point where the disqualification of those shares as "real estate assets" cannot endanger Z's ability to meet the diversification requirements.

The tentative regulations do not define the term "total assets." Clarification is needed as to the treatment of property subject to a mortgage, or to a tax lien or a mechanic's lien. The statutory language does not indicate an intention to count only the net assets, and a net asset interpretation would subject the trust to the undue burden of numerous recomputations throughout the year to determine such matters as whether the arrival of the real estate tax lien date in a particular state will automatically put the trust in possible violation of the diversification rules.

The definition of "rents from real property."[32] — As already mentioned, one of the basic requirements for qualification of a REIT for the conduit tax treatment is that, both for the 75 per cent and the 90 per cent income tests, only "rents

---

[31] Sec. 1.856-3(f).

[32] Code Section 856(d).

from real property," *as defined in the statute,* may be counted. There are three variations from dictionary definitions of the quoted language.

Profit-sharing and proprietary interest in tenant. — If the determination of the amount payable by the tenant depends, in whole or in part, on "the income or profits derived by any person from such property," such amount will not be counted as "rents from real property." However, the statute expressly provides that this taint does not attach to rents based upon a percentage of "receipts or sales," as distinguished from a profit-sharing arrangement. If the trust owns, directly or indirectly,[33] 10 per cent or more of the stock of a corporate tenant, or an interest of 10 per cent or more in the assets or net profits of a noncorporate tenant, rents received from that tenant will not qualify as "rents from real property."

The tentative regulations have been criticized as going outside the statute in these respects:

(a) If the prime tenant sublets any part of the premises to another on a profit-sharing basis, the prime tenant's rents (though having no relation to his profits or income) will be disqualified.[34]

(b) Where the tenant pays a fixed rent, but agrees to pay additional amounts measured by his profits if the profits exceed a stated amount, the fixed rent is disqualified whether or not the "overage" develops.[35]

(c) An allocable part of the prime tenant's rents are disqualified, even though the trust has no interest in the tenant, if there is a subletting of part of the premises to a subtenant in which the trust has a 10 per cent interest.[36]

If not changed, these regulations would impose on the trustees the burden of prohibiting subletting until they could

---

[33] See discussion, below, of attribution rules applicable in determining ownership.

[34] Tentative Regs. Sec. 1.856-4(b) (1).

[35] See footnote 34.

[36] Tentative Regs. Sec. 1.856-4(b) (2).

review all the provisions of subleases and investigate the relationship between the subtenant and the shareholders of the trust. Such a construction seems highly inconsistent with the statutory aim that the trustees have only a passive relationship to the trust property. One remarkable aspect of the tentative regulations is the use of the example of a corporate subtenant in which the trust has a 15 per cent ownership. Such a percentage would violate the diversification rule (discussed above), under Section 856(c)(5). As a practical matter, therefore, this regulation could have application only to cases where the trust owns exactly 10 per cent of the subtenant's stock. If it owned less, Section 856(d)(2) would not apply; and if it owned more, the trust would be disqualified by Section 856(c)(4).

Services to tenants and management or operation of property by the "independent contractor."—Section 856(d) (3) also disqualifies as "rents from real property" any amount received with respect to property if the trust "furnishes or renders services to the tenants of such property, or manages or operates such property, other than through an independent contractor from whom the trust itself does not derive or receive any income." The term "independent contractor" is, for the purposes of this provision, given a clear definition, as meaning:

(A) A person who does not own, directly or indirectly, more than 35 per cent of the shares of the trust; or

(B) If a corporation, not more than 35 per cent of its stock (or if not a corporation not more than 35 per cent of the interest in its assets or net profits) is owned, directly or indirectly, by persons owning 35 per cent or more of the trust's shares.

The rationale of this restriction is reasonably clear. If the same persons had a controlling interest in the management company and in the trust, the temptation would be to hold down the taxable income of the management company, by inadequate charges, thus swelling the net income of the trust which would be tax-free in its hands if distributed to shareholders. The tentative regulations, however, contain a provision which has been criticized by practically all those who appeared at the hearings, as being an indirect and unauthorized limitation on this definition of "independent contractor." In defining the term "trustee," these regulations say:[37]

"Furthermore, a trustee of a real estate investment trust may not be an officer or employee of, or have any direct or indirect proprietary interest in, any independent contractor which furnishes or renders services to the tenants of the trust property or manages or operates such property."

Critics of this provision of the tentative regulations point out that the term "independent contractor" is a term of art, specifically defined in the statute; that there is nothing in the statute which prohibits connection between a trustee and a contractor which meets that statutory definition; and that this restriction is, in effect, therefore, an unauthorized attempt to regulate the trustee's activities. It is to be noted that, when Congress dealt with the regulation of the mutual funds, it restricted the connection between investment advisers and the funds only to the extent of providing that not more than 60 per cent of the fund's directors could have an interest in the advisory group,[38] which offers a precedent if and when regulation of REITs in this respect is deemed necessary. As a practical matter, investors in the shares of REITs would expect some, if not all, of the trustees to be experienced in the management of rental properties. If, in addition, one or more of the trustees were active in the management of the trust properties, this should be an added protection to the investor, as some assurance that the property would be managed intelligently. If such a trustee were to attempt either tax avoidance by having the management company undercharge for its services, or over-reaching by charging too much for such services, the Commissioner has the remedy at hand under Section 482.[39]

---

[37] Tentative Regs. Sec. 1.856-1(d)(1).

[38] 15 USCA 80a-10(a).

[39] See GCM 2856, VII-2 CB 128.

The provisions as to rendition of services to tenants and as to management and operation of rental property by the independent contractor were stated by the report of the Ways and Means Committee[40] to be designed to assure that the bulk of the trust's income "is from passive income sources and not from the active conduct of a trade or business." The committee further said:

"A second restriction, intended to limit the definition of rents from real property to those of a passive nature, excludes from the definition amounts where the trust directly furnishes or renders services to the tenants or manages or operates the property. However, the bill permits these services, or management or operation of the property to be provided through an independent contractor. The independence of the contractor is assured by providing that: The trust may not receive any income from the contractor; the contractor may not own more than a 35 per cent interest in the trust; and not more than 35 per cent of the stock (or voting power) of a corporate contractor (or interest in the assets and profits if not a corporation) can be held by a person or persons holding a 35 per cent or greater interest in the trust."

The tentative regulations, above-mentioned, have been widely criticized as imposing unjustified restrictions on the right of the trustees to provide such services and property management "through an independent contractor," in the following respects:

(1) The regulations provide[41] that maintenance and repairs of the trust property, the cost of which is deductible under Section 162, must be "controlled and paid for by" the independent contractor, which indicates that the decision as to what repairs, if any, should be made is for the contractor and that he must bear the expense. The result would inevitably be that the contractor would raise his charges by an amount to insure himself against necessary but unforeseeable repairs, and would be in a position to refuse to make necessary

---

40 See footnote 10.
41 Tentative Regs. Sec. 1.856(4)(b)(3).

repairs, permitting the property to deteriorate without regard to the interests of the tenant or the owner.

(2) The statute says that the independent contractor must be one "from whom the trust itself does not derive or receive any income." The clear intent is that the trust may not have any proprietary interest in the contractor or any right to share in the contractor's profits, which are derived from managing the property and rendering services (such as elevator operation and cleaning) to tenants. The tentative regulations have been criticized as going beyond this concept in two respects: In the first place, they provide[42] that the trust may not receive any rent from the contractor, which means that the contractor may not be a tenant of the trust, even though he pays the going rate for space occupied. This provision appears to have no statutory basis, nor does there appear to be any policy reason for it. Furthermore, the same section of the tentative regulations contains the following somewhat ambiguous provision:

"If any services are performed for tenants, such services must be performed by, and the charges therefore (whether such charges are separately paid or included in the amount paid as rent) must be included in the income of an independent contractor."

Since rents are never broken down between the charge for space occupied and the charge for elevator and/or janitor service customarily supplied to tenants, a requirement that there be such a segregation, with the portion attributable to elevator and janitor service going to the contractor and the balance to the trust would be unrealistic and unworkable.

The customary and universal type of arrangement between the owner of rental property and a truly independent property manager should meet the letter and spirit of these statutory requirements. That arrangement is to pay the manager either a fixed fee or, more often, a percentage of the gross rents, with the owner having the sole discretion as to repairs, upkeep and improvements for which he pays.

---

[42] Tentative Regs. Sec. 1.856-4(b)(3).

Attribution rules. — *The Personal Holding Company Test.*
— Section 856(a) (6) provides that a REIT, among other
things, is one "which would not be a personal holding company (as defined in Section 542) if all its gross income constituted personal holding company income (as defined in
Section 543)." The committee report translates this involved
language into basic English, namely, that "no five individuals
may directly or indirectly own more than 50 per cent of the
trust." Even this is an over-simplification. The ownership
restriction in question (Section 542) applies only to ownership
"at any time during the last half of the taxable year," and
Section 544 spells out what is meant by "directly or indirectly
own." Under the rules there laid down:

(1) Stock[43] owned by a corporation, partnership, estate
or trust is considered as being owned proportionately by the
shareholders, partners, or beneficiaries;

(2) An individual is deemed to own stock owned by his
brothers, sisters, spouse, ancestors, lineal descendants and
partners.

Rents from real property. — As pointed out above, ownership by the trust of an interest of 10 per cent or more in the
stock, assets or net profits of a tenant will disqualify the rents
for conduit treatment, and a common ownership of more than
35 per cent of the trust and the "independent contractor" will
disqualify rents from the property managed by such contractor. Section 856(d) (3) further provides that the determination of ownership of these interests shall be governed by
the attribution rules of Section 318(a), with one modification,
with this result: [44]

---

[43] The term "stock" includes shares in an association. 1954 Code
Sec. 7701(a) (7).

[44] This is intended as a mere outline of these attribution rules,
as a complete discussion of them is outside the scope of this paper.
However, these rules, including the "double attribution" under Sec.
318(a)(4), need careful examination in connection with the organization and operation of REITs.

(1) An individual is considered as owning the stock of his spouse, children, grandchildren, and parents (but not brothers or sisters);

(2) Shares owned by a partnership or estate are considered as owned proportionately by partners or beneficiaries; and shares owned by a partner or beneficiary are considered as owned by the partnership or estate;

(3) Shares owned by a trust are considered as owned by the beneficiaries in proportion to their actuarial interests in the trust; shares owned by a beneficiary, unless his interest is a remote contingent interest (that is, five per cent or less of the value of the trust property), are considered as owned by the trust; and

(4) If a person owns 10 per cent or more of a corporation's stock, he is considered as owning the same percentage of shares owned by the corporation; and the corporation is considered as owning his shares.

The impact of local law. — *Definition of real property.* — As has been noted, the 1960 Act defines "real estate assets" and states that the term "interests in real property" includes certain things, but does not define "real property." A definition is of importance in connection with the determination of what are rents from real property and for application of the diversification rules. The tentative regulations[45] have this to say:

"(d) *Real property.* The term 'real property' means land or improvements thereon, such as buildings or other inherently permanent structures thereon (including items which are structural components of such buildings or structures). In addition, the term 'real property' includes interests in real property and interests in mortgages on real property. The term 'mortgages on real property' includes mortgages on leaseholds of land or improvements thereon. Local law definitions will not be controlling for purposes of determining the meaning of the term 'real property' as used in Section 856

---

[45] Tentative Regs. Sec. 1.856-3(d).

74

and the regulations thereunder. The term includes, for example, the wiring in a building, plumbing systems, central heating or central air conditioning machinery, pipes, or ducts, or other items which are structural components of a building or other permanent structure. The term does not include assets accessory to the operation of a business, such as machinery, printing press, transportation or office equipment, refrigerators, individual air conditioning units, grocery counters, furnishings of a motel, hotel or office building, etc., even though such assets may be termed fixtures under local law."

This provision has been criticized as inviting litigation over whether a particular fixture or structure is to be treated as real property, and, if not, the method of allocating values and rents; as to whether the examples of "structural components" is sufficiently comprehensive; and, more particularly, as ignoring the settled law of the situs as to fixtures which are to be treated as part of the realty. Since local law is governing in other areas, it is hoped that the regulations, in their final form, will provide a clearer and more practical definition, that taxpayers will understand and with which they can operate without unnecessary difficulty.

The status of the trust under local law. — While the so-called Massachusetts business trust has attained a definite status under the laws of some states, other state laws raise substantial problems, entirely apart from tax considerations.[46]

For example, in some states, the statutes appear to limit the creation of express trusts to specific situations, not including the purposes of a REIT. In others, the beneficiaries are held liable as partners, in some cases depending on the degree of control exercised over the trustees by beneficiaries. The tentative regulations under the 1960 Act[47] provide that an

---

[46] An excellent analysis of the laws of the various states appears in the July 1961 issue of *The Business Lawyer,* published by the Section of Corporation, Banking and Business Law of the American Bar Association. However, that article was written before adoption of some of the state enabling acts hereinafter mentioned, and does not discuss their effect.

[47] Tentative Regs. Sec. 1-856-1 (d) (1).

organization which is considered a limited partnership cannot qualify as a REIT.

In other states, the life of such a trust is limited to a specific term of years, or to lives of persons in being plus 21 years.

Since passage of the 1960 Act, in a number of states where the law as to the status of REITs and their beneficiaries was either hostile or uncertain, laws have been enacted to permit their operation in order to take advantage of the federal tax provisions. Among these are the states of California, Georgia, Kansas, New York, South Carolina, Tennessee and Texas. The State of Washington adopted such a statute even prior to the 1960 Act.

It is beyond the scope of this paper to analyze these statutes or the laws of other states in this regard. However, it is obvious that a REIT should not be created in, or acquire property in, any state without a preliminary study of the local law as affecting its status and operations and the liability, if any, of its shareholders for the REIT's obligations.

Reprinted by special permission of author and the publisher of *TAXES, The Tax Magazine,* Vol. 39 (December, 1961).

REAL ESTATE COMPANIES
AND INVESTMENT TRUSTS

By Dr. Ira U. Cobleigh,

Enterprise Economist

A swift summary of some of the features and things
to look for in realty company shares offering generous
tax sheltered incomes, and in the newer real estate trusts
which are rapidly gaining popularity.

Since 1950, a major American economic phenomenon has
been the widespread investment in real estate for income
and gain by private investors, implemented by syndications.
Syndications, simply stated, are partnerships, usually divided
among general and limited partners. The public buys limited
partnerships which permit holders to share in the tax sheltered
income, and possible resale gains, resulting from ownership or
leasehold of specific real property. Syndications have, however, certain drawbacks. Title to these limited partnerships is
difficult to transfer. Further, there is no broad or active
market for participations if the holder wishes or needs to sell;
and usually there's no diversification.

Syndicates Become Corporations

Syndicate participations, moreover, have proved "too
rich for the blood" of many individuals, since they commonly
require an outlay of not less than $5,000, and often $20,000
or $25,000. Thus, there arose a broad demand for the same
investment commodity in smaller, more negotiable, units
for the average investor. As a result, many of these syndicate
groups have incorporated, exchanging partnership interests
for share certificates. The resulting corporations, in a number
of cases have made public offering of their shares at popular
prices. These issues have been exceedingly well received,
enjoyed active trading markets, and, in certain instances,

increased in value by from 25% to 200% over their original subscription prices.

More than 150 realty companies sold stock in 1961, and today there are over 280 publicly owned real estate companies. The consequent demand for well situated income producing real estate has caused substantial advances in the price of urban and suburban apartments, office buildings, etc. — so much so that rather than pay dearly for older buildings, many realty firms themselves, have been assembling choice lottage and building new structures thereon.

Class A and Class B Shares

In many cases the equity capitalization of these real estate companies has been in the form of Class A and Class B common stocks. The Class A stock is the issue the public buys. Customarily, it has a priority as to dividends and becomes actively traded, either over-the-counter or on an exchange. The "Class B" stock is usually closely held and represents voting control. There are generally, however, specific corporate provisions whereby this Class B stock may, after a given date, be converted into Class A certificates.

A popular practice seems to be to pay monthly dividends to holders of Class A shares. These dividends may provide current yields of 7% or more, and are derived from net income and far more importantly, from payout of the "cash flow" generated by depreciation allowances. Since much of this distribution is a return of capital, these current dividends are largely exempt from Federal Income Tax.

Representative issues, falling in line with the pattern, just outlined would include the Class A stocks of First Republic Corp., Futterman Corp., Glickman Corp., Income Properties Inc., Walter J. Schneider Co., Tenney Corp., H. R. Weissberg Corp., United Investors, Wolf Corp. (This is just a random list, without any recommendation or endorsement intended.)

Factors to Consider

In consideration of such securities, investors should keep in mind the following points:

(1) Depreciation allowances do not continue indefnitely. Many real estate companies have come into possession of their properties after a substantial part of depreciation has already been used. (The cost bases used by the syndicate partnership members become their bases when they make a tax-free exchange of assets for stock.) Most syndicates use the "declining balance" method of depreciation, which quickly depreciates the carried value of property, and results in much smaller depreciation charges after a few years.

(2) Corporations are subject to 52% Federal Income Tax, so when depreciation allowances run low, the amounts available for distribution to stockholders may be reduced.

(3) While corporate real estate enterprises may substantially supplement their revenues from income producing properties by trading, buying and selling realty, there is nothing permanent about profits from this source, and they may dry up when the real estate market becomes less active or buoyant.

(4) Corporate real estate enterprises often build new structures. This involves a certain amount of risk as it may take two years to construct a high rise office or apartment building, and market and rental conditions may undergo major changes locally, regionally or nationally during such a period.

Further, most Class B shares of real estate companies become convertible into Class A shares within three years after issuance, and subsequent conversions of "B" into "A" could come at a time when depreciation charge-offs have become reduced, and a larger percentage of corporate income is subject to Federal Tax. Consideration of some of the foregoing points may prove useful in your evaluation of marketable real estate equities.

Real Estate Investment Trusts

A Federal Law, PL 86-779, effective Jan. 1, 1961, defines a real estate investment trust as an association or unincorporated trust with transferable shares, having one or more trustees. A major benefit enjoyed by such a trust is that, if it distributes 90% of its taxable ordinary income, it pays no tax on the distributed earnings. The law further specifies that such a trust (1) cannot deal in real estate as a business; (2) must hold real estate and/or mortgages for investment; (3) must derive less than 30% of its gross income from capital gains on real estate held for less than four years; (4) must not permit the organizer (who proposes to be manager) of a trust to own over 35% of the shares, or voting control of the trust.

From the above, you will note that trusts do not trade in the real estate market and are not designed for speculative profits. They do provide very definite tax advantages, since if a trust uses accelerated depreciation to cover cash flow, ordinary income when reported will not be taxable to the trust, and shareholders' income will not be reduced by corporate income taxes.

Real estate trusts usually have but one class of stock. The trustee has great legal responsibility which insures that the trust will be prudently and conservatively managed. The declaration of trust is an important document which prospective investors should examine. Look for the powers given to, and restrictions placed on, trustees and the provisions for dividend distribution.

In appraisal of a real estate investment trust consider:

(1) Trustees
(2) Promoters
(3) Limitation of trustees fees
(4) How soon income will start
(5) Type and quality of property in the trust. (Many trusts start either without any properties, or with properties to be constructed, and income deferred for a year or more).

Some 20 real estate investment trusts were formed in 1961 with nine offering their common stocks to the public.

There seems to be little doubt that this type of security will become widely popular among investors in 1962. Particularly attractive would be a trust, completely packaged, with income starting immediately. If such a trust could deliver a tax sheltered return of around 7%, it might well prove a rewarding investment with valid prospects for price appreciation. In today's economy, the investor has two things to contend with — high taxes and fear of inflation. The real estate investment trust gives him assured protection against both of these eroding factors.

Reprinted by permisssion of *Commercial and Financial Chronicle*, 110 Wall Street, New York, N.Y. 10005, Vol. 195 (January 11, 1962).

MORE ROOM AT THE TOP?

Real Estate Investment Trusts Have Come to Wall Street and Main Street

By J. Richard Elliott, Jr.

BOSTON — Real Estate Investment Trust of America, which can trace its roots in this city back to 1886 — and today has $35 million worth of properties tucked away in places like St. Paul, Kansas City, Hialeah, Fla., and Walnut Creek, Calif. — is an organization which can boost a unique record of achievement. Known as "REITA" by friends Down East, the trust is the biggest still intact of many similar New England groups which, over a century and more, have provided much of the capital to build the great cities of the West. It also is the only company of its kind with shares listed on a major stock exchange (the American), where they are trading at 20% above the price (then 30 time earnings) at which a secondary offering of stock was made only last summer. For the fiscal year ending next May, finally, REITA will post another enviable statistic or two. Because of a new Federal law, which frees realty trusts from the corporate income tax if they distribute at least 90% of earnings to shareholders, the conservative old firm should be able to report profits (and pay dividends) at more than double the rate of a year ago.

Trusts Busting Out

The law, P.L. 86-779 — the Real Estate Investment Trust Act of 1960 — happens to be the hottest piece of realty legislation to come down the pike in many a year, and not alone for its impact on the old-line "Massachusetts trusts" which long had lobbied for it. Far more significantly, P.L. 86-779 has started a parade of new real estate trusts which now are breaking financial ground all over the country. At latest count, over 40 have been formed. Like REITA, they offer to invest in high-yielding, prime urban properties, leases or liens,

82

and in similar fashion their shares are being snapped up by the public. Unlike REITA, but all the more remarkable, the majority have been going into the equity markets even before taking their first plunge in the marts where real estate is bought and sold. Thus investors, in effect, have written them a blank check for funds that already mount to nearly $300 million. Nor is the end in sight.

Boulevard or Bumpy Road?

Such enthusiasm in Wall Street is high tribute to the real estate industry's latest glamour avenue of mass investment — one that seems to pick up where the recently popular syndicates and realty corporations leave off (Barron's December 26, 1960). On the whole, the trust form is a less speculative means of capitalizing realty income than the others, and its returns on invested capital, at a time when traditional yields on property are meager, promise to be among the lowest of all. Obviously, then, it has become a popular vehicle for promoters. Finally, real estate trusts offer small investors a chance to share in the equity of prime properties, this time in the attractive form of the mutual fund.

For all its seemingly conservative appeal, however, the real estate trust may contain some hidden pitfalls for the public. For one thing the rules under which it will operate — necessarily detailed regulations to implement the Act — still are being drawn up by Treasury Dept. and Internal Revenue lawyers, who have been trapped in technicalities for over a year. Meanwhile, tentative regulations proposed by the U.S. and some states, if not revised, could be fatally restrictive. Second, owing partly to this delay, few funds have dared to convert many assets into anything more rewarding than Government bonds. Besides keeping them oddly unpropertied, and postponing the day when they can be accurately evaluated by investors, this status actually keeps them from legally qualifying as tax-exempt realty trusts.

Potentially most jarring of all is the increasingly tight supply and high cost of prime realty today. For the new trusts are coming on the scene as big buyers at a time when the real estate bull market seems to be approaching its inevitable top.

While their equity positions may be strong, they are not protected against a loss in property values. In a real sense, their risks — which they must run, having little choice except to buy — grow as fast as they themselves do. Indeed, the pressures of the situation already are producing a few questionable deals. For his part, the investor will be well advised to regard the whole field with something less than implicit trust.

Origin of the Species

To begin with, just what is a real estate investment trust? Actually, promoters have developed several varieties, but all trace their origins to a device which first came into use in New England during the nineteenth century. Private Boston capital sought a way to capitalize on the industrial revolution through investment in urban property. A corporation, however, could not then own realty unless it was an integral part of the business; only a company making adhesives, for example, could own the glue factory.

What soon evolved was the Massachusetts real estate trust — a form of beneficial ownership providing direct distribution of rental income to transferable shares. At first, these trusts were limited in scope, but before long participation was extended to the general public. As funds burgeoned, the soaring prices of downtown Boston realty sent trustees scurrying westward after the new railroads. Eventually, New England capital flowed through trusts into such fast-rising outposts as Chicago, Omaha and Denver.

Downed by the Levy

The trusts remained a dominant influence in realty investment until the Great Depression, when the courts suddenly declared them taxable as corporations. In the inflationary 'forties, the new impost cut deeply into earnings and stymied expansion. Through liquidations and mergers, most old-line Massachusetts companies fell by the wayside. For those left, the traditional appeal to investors was outweighed by both tax-sheltered realty syndicates and, even more, by the mushrooming mutual funds which the Investment Company Act of 1940 had made tax-exempt. Lobbyists for the realty trust demanded equal legislative treatment. After several false starts, such a bill was signed by President Eisenhower in 1960.

What the Law Allows

In brief, this complex amendment to the Internal Revenue Code defines a real estate investment trust as an unincorporated association managed by one or more trustees, having transferable shares of beneficial interest and organized in a form which would otherwise be subject to the 52% corporate tax. Further, there must be at least 100 beneficial owners, no five combined holding more than 50% of the shares. It must be "passive" — that is, the operation of properties must be turned over to an independent management company, in which no group of trustees or shareholders has 35% control. The operating firm (and affiliates) in turn cannot own over 35% of the trust shares.

Thus organized, the realty fund still does not qualify until 75% of its gross income is derived from real estate holdings. Such income can be rent, mortgage interest, capital gains from the sale of properties, dividends from other realty trusts and refunds and abatements or real estate taxes. However, rentals must come from properties not managed by the trust and in which no tenant is 10%-owned by the trust. What's more, only 30% of a trusts' revenues can come from capital gains on securities held less than six months or real estate held less than four years.

The rest of revenues may be derived from non-realty holdings, but 90% in all must come either from estate or from dividends, interest and stock gains. Thus up to 10% of revenues may be derived from any source at all. Finally, 75% of assets also must be in real estate equity, mortgages, cash or Government securities. The balance can be invested anywhere, so long as no more than 5% is in the stock of any one issuer, and the trust holds no more than 10% of the voting shares of any other company.

90% Payout a Must

The key requirement deals with dividends. By paying out at least 90% of net income to shareholders over a given year, the trust becomes exempt from corporate taxes on that amount. The tax is due only on the 10% (or less) of earnings retained. Presumably, more than 90% will be paid out by any prudent trust. For later readjustments (of allowable depreciation, for example) by IRS agents could drop the ratio below 90% — in which case the trust would become retroactively liable for full taxation. Also, only the trust pays taxes on capital gains retained for reinvestment, while only the investor pays the levy if the gains are distributed. (By contrast, a realty corporation must pay the gains tax, and shareholders must include net distributions as ordinary income.)

A trust's income and dividends, finally, enjoy the same tax shelter as other realty investments. That is, accelerated depreciation may be taken on newly-acquired properties (writing off 150% of the straight-line charge in the first year, less thereafter), to provide a larger cash flow than is reported as earnings. The trust even can show no earnings at all, as many realty companies attempt to do, and pay any amount of dividends out of cash flow; however, a trust cannot carry losses forward or back.

Accelerated depreciation on real estate, it should be noted, is under attack both in Washington and in some sectors of the industry — as a loophole, on the one hand, and a major cause of trafficking in realty, on the other. The omnibus tax reform bill which the Administration will offer Congress in the next session seems certain to include some revision affecting this shelter. In any event, to the extent that depreciation exceeds debt amortization (excluding interest) that portion of an investor's dividend is considered a tax-free return of capital. For promoters, it makes possible the generation of high cash "yields" from a thin equity capitalization — higher and thinner when the depreciation is accelerated.

While syndicates have thrived on this procedure, the 1960 Act tends to discourage trusts from taking too thin an equity position. Because 90% of reportable income already is committed, amortization costs, which also must be met out of taxable profits, are likely to be held down. The best way is to keep the mortgage itself low, automatically making equity relatively high. However, doing this virtually assures that the trust will adopt accelerated depreciation, in order to produce enough cash to meet all the payments — for in a typical venture, amortization alone frequently accounts for half of gross revenues. If depreciation is used to pay dividends, of course, it is lost as a means of improving property; hence, when the time comes for extensive renovation, the trust — supposedly a long-term investment medium — may be forced to borrow or sell more shares.

Whom Do You Trust?

So much for the law. Now let us see what this Act of Congress has bred. In Wall Street, it created quite a stir as analysts sought to discover which existing companies might qualify. Shares of existing trusts, like REITA, abruptly doubled in price. However, almost every stock that represented any sizable realty assets — syndicates, hotels, shopping centers, construction firms, even railroads, retail chains and mining concerns — also was appraised seriously as a potential trust. As it now turns out, it will be a cold day on Capitol Hill when such wholesale conversion to the tax-exempt trust form goes unchallenged, for the very notion thwarts the intent of Congress; the idea was to spur mass public investment, not to create new loopholes in the Federal tax code.

To be sure, some realty corporations may find a measure of tax relief under the present law, or under its contemplated liberalization. Most have studied the matter carefully. Says Jerome Deutsch, vice president of Realty Equities Corp.: "It could provide a haven for multi-propertied firms, where depreciation and 'losses' may be running out and cash will soon be scarce. In our own case, though, it's useless, since we're geared for quick turnover." The Kratter Corp., usually considered the syndicate-corporation likeliest to exploit it, now says: "We have nothing in mind on real estate trusts."

Room for Sheraton?

Sheraton Corp. of America, the hotel chain, is the company insiders — and outsiders — have speculated longest about. President Ernest Henderson, who often had said that Sheraton would use the device, announced at last year's annual meeting that the delay over regulations had forced his company to give up any such plans. However, it now can be reported that Sheraton has not given up. According to Ernest Henderson III, the treasurer, "the company may test on a modest scale the possibility of a spin-off of some hotel properties into a trust."

Added the president's son, in a recent interview: "We probably will make up a package that would cost us the least in capital gains taxes — perhaps three hotels, of varying financial strength, worth $10 to $20 million together. Sheraton would remain the operator on new five-year leases. Except for providing us with capital, though, there would be no direct benefits to Sheraton. Tax-exemption would be for the trust alone. Shares would be sold at less than full market value of the trust's assets, so the return on investment would be a little better than today. Our stockholders would get rights, but their proportionate ownership would come way down to stay within the law. Timing won't depend on regulations from Washington so much as on conditions in the money market. This will be an experiment, but not one in how to lose money." If it succeeds, other hotel-keepers undoubtedly will follow suit. Says a Hilton officer: "When regulations are issued, you can be sure they will be studied here very judiciously."

Hubbub in Hub

All this speculation, of course, has not totally obscured the bevy of new realty trusts which has emerged almost overnight. Experts had guessed that around $100 million might be raised in response to the 1960 Act in the first year or so; the estimate seemed high. Yet barely 13 months later, $200 million in trust shares are in the hands of the public and another $100 million are in registration. They range from the old-line Massachusetts trusts with a new lease on life, like REITA, to some whose assets are still in Treasury bills.

At the time of its $10 million offering last June, the big Boston trust owned 51 parcels in 13 states, carried on the books at a depreciated cost of $22.5 million, of which only $6.3 million was represented by mortgage debt. The properties — comprising much new construction, and even unimproved land, but no residential, motel or hotel buildings — are managed by a Boston firm from which all four insider-trustees resigned in 1960.

REITA is ultra-conservative by realty standards. "Our policy is to seek to increase the underlying value of our assets through reinvestment of depreciation," a trustee says. Last year, dividends totaling $724,312 were paid out to shareholders, even though reportable income, after taxes, came to only $485,629. The difference, however, was supplied by an overstatement of taxes due, rather than by accelerated depreciation. Cash flow was over $1 million.

Of the proceeds from its offering, REITA has invested about half in a Fort Lauderdale, Fla., office building and a California shopping center. The rest remains in Governments. "There is difficulty," says a trustee, "finding investments that meet our policy as well as the requirements of the Act." For the six months ended last November, REITA reported income of $564,179 vs. $267,827 the year before, equal to 44 cents a share (on nearly 1.3 million shares outstanding) vs. 36 cents (on 741,000 shares). However, this still does not reflect exemption from taxes, which REITA's cautious trustees refuse to include until Treasury regulations come out.

If the trust does only as well in the current six months — and almost any realty investment from the remaining $400,000 in new capital will upgrade profits — its real earnings for the full year (allowing for the exemption) would surpass $2 million, or some $1.60 per share, and cash flow would exceed $2.00 a share. (Net last year came to 66 cents a share, on the fewer shares then outstanding.) The current quarterly dividend of 30 cents, which will be boosted to comply with the 90% rule, if need be, compares with a quarterly payment a year ago of 18 cents.*

Bradley's Boost

A similar record is in the making for the only other old-line Massachusetts trust of any size, Bradley Real Estate Trust. If anything, Bradley is more circumspect than REITA, for it so far has resisted any impulse to invade the equity market with a new offering. (Slightly over 1 million shares are outstanding, trading over-the-counter at about $7.50 bid.) "There will be none from us," a trustee says, "until we see those regulations." Mortgage debt accounts for only one-third of Bradley's total assets.

Bradley was put together only last year from ten different trusts, some dating back to 1899. (Four other trusts under the same management were kept out of the package for tax reasons. The four, all trading over-the-counter: Business Property Associates and Commercial Property Associates, each a holding company for Bradley shares; and Wabash Avenue Trustees and Chicago Real Estate Trustees, each the owner of three buildings in Chicago.) Its latest report, for the seven months ended August 31, 1961, shows $126, 658 in capital gains (reinvested) and earnings of $184,205, or about 18 cents a share. (Bradley eliminated Federal taxes, except on the part, less than 10%, not paid out.) Although "trustees recognize that some of the present holdings should be liquidated and the proceeds reinvested where population and economic pressures hold greater promise of dynamic growth," Bradley has held off making any new deals pending issuance of the Treasury

---

*Correction — The six-month earnings figures for fiscal 1962 were stated correctly. However, these do reflect the exemption from taxes; the article said that they do not. Also, REITA has some $4 million in new capital remaining to invest, instead of $400,000. From these errors flowed some incorrect projections. Real earnings for all of 1962 will surpass $1 million, rather than $2 million, or about $1 per share instead of $1.60. Finally, the statement that the dividend will be boosted, if necessary, to comply with the 90% ratio gives an erroneous impression; actually, dividends, at the annual rate of $1.20 probably will exceed reportable earnings this year.

regulations. However, earnings have not yet reflected two properties which were being negotiated when the Act was passed and added after the merger. Including these, earnings now are at the rate of about $400,000, or almost 40 cents a share, a year — almost treble the pro-forma net, after taxes, of 1960-61.

Now arrayed alongside these old-line trusts are a host of new ones formed since the bill became law, and representing many a variation on the theme. One of the most interesting types is not an equity trust at all, but a purchaser of mortgages. Developed by veterans of the savings and loan business, such a fund will specialize in VA or FHA home mortgages and conventional construction-development loans. As such, it may yield substantially less than most realty investments, yet offer capital growth through the closest approach to an open-end mutual fund realty promoters have yet devised.

Pioneer in this field is First Mortgage Investors, a Boston-headquartered, Florida-operated venture. Last September it made an offering of 1 million shares, at $15, underwritten by Shearson, Hammill. In almost no time, the stock was bid up to $25 over-the-counter. (It has since settled down at around $19-20.) Moreover, the ink was hardly dry on the shares before another, almost identical prospectus appeared in Wall Street. Still in registration, this is an offering by Hemphill, Noyes, and Paine, Webber, Jackson & Curtis, of 1.7 million shares in newly-formed Continental Mortgage Investors. Others are said to be in the works.

As progenitor of the breed, First Mortgage Investors is unique on several counts. As a source of funds for the mortgage-banking business, it provides a one-stop service, combining the readiness of a savings-and-loan association to take VA and FHA mortgages, with the preference of banks for construction loans and that of speculative lenders for development paper. Besides supplying capital, FMI offers to provide mortgage banks with "warehousing" facilities for their paper; indeed, the trust hopes to be a working partner with local bankers while itself becoming a "banking institution on a nationwide scale."

The application of the trust form to mortgage-lending provides an investment medium substantially different from that of the Federally-chartered savings and loan, to which it may be loosely compared. Obviously, its portfolio can be more flexible than the S&Ls, which are subject to Home Loan Bank Board limits on the assets they can invest in development loans. FMI has set as its goal a portfolio divided about 50-50 between FHA-VA-insured home loans, on one hand, and development or construction loans ("meeting FHA or VA requirements") on the other. Of its $14.8 million capital, FMI so far has invested about $10.5 million, of which $8 million is in FHA-VA mortgages; and the rest in construction loans. Management hopes to invest the other $4.3 million largely in development loans. The differences among these three types of first mortgage, of course, lie in the yield: FHA-VA home loans guarantee over 5%; construction loans bear interest at about 10%, and development loans about 12%. Ideally, then, FMI would return a gross on its overall investments of 8-9%.

Also, whereas S&Ls must derive all new capital from their deposits (a source costing upwards of 4½% today) or, in the case of a stock company, sale of equity shares — and debt is limited to secured borrowings from Home Loan Banks of up to 17% of assets — the real estate trust plans to use its equity as a lever to attract long-term debt. First Mortgage Investors is about to announce lines of bank credit totaling some $25-30 million. Ultimately, management plans to issue senior debt securities, and believes it can acquire borrowed capital at a ratio to equity as high as 5-to-1 before having to sell additional shares. Within two years, it hopes to have about $60 million at work — earning perhaps 8% or more; $45 million of it borrowed at a cost of perhaps 6%, and the rest equity. Based on current rates of interest, FMI management says it can see earnings of $2.00 per share in two years. Policy will be to distribute 95% of that amount in dividends; an initial quarterly payment of around 10 to 15 cents probably will be declared next month.

Clearly, FMI is an unusual realty trust. Instead of owning an equity in high-rise, prime urban property, it holds Federally-guaranteed first-obligation paper on one-family dwellings. While property-holding trusts will be retiring their

92

mortgages and adding to their equity, FMI will be seeking an ever larger proportion of debt-to-equity capitalization. Depreciation, moreover, is not a factor; of far more concern is the rising rate of foreclosures on FHA-VA loans.

Finally, First Mortgage Investors offers a dividend reinvestment plan, by means of which it hopes in effect to pay substantially all its dividends in stock rather than cash. Any shareholder will have the option of taking dividends, and capital gains distributions, in cash, or automatically investing them in additional trust shares at prevailing market prices. In this way, FMI can comply with the Trust Act's 90% requirement, while allowing its cash earnings to be plowed back into still more assets.

One-Shot and Swap

Except for the mortgage trusts, all the new realty funds have been organized to invest directly in properties. One such type is the "one-shot" trust, formed to acquire a single building. A case in point is the $695,000 Gateside-Architect Building Trust. Organized by a group of New York syndicate promoters, Gateside Realty Co., it became effective last February when 139 shares were offered at $5,000 each. The offering was much like that of a typical syndicate because of the high share price, the single-property portfolio, and because the prospectus projected a return of 11% on invested capital. (According to the promoters, the trust actually is earning slightly more.)

The reason for organizing as a trust instead of a syndicate was to avoid any possibility of corporate tax. True, most syndicates now are exempt, since they qualify as limited partnerships, but the future of that exemption is by no means clear. Hence, Gateside determined to try the trust form as another means to the same end. No other properties will be acquired by Gateside-Architect Building Trust. Investors seeking diversification, according to the promoters, should invest in other Gateside ventures, whether syndicates or trusts.

Another variant, resembling the "swap mutual funds," is Liberty Real Estate Trust, a Florida-based venture which last fall registered $25 million in shares with the SEC. After three months of negotiating with prospective landlords who wished to exchange their holdings for shares in Liberty, the fund became effective in December by taking title to $11.4 million in assets. The portfolio includes 25 office, industrial, commercial and apartment buildings; three motels; a bowling alley; and the mortgages on two tracts, to be used, respectively, as the campus of a new college and the site of a subdivision of two-bedroom homes.

Spelling It Out

Still another, if equally rare, kind of trust is organized to purchase a specified group of properties, and a public offering is made to set it up in business. The SEC, when it came across an early issue of this sort, decided that a detailed physical description and five-year operating and earnings history were minimal requirements for disclosure. Hence, the prospectus of such a trust abounds with information for the investor. An example is First Union Realty, brought out last fall by Harriman, Ripley & Co. and Hayden, Miller & Co. The offering consisted of slightly more than 1 million shares, at $12.50, and all the net proceeds were committed to the purchase of a 21-story bank and office structure in Cleveland, the Union Commerce Building. (While this is the trust's sole acquisition to date, it is not a "one-shot"; other acquisitions of "long-term investment" value will be made from time to time, usually for cash, which "may be provided by the sale of shares.")

The Cleveland building was acquired for $25.5 million, with a $13.5 million Aetna Life 30-year mortgage, and immediately leased back to the Union Commerce Bank for 30 years. First Union is depreciating the property (less the $4.5 million attributable to land) on a conservative straight-line basis over a 30-year period, so that annual charges of $700,000 exceed amortization of $286,000 (in the first year) by over $400,000. Net reportable earnings will be $219,000 (21 cents a share), but cash flow comes to $755,000 (71 cents a share), and nearly full distribution has been pledged. Last month, the trust paid its first quarterly dividend of 17 cents a share, and the stock carries a bid of $13 in the counter market, making its "yield" — although two-thirds tax-sheltered for investors — around 5½ %, one of real estate's lowest. More ambitious is the neighboring Cleveland trust, U.S. Realty Investments. Conceived frankly as a "growth trust," according to its chief fiscal officer and trustee, Sheldon B. Guren, U.S. Realty sold $6.6 million in shares through Hornblower & Weeks last May, invested the money in properties which had been fully described in the prospectus, and then came back to file for a second offering, of $6 million, at the year-end. (The latter is still in registration.) Again, the prospectus presents a detailed picture of the fund's holdings, present and projected.

The Mixed Trust

Most often, new trusts are organized and the shares offered publicly without such specific statements of plans for the proceeds. In this respect, trusts, as the SEC interprets them, fall into a category much like open-end mutual funds. While a statement of general operating policy is required in the prospectus, unless certain acquisitions already have been contracted for, the promoters need not stipulate the actual assets they intend to acquire, any more than a fund is expected to spell out in advance exactly which stocks it may someday buy and sell.

In some cases, this kind of trust has at least one deal pending before it goes to the equities market, and the investor is given a full description of this part of the projected portfolio. Realty experts consider a "mixed trust" like this a happy compromise: the investor gets an idea of what's in store, while the trust retains some freedom of maneuver.

Such a venture is New York's First National Real Estate Trust, which also happens to be the biggest offering yet registered in the field. Last fall, First National brought out 2.5 million shares at $10 each, and, before the offering was completed, amended the prospectus to disclose its first acquisition: the $1.7 million Forest Park Apartments in Silver Springs, Md. (mortgaged for $950,000).

Participating in the venture are some of the best-known names in realty investment, law, corporate finance and mutual

95

funds. The underwriter is Aberdeen Investor Programs, Inc., sponsor of the Aberdeen Fund. Independent contractor, to operate the trust's properties, is Metropolitan Management Inc., a new firm formed around its principal stockholder, William F. Purcell, until 1960 a partner in Wien, Lane, Klein & Purcell, the law firm generally regarded as top real estate syndicator of major properties (120 Broadway, Plaza Hotel, Empire State Building, etc.). Other prominent insiders include A. Dana Hodgdon, president of the leading Washington stockbrokers, Hodgdon & Co., and H. Struve Hensel, former Assistant Secretary of Defense.

Blank Checks

Finally, the most common type of realty trust is the so-called blank check. They are so named because they make a public offering of shares before acquiring any properties — or even hinting at future acquisitions. Blank-check trusts normally seem to have the easiest time clearing the SEC. (Ironically, that's because they have nothing to disclose.) Of the $250 million currently being amassed by property-owning trusts, blank checks account for over 60%.

Since any investment in realty, according to noted authority, is 75% an investment in the people involved — management or promoters — the importance of top officials in a blank-check trust is paramount. Most are headed by men of long experience in real estate (if not as fiduciaries), who have acquired a reputation in their trade and, most likely, a following of clients or investors. In short, they can get enough signatures on their "blank checks" to attract a competent underwriter who is only too glad to sell the bulk of the issue.

The typical blank-check trust, while launched with relative ease, has not yet got far off the ground. A case in point is Philadelphia's Greenfield Real Estate Investment Trust, one of the first to clear the SEC when it offered 500,000 shares last March at $20 through Drexel & Co. Since Albert M. Greenfield's is a respected name among property-holders in the City of Brotherly Love — it long has been synonymous with Bankers Securities Corp., which has large interests in local realty, finance and transit — the $20 million quickly was oversubscribed.

Greenfield Real Estate Investment Trust so far has taken title to no realty. It assets, as of last September, (they remain substantially unchanged today) consisted of $9.3 million in Treasury bills and $200,000 in cash and miscellaneous items. Thus, for its first six months, the trust reported net income of $55,659 or approximately 10 cents a share. The current six months will produce about the same, even though an agreement to acquire a shopping center near Philadelphia may finally be heading for a closing.

As all the foregoing examples attest, a great variety of real estate investment trusts suddenly have appeared on the stock market. With many more still to come, they are beginning to make themselves felt, too, as a dynamic new force in the realty marts. What do their activities indicate about this new investment form? And what does the massive buying power of the trusts mean for real estate generally? From the facts available to date, Barron's next week will attempt to draw some conclusions.

Reprinted by courtesy of *Barron's National Business and Financial Weekly*, (February 12, 1962).

MORE ROOM AT THE TOP?

Investors in Realty Trusts
Should Carefully Appraise the Risks

By J. Richard Elliott, Jr.

Sometime this month, the shares of First National Real Estate Trust probably will begin trading nationally in the over-the-counter market. Although it will not be the first real estate investment trust equity to achieve this distinction — indeed, it will be the fifteenth — the New York venture easily may become the most widely held. In the largest offering to date of this new, tax-free form of investment, the company last fall registered 2.5 million shares at $10 apiece. Before the offering could be completed, however, the promoters and underwriters — including big names in both the realty and mutual-fund field — had to hurdle a number of regulatory roadblocks, while, in effect, temporarily dropping negotiations for property.

First National's experience serves to point up a few of the pitfalls which may confront investors in this new type of realty investment company. As noted in the list on Page 15 (and more fully described in last week's article), realty trusts run a wide gamut — from one kind to another, from large to small, from conservative to speculative. All of them, however, in varying degrees involve certain basic risks. In the first place, their operations may be hobbled by restrictive Blue Sky laws in various states. Even more far-reaching in its impact is the uncertainty which still surrounds the final spelling out of the basic Federal regulations. In the case of a few trusts, some question has arisen as to the role played by insiders. Finally, the view is widely held in the trade, not without foundation, that the trusts are venturing into the realty market at levels which are perilously high.

Blue Sky Laws

Let us first note a few difficulties which certain trusts have encountered from Blue Sky commissioners in a number of key states. Florida, for example, has demanded that trusts seeking to register there specify in the prospectus whether properties would (or could) be acquired from trustees or other affiliates. Until recently, California held out for competitive bidding to select the independent operating contractors.

Again, the influential Midwest Securities Commissioners Association, representing 14 states, meeting in February 1961, made a detailed pronouncement of policy that temporarily discouraged any trusts from entering its domain. Though the most stringent rules since have been modified, several major headaches remain. To illustrate, a trust may not sell shares in a Midwest S.C.A. state if, after its organization, it buys properties from its management company. Second, a trust may invest only 5% of its assets in unimproved land. Finally, it may acquire no property with more than a 66⅔% encumbrance; this provision eliminates many that could be FHA-insured at much higher ratios and even some conventionally financed parcels.

Rules of the Game

Of even wider concern is the uncertainty swirling about the long-awaited Federal regulations needed to implement the Real Estate Investment Trust Act of 1960. No form of business as complex as the real estate trust can be created by law alone. The Government agency charged with administering the Act must also establish the rules by which it means to govern. For realty trusts, this necessity has led to a delay which now is approaching 14 months.

After giving the law a quick reading shortly after passage, Treasury and Internal Revenue agents last spring published a tentative set of rules and asked for comment from the trade. The reaction was stormy. Realty experts pointed out these alleged defects: (1) by seeking to enforce the separation of trust and independent contractor, the rules would force management firms to skimp on maintenance and other tenant services, to the ultimate detriment of the trust's holdings, (2) they threatened to prevent trusts from obtaining even one trustee competent in the business, although, in the words of one expert, "REITs need specialized management even more than mutual funds"; (3) by prohibiting a trust from receiving any rents from its management company, they would stymie efficient operation by barring the operators from locating a branch office in a shopping center or apartment project; and (4) the spelling out of ways in which a trust could be disqualified, and so lose its tax exemption, retroactively, could ruin one guilty of debatable errors of judgment.

Shaken by the industry's adverse reaction, the T-men returned to headquarters to revise, and presumably soften, the first draft. However, the staff has been kept busy on other things and only in the past month or two, apparently, has any real headway been made. Current opinion in the Department is that final regulations will appear within 60 days.

Pitfalls and Potholes

Such roadblocks have halted the early progress of many realty trusts. Most, indeed, have held off investing their new capital until they can be more sure of the lay of the land. A number of others, partially or (like the old-line Boston companies) heavily invested, have even suggested to shareholders that their ultimate qualification for tax exemption may require changes in portfolios, or in management contracts.

In some cases, the long arm of regulation already has worked a hardship on investors. Thus, upon offering $25 million in securities last November, First National Real Estate Trust advised in the prospectus that its policy would be "to invest in properties of all types . . ., (but) it is not possible to state at this time what percentage of the trust's assets will be invested in each." In other words, the trust started selling stock on a blank-check basis. However, California — which the underwriters, Aberdeen Investor Programs, promoters of the Aberdeen (mutual) Fund, had counted on to take a large piece of the offering — held up clearance under its Blue Sky Laws.

Meanwhile, First National took title to its first property — a $1.7 million apartment project in a Washington suburb.

Since the offering was not completed — shares, as noted, still cannot be traded over-the-counter — this move proved to be a tactical error. The SEC promptly demanded that the prospectus be amended. The result was that thousands of First National shareholders had to be sent a copy of the amended literature and given a chance to change their minds, further delaying things for all hands. Now the legal hurdles seem to have been cleared and the promoters hope to close the offering this month. But the trust, in the interim, has had to sit tight on any other deals it may have in the works.

A Blank-Check Fund

Hung up in a different way is the Greenfield Real Estate Trust, which is still a blank-check fund. Greenfield's $10 million offering was one of the first to clear the SEC. The prospectus set forth a policy of acquiring "office buildings, shopping centers, industrial parks, industrial and commercial buildings, hotels, chain retail establishments, apartment houses and motels." Subject to a stipulation that properties be located in areas with a history of "growth or stability," it set the trust's investment objectives as "high cash yields."

This policy, however, remains to be put into practice, because, according to Robert Greenfield, one of the attorneys: "We haven't found any properties we want." Meanwhile, Greenfield remains a non-trust, the earnings of which stem solely from Treasury bills. What's more, even this meager income is subject to the 52% corporate tax. Offered at $20, the shares have suffered the steepest discount in the group, currently changing hands at around $15 bid.

Almost Open-End

Still another obstacle may be encountered by Nation-Wide Real Estate Investment Trust, which operates out of Boston and Syracuse. When its registration, of 750,000 shares at $10, cleared the SEC on December 19, Nation-Wide became the first trust to offer a monthly investment plan. Investors may sign up to pay $25 per month for a period ranging from 40 to 100 months, through the underwriter, REIT Securities Corp.

As in the case of the mortgage trust, First Mortgage Investors, re-investment of dividends also may be arranged.

To make available the necessary shares, Nation-Wide is seeking to sell only 700,000 now, retaining 50,000 in its treasury; should more be needed, the company would have to file again, since the SEC has decided that no trust investing in real properties can become an open-end (with an unlimited supply of registered shares). As of now, less than a third of the offered shares have been sold, predominently on monthly plans, and the trust is a long way from its initial goal of a $700,000 portfolio in realty holdings.

Other Risks

Nor do fully invested trusts escape pitfalls of their own. Take the case of the industry's most prominent "swap" fund, Liberty Real Estate Trust, which set up shop last December with $11.4 million in assets, represented by 25 properties and mortgages on two unimproved tracts in Florida. While Liberty's exchange of shares for property was tax-free, this procedure prevented it from acquiring a new depreciation base on which it could achieve a higher rate of cash flow. One consequence is that Liberty, while diversified in terms of properties, is equity-rich and earnings-poor. Mortgage debt of $5.2 million equals only 46% of total assets. Amortization ies $275,000, of which $20,000 is a deductible cost.

Owing to other factors, however, net return to investors will not be great. One is Liberty Trust's debt to its underwriter and promoter, Liberty Securities Corp., of Sarasota. In the first year, it will pay an instalment of $105,000 (one-sixth of the total due) "in lieu of the normal method of reduction of proceeds to the issuer." Partly because of this extended obligation, reportable net income in 1962, on a net cash investment of $6.1 million, will run to only $330,000, or 50 cents a share. Depreciation, totaling $368,000, will provide an excess over amortization of roughly $110,000. Thus the cash flow available for dividends will approximate $440,000, or 70 cents a share; a bookkeeping device may raise this to 86 cents in the first year.

In short, the shares (of which 626,252 are outstanding) will yield investors who acquired them for the equivalent of $10 apiece (the stock, by the way, now is quoted at $8 bid), slightly more than 7%, one-third of it a return of capital. "If in any given year substantial capital improvements are called for," the prospectus notes, "the Trust, if it is to remain qualified . . . may not make such improvements out of earnings (or depreciation reserves) but will have to either borrow money or sell additional shares."

Length of an Arm?

Prospective investors in realty trusts also should take a hard look at insider transactions. U.S. Realty Investments, a Cleveland fund which sold $6.6 million in shares last May, and made another offering of $6.15 million just last week, illustrates the point. In its prospectus, the trust carefully spelled out the projected investment of all its capital.

Many of the fund's start-up transactions and property acquisitions involved insiders to an unusual degree. According to the new prospectus, the three principal trustees (who are also its paid officers) are partners in the law firm which handled the trust's original registration, underwriting, realty and other matters; the firm, Gottfried, Ginsberg, Guren and Merritt, has received (or been pledged) at least $145,000 from U.S. Realty. In addition, Metropolitan Management Co., the trust's independent operating contractor (of which no trustee is an officer or employee) has retained the law firm, which also continues to represent the trust.

The management fee, of course, is one of the more important cost items for a trust, and its size, in turn, depends to some extent on legal expenses. Significantly, U.S. Realty has projected at $107,500 for the next 12 months its combined fees for management, "legal and audit" expenses, and trustees (the latter, if also officers, may receive an aggregate of up to ¼ of 1% of the fund's net worth). What's more, another trustee is "a substantial shareholder" in the construction and engineering company which holds the contract to build the Tulsa Airport Motel, a major property which U.S. Realty plans to build.

Inside the Portfolio

The trust's original portfolio was acquired for the most part from sellers in which "the sponsors and some of the trustees had varying interests." Again according to the new prospectus, insiders held a 4.7% interest in a firm called Radiart Realty, which sold to the trust, for $435,000, a 1926 apartment house with street-floor stores and an industrial property with lease expiring in 1969, depreciated to a net combined value of $161,000. They owned 11.4% of a shopping center sold to the trust for $550,000, and the three officer-trustees sold an adjacent, unimproved lot (which they owned outright) "to complete the addition to the . . . shopping center" for $90,962.

Insiders also owned a 20% stake in the Forest Hills Park Co., from which the trust acquired of $3.9 million an apartment building, a shopping center and a variety store unit, carried on the books at a net $2.9 million. They held 35.9% in Capital Investment Co., which sold a large apartment tower, written down to $1.8 million, to the trust for $2.2 million. They held 30% and 50% interests, respectively, in two of three office buildings acquired by the trust for a total of $2 million, in which 43% of the total rentable space carries leases expiring, without renewal options, this year.

Moreover, trustees Ginsberg and Guren transferred to U.S. Realty a building which they themselves owned. The property, an industrial showroom and service garage, was built in 1913 and is leased by International Harvester through 1971 at an annual rental of $33,000. After debt service, taxes and other expenses, which the landlord must pay, the net yield appears to be around $15,000. To acquire it, the trust paid $310,000, — although the building's cost to the sellers in 1947 had been $115,623, and it had been depreciated since then to a net $42,911. The trust was able to get a mortgage (6%, 10-year) for $175,000, making its cash outlay $135,000 or slightly less than ten times net yield. (Similar industrial properties frequently sell for three to five times net yield.)

In none of the deals involving trustees as sellers, according to the prospectus, did the trust call for an independent appraisal. As for the International Harvester garage, the prospectus concedes that "the price was not determined by arm's-length negotiation, but reflected the opinion of the above three trustees (Messrs. Ginsberg, Guren and Gottfried) as to the then fair market value of the property."

New Offering

For one reason or another, the portfolio of U.S. Realty Investors has failed to generate what its trustees consider an adequate income. Hence, with the proceeds of the second offering, the company plans to expand its holdings. This time, however, it is seeking higher-leveraged properties: two new Cleveland office buildings (occupied by B. F. Goodrich Co.); a parking garage in St. Louis; a Madison, Wisc., shopping center; office buildings in Miami (one-third occupied by the U.S. Government on a lease expiring this year) and Manhattan (390 Fifth Ave., vintage 1903); a Howard Johnson motor lodge under construction in Erie, Pa.; and two other motels planned for Columbus, Ohio, and Tulsa, Okla.

"Motels and hotels are less conservative than the types of properties presently owned by the Trust," Mr. Guren told a group of security analysts last summer. "As this type of use is regarded as more speculative . . . we will not become topheavy with the motel-hotel group, but nonetheless a fair number of units of this type will give us greater diversification and enable us to increase the return to investors." In effect, it seems that the new properties also will provide cash to pay the old dividend. On a pro-forma basis, for the 12 months beginning November 1961, U.S. Realty's latest prospectus projects a cash flow for distribution from all holdings, present and prospective, of $930,000 — or about seven cents per share a year more.

Inflated Market

As all the foregoing discussion suggests, finally, the main challenge confronting every trust today is the inflated realty market. Comments John C. Williamson, secretary-counsel of the National Association of Real Estate Boards: "The proliferation of real estate public offerings, beginning with the

REAL ESTATE INVESTMENT TRUSTS

Trust	Location	Type(a)	Approx. Assets (000) (b)	
American Realty Trust	Washington, D.C.	B	$5,000	
Anaconda R. E. Inv. Trust	Ft. Lauderdale, Fla.	P	1,636	(c)
Bradley R. E. Trust	Boston, Mass.	M	10,904	
Business Property Assocs.	Boston, Mass.	M	1,271	
California Properties	San Diego, Calif.	B		
California R. E. Inv. Trust	Los Angeles, Calif	B		(c)
Chicago R. E. Trustees	Boston, Mass.	M	3,200	
Commercial Property Assocs.	Boston, Mass.	M	487	
Commonwealth Realty Trust	Philadelphia, Pa.	P	4,305	
Continental Mortgage Investors	Boston, Mass.	L		(c)
Continental R. E. Inv. Trust	Baltimore, Md.	B	3,000	(c)
Dennis R. E. Inv. Trust	Albany, N.Y.	B	10,000	(c)
Denver R. E. Inv. Assn.	Denver, Colo.	B	8,000	
First Atlanta Realty Fund	Atlanta, Ga.	I		(d)
First Contl. R. E. Inv. Trust	Chicago, Ill.	B	10,000	(c)
First Diversified R. E. Assn.	Dayton, Ohio	B	2,000	
First Mortgage Investors	Boston, Mass.	L	15,000	
First National R. E. Trust	New York, N.Y.	PB	25,000	
First R. E. Inv. Trust of Iowa	Cedar Rapids, Ia.	I		(c)
First R. E. Inv. Trust of N.J.	Hackensack, N.J.	P	677	(c)
First Union Realty	Cleveland, Ohio	P	13,250	
Flato Realty Trust	Corpus Christi, Tex.	S	20,000	
Franklin Realty Trust	Philadelphia, Pa.	B	10,000	(c)
Gateside-Architect Bldg. Trust	New York, N.Y.	O	695	
General R. E. Inv. Trust	Omaha, Nebr.	B	350	(c)
Great Southern R.E. Trust	Atlanta, Ga.	B		(c)
Greenfield R. E. Inv. Trust	Philadelphia, Pa.	B	10,000	
Liberty R. E. Trust	Sarasota, Fla.	S	11,416	
Metropolitan Realty Trust	Washington, D.C.	P	6,500	(c)
National R. E. Inv. Trust	New York, N.Y.	B	15,000	(c)
Nation-Wide R. E. Inv. Trust	Boston, Mass.	B	7,000	
North American R. E. Trust	New York, N.Y.	B	20,000	(c)
Pennsylvania R. E. Inv. Trust	Philadelphia, Pa.	P		
Perpetual Inv. Trust	Washington, D.C.	B	(c)-(f)	
R. E. Inv. Trust of America	Boston, Mass.	M	32,722	
Stephen Realty Inv. Co.	Denver, Colo.	B	7,000	
U.S. Realty Investments	Cleveland, Ohio	P	28,124	(g)
Wabash Avenue Trustees	Boston, Mass.	M	988	
Washington R. E. Inv. Trust	Washington, D.C.	PB	3,000	
Western Land Trust Fund	Oakland, Calif.	B	2,000	
Western States Real Inv. Trust	Aurora, Colo.	B	200	(c)
Wisconsin R. E. Inv. Fund	Milwaukee, Wisc.	I	2,000	(h)

(a) Type: M-Massachusetts trust (existing, old-line); O-One-shot fund (syndicate type); S-Swap (exchange) fund; P-Properties described in prospectus, accounting for entire proceeds, to be acquired; B-Blankcheck (projected use of any proceeds not delineated); PB-Partly blankcheck, some property to be acquired, described in prospectus; L-Liens, mortgages to be acquired from proceeds, rather than equity investments. I-Intra-state. (b) Per latest balance sheet (not necessarily market value of holdings); in case of newly offered trust, value of offering; where both factors applicable, total of the two. (Note: properties to be acquired, under mortgages, will have higher asset value than represented by capital available for investment.) (c) SEC registration not yet effective. (d) Offered to Georgia residents only. (e) Offered to Iowa residents only. (f) Name to be changed. (g) Proforma balance sheet, including investment of second offering now in registration. (b) Offered to Wisconsin residents only.

syndicate and catalyzed by the real estate investment trust, may prove to be a mixed blessing unless the warning signs are heeded by promoters. One such sign is the high price of good income-producing real estate as syndicates, trusts and corporations bid for it."

Other signs abound today that realty investors — trusts and others alike — are perched on precarious heights. Vacancy rates in both office and residential buildings are mounting. In most cities, meanwhile, new construction continues apace. Hence the risks are getting greater day by day. Sheraton Corp. last year repossessed no fewer than 13 hotels that had been sold to syndicates, only to fall into neglect. "In hotels, where occupancy is a day-to-day business, the effects are immediate," Mr. Henderson observes. "In apartment and office buildings, where leases take a little longer to expire, the effects are merely postponed."

In this situation, the dilemma for realty trusts is obvious. "They are coming in at the worst possible time," says a prominent real estate executive. "Their function will be to take losing properties off the hands of syndicates, corporations and everyone else." Many responsible trustees are aware of the hazards, as indicated by the go-slow investment policies of trusts from the old-line Massachusetts types to the new blank-check funds. However, as an SEC commissioner implied not long ago, public investors in realty, despite all the warning signs legible between the lines of full-disclosure, usually are the last to know. The toughest decision for a beleaguered property owner, he remarked cautiously, soon may be "whether to petition in bankruptcy or go public."

Reprinted by courtesy of *Barron's National Business and Financial Weekly*, (February 19, 1962).

REAL ESTATE FOR SMALL INVESTORS

That's the appeal being used by the real estate investment trusts that have been set up in recent months. A look at how they've been doing

First it was syndicates, then real estate corporations. Now it's the real estate investment trust, latest means available to the small investor who wants to put some of his money in realty. The trust itself is not new; it was around long before the turn of the century. But a change in the federal tax law, effective at the start of 1961, gave it a decided advantage that it never had before.

The new law stipulates that realty trusts which pay out at least 90% of their net profits to shareholders are exempt from federal income taxes on the portion distributed. Obviously, this eliminates the double taxation inherent in the ownership of shares of real estate corporations which must first pay regular corporate taxes on profits before disbursing dividends. In this respect, therefore, and in certain others as well, the trust is very similar to a mutual fund except that it is invested mainly in real estate instead of securities and it is a closed-end affair.

Trust Defined

Basically, the trust is simply a device which enables many small investors to pool their savings to buy mortgages and pieces of property — office buildings, apartment houses, hotels, shopping centers and the like. They are therefore able to take advantage of the high rate of return characteristic of realty investment and at the same time keep risks down by means of diversification and experienced management.

Certain strict requirements must be met, however, if the real estate investment trust — "REIT" — is to qualify for special tax treatment. It cannot deal in real estate as a business and cannot operate or manage the properties, but must assume a purely passive role in realty investment — much as a mutual fund remains aloof from the operations of firms in which it has invested.

Furthermore, it must derive at least 75% of its income from rents, interest on mortgages, capital gains from property sales and like; 15% can come from non-realty holdings. And not more than 30% of the trust's gross income can be contributed by sale of securities held less than six months or by disposal of property held less than four years.

These restrictions assure, among other things, that the REIT will be a relatively long term holder of real estate rather than a short term trader. This means of course that there may be less chance of achieving much in the way of capital gains from the sale of real estate, at least during the first few years of a trust's life. But if this seems something of a drawback to the speculatively inclined, there are some very distinct advantages for the average investor in this type situation.

Not only is there more money available to shareholders because of the trust's tax exemption, but at least a portion of the pay-out itself may be tax-free. Ever since 1954 when rapid property write-offs were first allowed, practically every real estate operation has benefited from substantial deductions for depreciation. The trusts are no exception. In most cases, a large cash flow is available from depreciation, and any distributions made from it are not subject to ordinary income taxes. Instead, such payments are treated by the Internal Revenue Service as a return of capital and are used to reduce the investor's cost basis.

Of course, the end effect of this is to postpone any taxes until the shares are sold, at which time capital gains rather than ordinary income taxes will apply. For some trusts, the return-of-capital portion of the payout may amount to as much as 50% or more of the total. There will also be capital gains distributions from time to time, taxable also at the maximum 25% rate. And, finally, a portion of the trust's distribution is ordinary income which is subject to an individual's regular tax rates. Holders receive a statement from the trust explaining how much of each kind of income is involved.

The REIT also has other advantages over some traditional types of realty investment. Most offer a considerable degree of diversification, something that syndicates usually lack. In addition to holding various kinds of property, the trusts can diversify geographically. Furthermore, their shares are quite low priced and are traded over-the-counter, making for good marketability. The number of participants in a syndicate, for example, often is quite limited and an investor frequently has difficulty liquidating quickly at anywhere near the price expected.

Thus far, some 40 or more REITS have registered with the Securities and Exchange Commission, and at least 15 have already offered shares to the public. There is considerable variation among them. Greenfield Real Estate Investment Trust, the first to go public upon enactment of the new law, intends to be extremely diversified as to type of property. First National Real Estate Trust, operated by Aberdeen Investors Program which is a mutual fund, also expects to be broadly diversified. First Mortgage Investors, on the other hand, will specialize in a single kind of investment — first mortgage development loans.

Still in Infancy

The trouble with most of the trusts which have been organized to date is that they are just getting started with their investment programs. Consequently, it will be some time before it can be determined whether they are achieving their objectives, either as to suitable properties or income and dividends. Among the prominent names in the field today, long-established Real Estate Investment Trust of America (it made a new offering in mid-1961) is the only one with a record to stand on and a full portfolio of properties.

Few are paying any dividends as yet, although their aim is to achieve a return of 7% to 9% annually. Obviously, the absence of income for an indefinite period is a big drawback from the standpoint of shareholders, present or prospective. Initiation of dividends will depend, of course, largely on how soon suitable income-producing properties can be acquired.

REAL ESTATE INVESTMENT TRUSTS

	Offered	Amount (millions)	Offering Price	*Recent Price
American Realty Trust	Oct. 9, '61	$ 5.0	$10	$10
Commonwealth Realty Trust	Feb. 8, '62	4.3	10	10
Denver Real Estate Investment Trust	July 26, '61	8.0	10	11¾
First Mortgage Investors	Sept. 22, '61	15.0	15	20
First National Real Estate Trust	Nov. 8, '61	25.0	10	10
First Union Realty	Oct. 26, '61	13.3	12½	13
Greenfield Real Estate Investment Trust	Mar. 29, '61	10.0	20	15
Liberty Real Estate Trust of Florida	Sept. 25, '61	25.0	10	8¾
Real Estate Investment Trust of America	June 15, '61	10.0	20	a23
Stephen Realty Investment Co.	Apr. 12, '61	7.0	5	5
U.S. Realty Investments	May 25, '61	6.6	10	10
Washington Real Estate Investment Trust	June 7, '61	3.0	5	5½

*Over-the-counter, bid. a–American Stock Exchange.

For the small investor exploring REIT possibilities, a few questions are in order: (1) When will income commence? (2) Is there an existing portfolio of properties? (3) Are they diversified both as to type and geographically? (4) Perhaps most important of all, what's the financial acumen of the trustees?

All of these factors have an important bearing on future performance. At this early stage of development, few of the trusts are susceptible of appraisal. Nevertheless, as a group, they do appear to offer the small investor interesting opportunities for income and they could also prove to be a satisfactory inflation hedge over the long run.

Reprinted by permission of *Financial World,* Vol. 117 (February 21, 1962).

FACT AND COMMENT

By Malcolm S. Forbes

Multiplying Your Money in Real Estate

Most of us, when we think of investing, think in terms of buying stocks and bonds in companies making and distributing things or services.

But many a man has made and is making multiple millions in real estate.

One of the more concentrated, dazzling examples is illustrated above. That scrubby, barren, virtually valueless strip of sand now sells — when any is available — for thousands of dollars per ocean-front foot. In a few decades the 3,322 initial residents of Miami have seen their village become a city of a million residents, swelled the year round by additional hundreds of thousands of vacationers. Nor is Miami unique. Much of the rest of Florida burgeons at a pace good trotters would envy. So, too, Arizona . . . California. Nor is the soaring value in real estate confined to the sunny states. Look around you in your own suburbia or city block: Anywhere, U.S.A. Consider what you paid for your country acreage or your city plot a few or many years ago. With rare exception, today it would command a far higher price.

In recent winters I have visited many islands in the Bahamas. Each succeeding year I can be certain of only one thing: Many of last year's quiet little island anchorages will have changed hands, and new developments will be under way. Four years ago we visited a lovely small cay, uninhabited. The next winter we stopped by and there was a house on it, with a small harbor developed. An American had purchased it and created for himself a small "hideaway" at a total cost of about $50,000. When we stopped by a year ago bulldozers were busy, and men were all about with blueprints. It seems the American had sold it to another executive for $250,000, and this fellow had more elaborate plans. This year we've been told a syndicate has bought it for over $1 million and plans a full-fledged resort, golf course, landing strip and the whole works. That four-year cycle in the life of one island is not unique in the Bahamas today.

E. P. Taylor, the dynamic Canadian tycoon (Forbes, Feb. 1, 1959), four years ago bought 4,000 acres about a 20-minute drive from Nassau for $2 million. He told me he'd planned to invest a total of about $6 million in creating an attractive club, Lyford Cay. It is now almost $16 million. Out of barren land he has created one of the most attractive resorts anywhere in the world. Lovely club house, magnificent marina, golf course — and within the Club's 800 acres are a growing number of substantial winter homes belonging to some of the most prominent men in American business.

Any return on the investment? "I'm in no hurry," says Mr. Taylor. But I'm told that a lady who has a mere 22 acres adjoining the Lyford Cay development now wants $1.5 million for it. And Mr. Taylor has some 3,200 acres in reserve. By the careful, first-rate development of part of his land, he has skyrocketed the value of the rest.

Does all this mean that buying real estate is a sure way to multiply your money?

Personally, I'm a skeptic. It goes back to a couple of those childhood experiences that psychologists make so much money interpreting.

My mother and father were close friends of a couple who had made literally millions in the initial Florida boom of the Twenties. They used to arrive at our home in Englewood, N.J. in a seemingly endless, chauffeured limousine and distributed to us children the most wonderful big presents. Then came the Florida bust in 1927. Within weeks they were stony broke and dad was lending them money to pay the rent on a small two-room New York apartment.

My other youthful memory of money in real estate goes back to the beginning of the George Washington Bridge construction. Everyone apparently was sure that at the Bridge's completion all the wooded land on the New Jersey side for miles around would be promptly inundated by the Big City cliff dwellers. Rough roads were cut through the woods, and buses would arrive from New York, while real-estate promoters under great tents would auction off numbered lots. It was all very exciting.

After a few months nothing more seemed to happen. The "roads" again grew green. The Depression arrived. And it wasn't until 27 years later that what had been foretold did take place. Now the whole area is a ranch-house-studded suburbia with a vengeance. But I'll wager not one in a thousand of the initial investors still held title to a square foot of the property they so eagerly bought in 1928.

Look, too, at what can happen within a city. There was a time when New York's 14th Street was infinitely more valuable business property than the Fifties on Fifth Avenue. Today most of it is occupied by one- and two-story "tax payers" and neglected loft buildings.

I guess for those who know what they're doing — and doing it themselves — real-estate investing and developing has been, is, and will continue to be quite a bonanza. But unimaginative, unknowledgeable me will string along with more mundane investments — like AT&T.

Besides, I don't think holders of Webb and Knapp common feel they've been turned loose in any melon patch.

Reprinted by permission of *FORBES Magazine,* Vol. 89 (March 1, 1962).

TAKING ANOTHER LOOK AT INVESTING IN REAL ESTATE

By Richard H. Swesnik

President, Swesnik & Blum, Inc.,
Washington, D.C. and Chairman,
Federal Tax Subcommittee, Realtors Washington
Committee, National Association of Real Estate Boards.

Specialist in real estate syndicates alerts the investor and security analysts to the long-run opportunities in properly organized and managed trusts, and to the disadvantages they may not be aware of in the corporate form of owning real estate. Criticized, for example, is the realty corporation's constant buying in order to continue tax write-offs to avoid double taxation. The original limited partners and the corporate promoters are depicted as gainers in the exchanges and sale of newly formed corporations' stock, and not the investing public who subsequently buy (1) a "tax liability" and, also, (2) find they may not have bought well managed conservative income-producing real estate. The writer notes that very few experienced syndicators have formed trusts under the January, 1961, Real Estate Investment Trust Act, and warns that Congress will undo any damage its laws may have caused.

Starting in 1951 when the first syndication was accomplished by the writer in Washington, D.C., the problem was to determine the correct owning vehicle so as to couple the safety of owning large income-producing properties with the tax advantages of allowing the depreciation to flow directly to each of the investors. When we considered the tax advantages as a result of depreciation, the corporate method was ruled out and the limited partnership method as an owning vehicle was used. The odds-on favorite method of syndication in the decade of the 50's was the limited partnership.

In October, 1960, the Internal Revenue Service clarified the criteria which they would use in evaluating whether or not an owning vehicle would be taxed as a corporation, thus solidifying the position of properly organized limited partnerships as the favorite method of syndication. There are, of course, disadvantages to owning limited partnership interests in a syndicate — lack of a formal market in depth for the syndicate shares, lack of diversification, and usually the need of a minimum of $2,500 to invest before one can participate. However, the tax advantages, growth through amortization of debt, and better-than-average income far outweigh the disadvantages of owning a limited partnership interest.

Requires an Act of Congress

The only other method of owning an interest in large income-producing property through 1960 was either to be an association or a trust which was taxed as a corporation or to own stock in an owning vehicle organized as a corporation. The corporate form allows tremendous administrative ease of operation for its President. It allows for free and easy corporate borrowing in addition to the regular mortgage financing and, if it is large enough, it provides a market in depth for the investor, and diversification. No matter how carefully a corporation is organized and whether or not debenture techniques are used, nothing will save the corporation from its present tax disadvantage except an Act of Congress, which does not appear to be forthcoming.[1]

There are obvious advantages in the use of the corporate form as an owning vehicle in such areas of the real estate field as the activities of a construction company either contractual or speculative, a land development company engaged in the acquisition, subdividing and subsequent resale of land, or the conducting of other businesses such as mortgage banking. However, it is extremely difficult to perceive why a corporation should be used as the owning vehicle for passively receiving the income of select office buildings, apartment houses, and shopping centers. After all, the main consideration which gave impetus to the formation of syndicates in limited partnership form was the tax advantage of the syndicate itself being excused from the payment of any taxes, thus avoiding the double taxation that occurs when

---

[1] Reliable sources have indicated to the writer not to expect any action "on real estate" during this session of Congress.

properties are owned in corporate form — once at the corporate level and once at the point of receipt of money from the corporation to the individual stockholder.

Notwithstanding the disadvantages, during the past few years many limited partnership interests were exchanged for stock in new publicly owned corporations on a "tax free" basis and many of the individual syndicates which were held in limited partnership form were thus consolidated into publicly owned corporations. Simultaneous with these exchanges, many of the new corporations issued stock to the general public. In a given number of instances, especially in the New York area, the new publicly owned corporations saw a rapid increase in the market value of the stock. The investing public hungrily bought the new stock and some of the former owners sold their newly acquired shares. The new buyers sought to invest in real estate and still retain the liquidity that, up until that time, only a corporation could give.

Disadvantages of Corporate Form

The disadvantages to the long-term investor in owning real estate in corporate form have not been too carefully examined by either the security analysts or the general investing public. One must be reminded of a "perpetual motion" machine when examining the tax policies of the publicly owned corporation. For, in order to avoid the ultimate payment of corporate income tax, these corporations must continually be in the market to purchase and must use ultra-rapid methods of depreciation in order to distribute money to its stockholders which will not first be taxed at the corporate level, and part of which may be "tax free" when paid out to the stockholders. The frenzied manipulations of some of these corporate moguls with respect to the buying, the taking of fast depreciation, and then the sale of properties makes one wonder when the Internal Revenue Service will tax the sale of these properties as ordinary income rather than as long-term capital gains, as this buying and selling often seems to be the principal activity of these corporations. And one must also wonder what happens in a soft market when these corporations must continue their buying in order to continue the tax write-offs to insure avoidance of double taxation. It is apparent to many astute leaders in the field that the purchaser of corporate stock may eventually conclude that perhaps he should have been the original owner of the limited partnership interest when the original exchange was made and have sold out long ago, as he is liable one day to find he is at the end of the trolley with all the doors closed. What may have been a good opportunity for the original limited partners and was an excellent opportunity for the corporate promoters, who formerly were the syndicators in most cases acting as General Partners, was not necessarily a sound opportunity for the investing public. In practically all the mergers the exchanges were tax free so that the new cash buyers were buying, often at higher prices, a tax liability to the extent of any prior depreciation taken on the properties exchanged.

Tax Liability Examples

Consider that a new corporation was formed and it was exchanging its stocking for all of the interests in a limited partnership which had owned a property for six years. In order for the exchange to be on a tax-free basis, the property owned by the partnership is brought into the corporation at its book value, which is what the partnership originally paid for the property *less* the total amount of depreciation taken. For example, if the property was purchased by the partnership six years ago for $3,000,000 in cash and the property was exchanged for stock in the new corporation which was formed, there is no tax despite the fact that on the books of the partnership the property is carried at its depreciated basis, which in the case of this six-year-old building would be approximately $2,350,000. Note there is no tax to anyone *even though* the corporation was exchanging stock certificates which would have a market value based on the building's value of $3,000,000 as soon as the stock certificates are traded.

The net result of this exchange is that when new stock is issued, the new investors are buying into a corporation

119

with a property value of $3,000,000 which the corporation must carry on its books at $2,350,000. The new investor, therefore must consider the fact that there is a tax liability to the corporation based on $650,000 profit in the event of sale of the property for $3,000,000. The new investor did not share in any of the benefits of the prior depreciation, yet must share in the tax load. In other words, the new investor is paying "retail" for his share of a building which is being carried on the books at "wholesale."

What makes this extremely difficult for one to understand is that many security houses sold these stocks to their clients — although when one compares some of the other stocks that were sold to the public these corporate realty stocks must have looked good. When one talks to the heads of the present realty corporations you come away with the feeling that they are very well aware of the tax consequences of their prior moves and are seriously considering building and developing new properties, rather than purchasing existing properties. While this creative real estate is frequently more speculative than acquiring existing properties, the realities of depreciation are such that "creative" properties may be written off faster, thus helping the corporate tax picture. Other corporate realty firms have gone far afield and have started the highly speculative business of building and selling tract houses. This appears to be a substantial departure from filling the long-term investor's needs of owning conservative income-producing real estate.

Who Pushed the Greed Button?

The question one must ask is this: Who pushed whose greed button? Was it the syndicator who was tired of syndication and relished the power, salary, security, and personal liquidity corporation ownership would give? Or was it the limited partnership investor who sensed that perhaps his to-be-acquired corporate stock in exchange for his partnership interests would increase in value (at somebody else's expense) once it was publicly marketed? Or perhaps it was the security houses who only knew how to market securities in terms of corporate stocks and could not resist marketing stock which represented equity interests in something as wildly sought after as prime real estate.

In April of 1961 the Secretary of the Treasury asked the Congress to do something about what the Treasury felt were apparent abuses by the corporations in the use of accelerated depreciation for avoiding the payment of corporate taxes. While the heads of some syndicates which were organized as limited partnerships were also using accelerated depreciation, the excessive use of such depreciation was not necessary by virtue of the method of ownership.

National Real Estate Association's Position

Recognizing that the Treasury Department may have some merit to their position, the National Association of Real Estate Boards at its annual convention in November, 1961 adopted the following policy statement:

"In order to encourage construction and investment in real estate, we recommend the retention of the application of accelerated depreciation, but in order to prevent abuses we urge the Congress to amend the Internal Revenue Code so as to require that property subject to accelerated methods of depreciation be recomputed to the straight-line method on sale of the property within three years of acquisition or completion of construction."

If this resolution is adopted by the Congress, much of the machinations of the corporations would, of course, be stopped. On the other hand, if the regulation as proposed by the Secretary of the Treasury were adopted, the entire real estate industry, along with the construction industry, would grind to a near halt, causing severe economic hardship.

When we consider the disadvantages of limited partnerships, namely, the turbulence that occurs if the general partners die, the difficulties of general borrowing because of the unlimited liability to the general partners even for nominal amounts, the necessary restrictions of the transferring of limited partnership interests, and the initial cost to invest in real estate syndicates in limited partnership form, along with the lack of liquidity, plus the lack of diversification as limited partnerships are usually one-shot deals in order to avoid being taxed as an active real estate corporation, one would wonder if, indeed, the disadvantages do not outweigh the advantages.

Present Tax Position Under January, 1961 Law

The Real Estate Investment Trust Act which became effective in January, 1961 has been carefully evaluated by those in the multiple ownership field to determine whether or not this new vehicle retained the advantages of the corporate form and eliminated most of the disadvantages of the limited partnership form. Without getting into the technical provisions of the Real Estate Investment Trust Act, the all important item is that it will not be taxed as a corporation if it is properly organized and operated.

The increase in syndicated investments, despite the fact that the Real Estate Investment Trust Act is now in its second full year of operation, indicates that the public still feels that syndication in limited partnership form is here to stay. Indeed, because of the uncertainty about what the final regulations will contain when the Internal Revenue Service issues them, many syndicate managers and others experienced in the multiple ownership field have been hesitant to form real estate investment trusts. Under the new Real Estate Investment Trust Act, Congress endeavored to make possible the elimination of many of the disadvantages of owning real estate in either corporate form or in the limited partnership form. Initially, the trust may be worked in such a way as to virtually guarantee its perpetuity as trustees may name their own successors, therefore eliminating the ending that trust business in the event of a trustee's death. Unlike the general partners in limited partnerships, the trustees could borrow monies from time to time to meet emergencies and such borrowings would not become their personal responsibilities, the lenders looking at only the physical assets of the trust and not the trustees.

The transfer and mobility of the certificates would be easily handled through transfer agents, just as readily as stocks and bonds. It is entirely probable that shares in trusts with desirable income-producing properties and with large numbers of investors could be traded. Of course, this would depend upon the total cash worth of the trust and the number of certificate holders. Some of the larger trusts eventually could probably be traded on the New York Stock Exchange, some on the American Exchange, while others would be quoted in the less formal over-the-counter markets.

If the trust held a number of diversified properties such as shopping centers, apartment houses, and office buildings, the certificates would represent this diversification and its owners need have very little cash invested. In fact, for as little as $25 they could achieve the diversification or "mix" that could cost as much as $20,000 in a series of purchases in limited partnerships.

Tax-wise, the trust would do the same things for the investor that limited partnerships now do, that is, avoid the corporate tax and generate some "tax-free" income. We are still a long way from Utopia, however, as the new Real Estate Investment Trust Law has some disadvantages, too. It is not possible, for example, to own property in trust form and create tax loss. The best that could be done would be to pay a return to the investor that is entirely "tax free." This tax loss (in excess of actual cash returns) rarely happens, however, in properties that are well capitalized and that are fairly new. This event usually occurs where extremely rapid depreciation is taken on older buildings which have shorter economic life. It can also occur in situations where the cash down payments on buildings are small and the repayment of the mortgage is on an interest-only basis or the mortgage requires little repayment of its principal. This slight disadvantage is specious inasmuch as the majority of the leaders in the industry are not particularly charmed with ultra rapid depreciation of older properties because of the speed with which such depreciation forces them to dispose of the property.

The speedy depreciation ultimately causes taxable income on dollars the investors are not receiving, which is the opposite situation which most investors desire. Further, if conventional methods of financing are used and sensible ratios of land to improvements are followed, such losses as may be developed through fast depreciation usually occur only at the outset, and usually last for only a year or two. Additionally, while a speedy tax depreciation may be desirable for a particular property when this property is mixed with the other properties held by the trust, it is highly improbable that a tax loss in excess of actual cash distributions could be developed.

My original thoughts in early 1961 were that the most successful new real estate investment trusts would be those which are mergers of existing limited partnerships or those which were held in corporate form prior to the new law. Since that time, however, we have concluded with respect to exchanges that the cash purchasers of shares of a real estate investment trust that was exchanging properties would be taking on a future capital gain load which, in truth, they had no right to shoulder. The exchange of a limited partnership interest for real estate investment trust certificates could be made on a tax free basis, but the new trust, although exchanging certificates at market value, would necessarily have to carry the properties on its books at their then depreciated value. So, obviously, the new investors would be taking on potential capital gains to the extent that the market value exceeded the depreciation value at the time of the original transfers. However, the exchange type of trust, even though it has its disadvantages, has the major advantage of producing immediate income for the investor, as opposed to the "blank check" type of trust, which merely seeks to raise funds and then search for properties. Ideally, of course, a new trust which could purchase well selected properties, and could start depreciation at the cost of such properties would be most beneficial to the trust certificate holders.

We have seen something occur during the past year (1961) which is curious indeed. *Very few* experienced realty promoters and especially those with multiple-ownership backgrounds, such as syndicators or heads of realty corporations, have developed a real estate investment trust. While the Internal Revenue Service regulations have not become final, the briefing conferences such as the one sponsored by the National Association of Real Estate Investment Funds in Washington in November of 1961, helped to pinpoint and clarify some of the areas of doubt or confusion.

Treasury, Securities Exchange Commission, and "blue-sky" officials who attended the conferences helped in the clarification of these problem areas. So, as of this writing there is nothing substantially deterrent to the forming of a trust.

Experienced Syndicators Avoid Forming Trusts

One may ask why the experienced syndicators, for example, have not formed a trust. The answer is painfully simple — the emoluments to a promoter of a trust are not as extensive as they are when, all things being equal, a syndicate is formed. The promoter *cannot* be both trustee and independent contractor, which he most handily can be in a limited partnership. That is, he may be both general partner and he or his company can act as managing agents. Secondly, his personal tax position is not as attractive. In a trust he will receive ordinary income either as trustee or as the independent contractor. While in a syndicate, if his "fee" is taken as interests in profits, his income is subjected to the tax advantages of depreciation. To be competitive as a trustee, he must share in a maximum of three-quarters of one percent per annum of the gross assets. This is somewhat less than what is par for the course in realty syndications.

A Fine Investment Opportunity

However, the investing public has a fine investment opportunity in a properly organized and managed trust and it is the *responsibility* of the ethical real estate industry to provide this.

What Congress gave, they can take away. If the stench grows heavy as a result of sadly paying trusts administered by publicly known names who are unoriented and inexperienced in real estate, you may count on Congressional indignation and action against the entire industry. Surely those of us who have earned a little in this field can put a little back in terms of slightly lesser incomes for the good of the industry, which ultimately benefits us all.

The public must be told, however, that no matter in what form — that is, corporate, limited partnership, or real estate

125

investment trust, real estate is a long-term investment, usually eight to 12 years. For one to realize the true advantages of owning real estate he must patiently wait until such real estate is eventually refinanced or sold. All of the machinations of the real estate investment trust market, and all the manipulations of the corporate realty stocks, and all the exchanging of limited partnership interests will not alter this fact.

With respect to the new real estate investment trust, the hullabaloo caused by the stock market professionals who are underwriting the new trusts is merely the curtain that covers the stage upon which must be sound income-producing property, carefully selected and operated by experienced and responsible persons. When the curtain opens, the intrinsic values of the properties and the wisdom of the men who select and operate them will govern the ultimate value of the shares. You may be sure the holdings of any trust will be ultimately examined by technically competent realty personnel. Those trusts organized and operated by get-rich-quick promoters who thought this was a field easily learned and mastered will certainly be re-valuated by perhaps a dollar-wise but unhappy but re-educated public.

Reprinted by permission of *Commercial and Financial Chronicle*, 110 Wall Street, New York, N.Y. 10005, Vol. 195 (March 8, 1962)

WHAT THE INVESTOR SHOULD KNOW IN BUYING REAL ESTATE ISSUES TODAY
—And the Risks Involved
By George J. Bradford

NOTE: This most interesting story appears when so many new real estate issues are about to be offered to the public — and at a time when the number of vacancies in office buildings and apartment houses is increasing.

For the past ten years or more, real estate operators — financed by the taxpayer through federal loans of one kind or another, have made fortunes on a shoestring — and the likelihood exists that they are now ready to cash in further by offering the public shares in their enterprises based on today's inflationary real estate values.

This practical article tells you what the investor should know in buying real estate equities at any time — and especially now. It calls attention to the pitfalls in accounting, the involved tax considerations, cash flow, depreciation — and other complicated factors creating problems for even the most sophisticated investors in arriving at real asset and resource values, and notes the serious problems that can arise from management by the promoters themselves vs. practical professional operation.
— EDITOR

Three years ago, in April 1959 to be exact, when Kratter Corporation came on the scene, Wall Street was introduced to a new investment vehicle, the incorporated real estate syndicate. Unorthodox accounting principles combined with mysterious terminology relegated these securities into a classification spurned by most analysts. And yet, attractive profits were made in stocks like Kratter, Futterman, Wallace, Glickman and Uris Brothers.

As recognition of this became more diffused, investors showed a continuing appetite for this type of security. When Congress passed the Real Estate Investment Trust Act of 1960, the new legislation literally opened the flood gates, and a new type of publicly owned real estate venture was born.

In the past fifteen months, the proliferation of real estate stocks witnessed by the investment community has only been exceeded by electronics stocks and scarcely matched by such spasmodic outbursts as the boat and shell home stocks.

Huge sums of money have been invested in these securities; in many instances by individuals whose commitments were largely motivated, not by understanding the intricacies of the new medium, but by the visual influence of large billboards announcing the erection of a new "Glickman Building."

AND NOW — NEW ISSUES TO BE OFFERED AT TOP OF MARKET?

Since the new Real Estate Investment Trust Act (REITA) went into effect in January 1961, $200 million in trust shares was distributed to the public and another $100 million of securities are in various stages of registration. Today, three classes of securities comprise the bulk of public real estate investment media: 1) real estate syndicate participation, 2) the diversified real estate owner-manager corporation, and 3) real estate investment trust certificates. From an analyst's standpoint, only the last two are significant. Reflecting the substantial investor interest in the new species, this is an opportune time to reappraise the fundamental nature of these investments in the light of today's real estate market situation.

The Concept of the Real Estate Corporation

The investor willing to undertake the risks in this class of securities must have full comprehension, at least, of their basic nature and of the risks involved. For greater security they must possess the following characteristics:

1) A liberal, tax-sheltered dividend.

2) A measure of long-term growth reflecting appreciation of value of real estate assets held in the portfolio.

3) An access to substantial lines of credit for further development of the business.

4) The spreading of risks due to broad diversification of assets and their geographical locations.

5) Professional real estate management.

6) Liquidity resulting from daily trading in the company shares, either over-the-counter or on one of the exchanges.

Let us critically examine these principles, so that when you are considering a commitment in this field, you can make a realistic evaluation of the intrinsic merit of the given security.

1) The Nature of the High Current Return — The fundamental nature of the liberal tax-sheltered current dividend must be clearly understood.

These distributions, most of which are made on a monthly basis, are not tax-exempt in the sense of municipal bonds. They are accorded, at best, tax-sheltered treatment as a return of capital.

This stems from a high degree of leverage derived from the use of sizable borrowed funds and favorable tax treatment of operating earnings due to rapid depreciation allowances.

>**Thus, in assessing the profitability of any real estate project, we focus on the cash flow — net operating earnings and depreciation — for this figure will determine the size of potential dividend distributions.**

After interest and debt amortization expenses and maintenance charges are deducted from rental income, the balance is available for the stockholders.

• **Since depreciation is a tax-deductible expense, if it is high enough to offset net operating earnings, the property is operating at a loss for tax purposes and any return to the participants in such a venture is treated as a return of capital, which is tax-free until the investor's original equity is retrieved.**

When his basis price has been reduced to zero, any subsequent payments are treated as capital gains, taxable at the maximum rate of 25%. If the investor sells his shares at that point, he will incur capital gains taxes on the entire proceeds.

>This seemingly ideal situation has two very serious drawbacks. *First, the favorable tax treatment of real estate operating earnings may be shortlived. It represents a loophole which many people believe will be at least partially plugged in the next session of Congress.*

Such change would not operate retroactively and would not affect any of the existing properties, but would nevertheless have a material effect on real estate earnings and dividends.

>**The second drawback is inherent in a rapid depreciation schedule. As the depreciation curve slopes downward, the property must be sold or refinanced; otherwise the depreciation charge is insufficient to offset net operating earnings, thereby subjecting the property to taxes and materially diminishing the fund available for dividends.**

In the face of perceptible over-development in many metropolitan areas, as indicated by rising vacancy rates, such property sales may be becoming increasingly difficult. This leads us to the second feature.

2) Long Term Asset Appreciation — The post-war period has witnessed an unprecedented rise in real estate values. Many corporations which have depreciated their portfolio assets were able to sell their properties at prices far above their adjusted book values. **It is alleged that the true values (market values) of assets presently on the books of real estate companies far exceed their written-down costs.**

In the absence of accurate appraisal, no investor can make a valid evaluation of any such discrepancy.

On the other hand, it is known that one of the industry's largest entities was forced to sell several parcels

of commercial real estate in 1961 at a substantial loss. The type of property involved, its location, and the demand for it may give some clues as to its intrinsic value.

3) **Access to Substantial Resources** — It is axiomatic that a large diversified real estate company would have easier access to future financing than an individual syndicate. **At the same time, it must be noted that many of these companies are already top-heavy in debt, with capitalization ratios of 70% funded debt to 30% equity capital, not uncommon. With no reinvestment of earnings (all, or substantially all, cash flow is paid out in dividends), future growth must come from equity financing accompanied by dilution. Moreover, it must be realized that leverage maximizes losses as well as profits.**

Therefore, should we witness a real slump in demand, not only the dividends in these companies, but also the fixed charges would be seriously impaired.

A few of the more conservatively operated companies have faced this problem by amortizing their debt at a rate in excess of mortgage requirements. This form of self-imposed saving has the salutary effect of a true increment in the book value of the stock.

4) **Diversification of Risk** — Diversification of properties and locations affords the investor a measure of protection against unforeseen economic setbacks of a particular area or type of property. •As an example, consider the disastrous experience of the investor in textile properties in New England. •By the same token the management of a real estate company must be thoroughly familiar with the operation of the type of property in which the company invests.

• The successful operation of a major metropolitan hotel is essentially different from that of a resort hotel or motel; that of a motel from a shopping center. **When a real estate company invests its money in any venture, it must have the experience, the talent, and the capability to run the project if need be and to run it successfully.**

>Moreover, the investor would be well-advised to examine what interests the company invests in. *As attractive*

real estate becomes more scarce, a brisk market in interests less than full ownership develops. Thus, we find a number of companies purchasing merely leasehold or net lease interests. **The value of such diversification is small. The lessor obtains no benefit of depreciation or potential increment in value but merely a pre-determined rate of return for a term of years. The security of such an investment is largely determined by the quality of the tenants and the duration of their leases.**

5) Professional Management — Professional, experienced real estate management is exceedingly difficult to find. The far-flung interests of a diversified real estate company require the services of a pool of professional talent, embracing finance, law, accounting, and many specialties. Even the successful syndicate did not entail the scope of the new activity.

•It must be borne in mind that the industry today is still highly promotional, and that most real estate managements are recruited from the ranks of imaginative syndicate promoters. In many instances, the broadened horizons of expanded activities have led directly to empire building. Some such ventures were disastrous, others are struggling with projects which were ill-conceived from the start.

>**Finally, it should be borne in mind that the incorporation of a real estate syndicate and its subsequent distribution to the public should not be for the private gain of its promoters. The investor should carefully scrutinize the nature of the transactions between the management and the company.**

The Real Estate Investment Trust
(The Set-up and Numerous Technical Provisions)

The Real Estate Investment Trust Act, which became effective in January 1961, is intended to provide comparable tax treatment for real estate investments to that accorded the mutual funds. As a consequence of such favorable treatment, the trusts must comply with the enabling statute in their investments and operations, and to submit to the full regulatory power of the government.

The real estate investment trust is an unincorporated association of no less than 100 beneficial owners, no five of whom control more than 50% of the shares.

•Its distinguishing feature is that the trust must be "passive," an investment, divorced from the management of the properties owned.

•The management company must be independent, although a measure of cross ownership (no more than 35%) is permissible.

•Investment policy is left to the discretion of the trustees although the nature of eligible investments is closely prescribed.

•Thus, 90% of gross revenues must be from real estate, dividends, interest and stock gains; 75% of the gross revenues, however, must be attributable to real estate holdings.

>**The key provisions relate to the distribution of income. The trust must distribute at least 90% of its income in order to preserve its corporate income tax exemption. Presumably, the trusts will distribute 100% of income.**

•Capital gains may be retained for reinvestment, in which case the trust is liable for taxes. *This is another feature, distinguishing it from the real estate corporation which is liable for the gains while the distribution of the gains to the shareholders subjects them to ordinary income tax rates on that portion of the dividends.*

Why the Investor Must Be Wary

The foregoing provisions are incomplete and serve only to indicate the extent of the technicalities inherent in the new law.

Moreover, detailed Treasury regulations implementing the Act are nearly a year late. The result of this colossal administrative indulgence, has been that the majority of the new trusts have the bulk of their assets in temporary short-term Government investments.

133

Let the Buyer Beware

>Beyond these technicalities a few crucial questions concerning the basic concepts of the trusts must be noted.

>**Uppermost is the concern over the timing of these new enterprises. The trusts are coming to the market at the height of the real estate boom.**

•To comply with their intended purposes, they will have to compete with the syndicates and corporations for the few remaining parcels of relatively attractive income producing properties.

•The potential price spiral in existing properties may lead to undesirable speculation and in the face of rising vacancy rates it is doubtful that such excess costs will be retrieved from would-be commercial, industrial, and residential tenants.

• **In case of a temporary set-back, the effect on portfolio values could be extremely damaging.**

•In this connection, it should be pointed out that the trusts are limited to only 30% of their revenues from any short-term capital gains, which (with regard to real estate holdings) embrace a holding period of less than four years.

• **Another, factor worth considering is the trusts' ability to effect necessary renovation, remodeling and extraordinary maintenance. With all income paid out in dividends, the only way such projects can be undertaken is through new financing, presumably through additional shares. Thus, it is reasonable to expect some measure of dilution, in many respects similar to the open end mutual fund.**

• **Finally, a word about insiders' or promoters' trading with the trust.**

These enterprises are trusts only in form, and not in the relationship between the trustees and the beneficiaries. Indeed, the trustees may exercise effective control, benefit from increase in value and engage in numerous transactions which private fiduciaries are prohibited.

Hopefully, these managers will be guided by principles of prudent business conduct in their relationship with the trusts under their administration. *Quite regrettably, such has not been the uniform practice in many of the newly organized trusts.*

In Sum

The Real Estate Investment Trust Act has greatly expanded the project for public buying of real estate issues. It has not solved the basic requirement of extreme selectivity.

This article has attempted to delineate the necessary analytical processes which the investor must follow in making commitments in a relatively new area. A number of exceptionally well operated trusts and corporations are available for the investor's consideration. A review of the most attractive selections in this field must await a future study. If the reader is helped to avoid some pitfalls as a result of this article, we will have achieved our immediate objective.

Reprinted from *The Magazine of Wall Street,* Vol. 110 (April 7, 1962) by permission of Colonial Communications Corp.

MANAGEMENT'S DUTIES
IN PUBLICLY OWNED REAL ESTATE

*By Louis J. Glickman.**

*President and Chairman of the Board
Glickman Corporation, New York City*

Changes in real estate managerial responsibilities
wrought by the transition from personal, limited ownership to the present new era of public ownership — via
syndications, real estate corporations and investment
trusts — are traced by expert intimately involved in real
estate operations for 35 years. Three areas requiring
progress are: custodianship, technology, and knowledge
of real estate in particular and the economy in general.
Mr. Glickman notes that competition for good properties
are increasing and profit margins narrowing — hence,
the need for research and development, revolution in
real estate technology, and keeping properties long life
income producers, Mr. Glickman also addresses himself
to the charges made that real estate has lowered its
standards, and caused booms and busts.

There is no professional association with which I can
identify my life's work more closely than that of the Building
Owners and Managers. After all, for 35 years, I have made
a comfortable living by owning and managing buildings — for
myself, for my syndications, and now for the corporation I'm
privileged to head. While I have witnessed many changes in
the real estate industry in the course of these 35 years, none
have been as significant and as dramatic as those which
developed as we entered the era of public ownership of real
estate.

And, indeed, we have entered a new era. An era in
which man has taken some of the most aggressive and most
far-reaching steps in search of a better life. An era in which

---

*An address by Mr. Glickman before the convention of the
National Association of Building Owners and Managers, San Fran-
cisco, Calif.

tremendous strides have been made in the fight against disease. An era in which man has attained the virtual conquest of space. An era, also, in which man has begun to realize his desire to share the basic wealth of our country — its land and the structures above it.

Let us not underestimate this new complexion of property ownership. This shift in the ownership of real estate — from the hands of the wealthy few to the domain of the millions — has been an evolutionary change on the American scene, in fact, it has been revolutionary in its scope. And this has been a natural and predictable development. Why? Because the values of properties have risen to such an extent that the individual investor can no longer afford to own large prime urban real estate alone. For some years now, the multi-million-dollar individual investor has been fading from the scene because of our national tax structure and is now practically extinct. To replace him in the real estate market, we now have group ventures, such as syndications, publicly owned companies and investment trusts, which have stepped in and taken up the slack. And this is as it should be.

Now what does this revolution mean to those who manage buildings of all kinds? It means that those who do not already manage properties for large group ventures should look forward to the day, perhaps very soon, when you will be doing so. And it is this new dimension that I want to discuss in some detail. Basically, it can be broken down into three essentials. One is a new look at the custodianship in managing properties for thousands of absent and faceless owners. Second, is the absolute need to adopt modern technology; just as every industry has to do as it faced the challenges of the Twentieth Century. And third, we will have to become even keener judges of the real estate market and the economy in general than ever before.

Custodianship for Absentee Owners

Let's look at the first of these — custodianship. Managing properties for syndications, real estate corporations and trusts, means serving a new type of master. That master is the millions of thrifty Americans who have set aside a part of their incomes to invest in the skylines of our cities. And I am one who believes that this is a trust. We cannot default. I became alert to it when public syndications began about a decade ago, when hundreds and sometimes thousands of people — strangers to each other — became partners in the ownership of large properties. I realized then that I was no longer managing properties for my own account, but that I was the guardian of the cherished investment of others. This same feeling has become intensified since my enterprise, like many others, became a publicly held stock company in which people from all walks of life can invest their hard-earned money without even the benefit of direct contact with the man at the wheel.

Let's look at a simple example of where the burden of this custodianship has changed with the advent of public ownership. A responsible and far-sighted managing agent may know that a major renovation of a particular building is in order. He knows what the job will cost and also what that cost will do to the cash flow of that property. What's more, he knows the consequences of delaying the needed renovation. Now, in managing that building for an individual or a small group of owners whom you know personally, you can call them in and lay the cards on the table. The chances are that they'll rely heavily on your judgment and tell you to do what you think is best. But, at least, they have been consulted and, regardless of the outcome, there is a sense of shared responsibility between owner and manager.

But you can't call in 16,000 stockholders and discuss management problems with them. You have to make these decisions for them — courageously and in good faith — and you can't palm off any of the responsibility for the consequences of your decision. In the case of the renovation I've used as an example, I say that if you are thoroughly convinced that the costly pill of renovation, if swallowed today, can bring about a brighter day tomorrow, it is your responsibility to have the courage of your convictions — and renovate. It's the same kind of courage a doctor needs to muster when it would be easier to spare an anxious patient some unpleasant therapy. We are professionals too, and our investors look to us for the same kind of professional judgment and courage in the custodianship of their properties.

Real Estate Industrial Revolution

Next we must consider the means by which we can become as modern in our techniques as the modern look of our industry requires. And what are the hallmarks of modern industry? One is the broad base of ownership. We have that. Another is automation. We don't have it yet. And then there is research and development. Another field in which we are lacking today. Let's face it, the development of the publicly owned real estate company is only the beginning of what may be considered the industrial revolution of property ownership and management.

We are already seeing some strong competition developing among these groups for desirable properties and several hundred million dollars is in the market looking for sound investments. The narrowing profit margins will bring about the next major change in property ownership. While ingenuity, imagination and know-how have always been of prime importance in the management of property, this growing competition will compel us to apply new, Twentieth Century technology. This new technology is needed not only to cut costs, but — and this is far more important — it is needed to make our operations more efficient and to provide better service in order to remain competitive.

An important step in this direction is automation. Since the first of this year — after many months of planning and preparation — our company has been feeding all figures relating to the operation of our properties into giant computers. Since the first of May, all tenant billings, payments, and arrears followups have been handled automatically by our data processing devices. But this can be only a beginning. Research and development is our biggest challenge today. In other industries a company is judged largely by the research and development it carries on. We, too, will be judged in the same way mighty soon, and we must be ready for it.

Some may ask — Where does research and development fit into a program of property management? The answer to this is important and, what's more, the lack of an answer can be fatal in managing properties for publicly held ventures. The competition for good properties is mounting now and will continue to mount. This means that profit margins are likely to narrow, unless we can compensate elsewhere in the balance sheet. That elsewhere must be found and the degree of compensation must be increased. And this means constant research into both physical and financial technology. It means not only searching for better ways to operate our buildings and serve our tenants. But it also means finding more efficient means of minding our own stores to reduce overhead without diluting our effectiveness. It means finding even better ways of using the purchasing power that large property portfolios give us. Only if we tackle our jobs with the modern approach, through research, can we make this public ownership principle meaningful and beneficial to the millions who cast their lot with us.

Our third important task is to become keener judges of the economy in general and of the real estate market in particular. Our industry has come under some sharp criticism during recent months — both in highly respected journals and even in the corridors of government. Charges have been leveled at us in the real estate industry for riding the crest of a boom, completely oblivious to the bust which is said to be just around the corner. And charges have been leveled at us that we have diluted our high standards in our financial dealings, in construction and in other phases of our business.

Denies Real Estate Caused
Booms and Busts

Now, I have never found that real estate has been identified with frequent and artificial booms or busts. I have never subscribed to the idea that the vast construction of the post-war years has been a boom in any sense of the word. First of all, it was necessary to make up for the under-building of the 1930s and during the war years. Beyond that, it was a natural expansive movement, no more than in line with the expansion of our population and our economy.

Our nation's population is expanding to a point where the figure of 200 million people is only a decade or so away. Our gross national product has soared over the $500 billion mark and is still increasing steadily. For 200 million people to produce and consume $500 billion worth of goods and services, we will need more space of all kinds, and common sense tells us that we must be ready for it by creating this space in the years immediately ahead, beginning right now. And may heaven help us if we do not keep pace with the growth of our country.

Poor Construction and Lowering
of Other Standards

The second charge, that of dilution of our high standards, should concern us just as much. Our industry has been charged by its critics with undermining the vitality of the central city by developing the suburbs too much. And it has been charged, at the same time, with overcrowding our central city. Our industry has been accused of producing chintzy office buildings by hanging flimsy curtain walls around thinly disguised loft space. And, at the same time, it has been accused of trying to hide the age of our older buildings behind the cosmetics of remodeled lobbies and elevators. We have been maligned for building too much, too quickly. And we have been chided for building too little and too late.

In other words, to listen to our critics we're damned if we do and we're damned if we don't. But isn't it just possible that some of those who snipe at our industry are out of touch with reality — with the reality of the times we live in? Let's look and see for ourselves.

What has really happened during the past decade is a twofold development. First we have had, as I mentioned before, a phenomenal expansion of our economy. From our point of view, as owners and managers of office buildings, this has meant a tremendous demand for office space to accommodate new industries as well as new and growing companies in existing industries.

Second, through syndication, publicly held real estate companies and now the investment trusts, a growing number of office buildings in and around our cities have become the property of millions of people who have no experience in property management. These people look to you to make and keep these properties productive through imaginative leasing practices, resourceful financing and a keen sense of the markets in which to buy or sell properties for these portfolios.

Vacancy Rental Rates

That we have done a good job so far is self-evident from the available statistics. Figures gathered by the National Association of Real Estate Boards tell us that in 71% of our prime urban office buildings, the vacancy rate is no more than 5%. Indeed, it is 2% or less in 34% of our prime urban office buildings. And what about residential properties? The same source tells us that in 25% of all rental multiple family units — and I'm speaking only of habitable units — in 25% of all rental multiple family units the vacancy factor is 2% or less. And it is 5% or less in nearly two-thirds of all these dwelling units. I think we can look anyone squarely in the eye and say that we have kept our inventory of buildings productive.

But where do we go from here? Let's look first at our existing inventory of buildings — I don't like to call them old because age has little to do with quality. I am convinced that a prime property can be kept prime through imaginative management, regardless of its age. Let us remember that buildings become prime real estate because they're put up for the right use at the right place. We can keep them prime by applying the modern technology of which I spoke before. This is where research and development comes in. Our research should delve into finding methods of predicting, with a measure of certainty, who the future tenants of these buildings are likely to be, what their needs are and what services they would reasonably expect.

Threshold of Real Estate Technology

Our research should stay a pace, if not a step ahead, of the changing patterns in the lives of our cities, to make certain that we are prepared for changes when they come. And our research should determine well in advance what physical amenities it will take to keep our prime properties prime. Today we talk about automated elevators and central air conditioning. But if we apply ourselves diligently to our research, these may be only horse-and-buggy conveniences compared to the ones we may someday offer our tenants. In the fields of communications and transportation, to name just two, lie untold advances by which we may someday equip our buildings with time-savers, money-savers and tenant-savers. As I said before, we're only at the very beginning of a new era of real estate technology.

Prime real estate, if properly managed, can produce steady income for a long time. But income is only part of the picture. What we are sometimes tempted to forget — and something which we must never, never forget — is that income is only one of the benefits for which the investor buys real estate through publicly held group ventures. Far more important, I think, is growth of equity, and it is growth we should keep in mind when we plan and when we execute our plans.

So, as we manage properties for public ownership, our strategy remains the same, but our tactics may change. Where older prime buildings once commanded the tenancy of our largest and most highly rated tenants, they now command the patronage of the smaller and newer enterprises that make our economy grow. And it is an old axiom of leasing practice that the rents per square foot are higher for small tenants than they are for giant space users. Consequently, I have no fear for the well located and well managed skyscraper built a generation or two ago.

What about the new towers that grace our city skylines? Are they chintzy? Are they a drug on the market? Not in my book. Criticism, especially in the fields of art and architecture, must be subjective and controversy just can't be avoided. But the new towers, sheathed in various combinations of metal, glass and masonry are representatives of a new technology and, in most cases, of new concepts in space planning.

Most certainly they are needed. Again, I point to our economic expansion. If the lure of new buildings has caused a certain degree of fluidity in the commercial leasing market, I welcome it. It makes it possible for us to engage in imaginative planning and leasing of the type that keeps buildings productive. The fact that the concentration of these new structures has created entire new business neighborhoods is also a healthy sign. I consider them no threat whatsoever to our established financial and mercantile districts where the older buildings stand.

But those of you who manage these gleaming new towers must use foresight also. Today, these new buildings, many of which are publicly owned, are new and shiny. But they, too, will be superceded by others and they will pass into the realm of the old-fashioned. Therefore, you, too must undertake serious research into methods for keeping them competitive and productive. In short, you must prepare today for tomorrow just as those whose properties have already been steam-cleaned once or twice. Your time for research and planning is now, especially if you bear the responsibility of running these properties for thousands of unseen stockholders.

Perhaps the government, in its desire to define corporations for tax purposes, has put its finger on a principle which we, as property managers, would be wise to consider. One of the characteristics of a corporation, government tax manuals say, is continuity. And it is continuity which we should keep in mind in managing properties for our stockholders in the modern economy. They have invested their funds in real estate because they consider it less fickle, less volatile and considerably more stable than many other investment opportunities offered to them.

Neither Fickle Nor Volatile

It is our job, then, to live up to these expectations. Real estate, if properly managed, is not fickle or volatile. In fact, I'd say it is one of the most stable industries I know. There is not an industry which does not have its ups and downs; which does not react to the vagaries of the national economy and foreign developments; and which does not, to some degree, affect the national economy in turn. We, in the real estate industry, also have our ups and downs, and I think we are all aware of the fact that a major disaster in our economy is certain to affect us in due time. But I look for no disaster in our economy and, as a result, I do not look for a disaster in our industry. As a matter of fact, historically, real estate is the last facet of our economy to react to recessions — although, admittedly, it is also late in responding to the upturn when it comes.

As long as we act responsibly in the ownership and management of properties, as long as we use the tools of modern technology, as long as we prepare for the future through research and planning, we can insure the stability of our industry. Let no one forget that the real estate industry is stable and sound, and that it deserves the respect of the community and the public. We are not saints and we are not masterminds. But we have a long and honorable heritage, and it is about time we blew our horns about it. I know that ours is an industry which is only on the threshold of a bright new age.

Reprinted by permission of *Commercial and Financial Chronicle*, 110 Wall Street, New York, N.Y. 10005, Vol. 196 (July 19, 1962).

CASH-FLOW PRESENTATION IN REAL ESTATE INVESTMENTS

By Julius Peltz

The author is a certified public accountant in New York City.

THE IMPORTANCE of cash-flow effects in manufacturing and natural resources enterprises is a well-established fact of financial life. Consequently, such presentation in financial statement form, for management and investor alike, has been quite thoroughly explored — even to the point of "cash flow per share" computation.

To the average real estate investor, however, cash flow is not so much a matter of funds available for possible reinvestment in expansion and research, for example, with resultant future capital (and market) value increase in his investment. To such investor, cash flow is a matter of immediate and primary importance, determining the actual current return on his investment — in dollars and cents — and upon which many such investors depend daily. (And with the advent of the far-reaching real estate syndication investment medium during the past decade, this is now more the case than ever.)

With the popularization, so to speak, of real estate investment, therefore, goes the problem of cash-flow presentation in such a manner that even a lay reader of financial statements can understand same.

The commonly used form for presenting cash flow — the Application of Funds Statement — is generally prepared separately as a supplement to the usual statements of condition and operation. In real estate financial statement analysis, the same procedure is invariably followed, resulting in adequate information — to the *experienced* peruser of such statements. The uninitiated investor, however, may be hard put to determine just what is the cash profit available for distribution to him — what he is first, last and foremost

TABLE 1

ABC REALTY CORP.
COMPARATIVE BALANCE SHEETS

Assets	9/30/61	9/30/62	Changes*
Cash in bank	$ 6,200	$ 5,600	$ (600)
Property	527,800	527,800	—0—
Ppd. exp., dep., etc.	800	1,600	800
Total Assets	$534,800	$535,000	$ 200

Liabilities and Capital			
Expenses (and taxes) payable	$ 12,600	$ 15,200	$ 2,600
Mortgages payable	299,900	287,700	(12,200)
Notes payable	64,600	56,600	(8,000)
Accrued interest on notes	4,200	3,700	(500)
Capital stock	27,300	27,300	—0—
Earned surplus	48,500	56,900	8,400
Allowance for depreciation	77,700	87,600	9,900
Total Liabilities and Capital	$534,800	$535,000	$ 200

*"Cash" profit consisted of **earned surplus** increase of $8,400
plus **allowance for depreciation** increase of 9,900
plus **accrual for interest** on stockholders' notes of 3,700

For a total cash inflow (after income taxes
of $3,600) of .... $ 22,000
This amount was applied towards **mortgage**
payments of $12,200
plus **interest** payments to stockholders of 4,200
plus **note** payments to stockholders of 8,000

For a total cash outgo of 24,400

Resulting in a net decrease of total assets less expenses
payable of .... $ (2,400)

TABLE 2

ABC REALTY CORP.

STATEMENT OF INCOME AND EXPENSES
10/1/61 to 9/30/62

		Percent Return on Investment*
Rent income	$105,500	
Total general expenses (per Sched. A) _____$72,900		
Total repairs and maintenance (per Sched. B) 7,000		
Total Operating Expenses	79,900	
"Cash" profit (before **amortization and taxes**)	25,600	
Less: amortization	12,200	
"Cash" profit (before **taxes**)	13,400	9.8
Less: federal income taxes	3,600	2.7
"Cash" Profit Available for Stockholders	$ 9,800	7.1
Less: Paid versus "notes" _____$ 8,000		
Paid versus "interest" on "notes" ____ 4,200		
Total Paid to Stockholders	12,200	8.9
Insufficiency of "Cash" Profit	(2,400)	(1.8)
Add: "note" payments _____$ 8,000		
Add: amortization minus depreciation _____ 2,300		
Add: "interest" paid minus "interest" accrued 500		
Total adjustments for tax return purposes	10,800	
Increase in Earned Surplus	$ 8,400	

* of $136,500

usually interested in. Too (and what may be even more important to him as a criterion of the value of his investment — no matter how uninformed he may be analysis-wise), he wants to know what the profit return on his investment is, *percentage-wise*. Such a figure he *can* understand.

In my practice, I have formulated a presentation which seems to attain the foregoing objectives simply and succinctly — and in a manner which integrates the information directly into the financial statements themselves.

While, obviously, no startling innovations are involved, the rearrangements utilized do present the data so that — at a glance — the lay investor can see not only how much cash is available for distribution to him and how much thereof was actually so distributed, but also what percentage return these amounts constitute on his original investment. This information is presented as an integral part of the Statement of Operations, which still concludes with the book value increase or decrease in Net Worth, and consequently still ties in with the Balance Sheet. The latter statement is presented in a two-year comparative form, so that a simplified Statement of Source and Application of Funds can be prepared therefrom — and in such manner that the data contained in this cash-flow summary can be related directly to the Statement of Operations.

Presented on the preceding page is a specific example of the foregoing — drawn from actual experience, and shown just as originally reported to the investors. The illustration involves a so-called "thin" corporation, with the Notes Payable being held by the stockholders in direct proportion to stockholdings — a not too atypical situation. This thus allows for demonstration of the handling of the payments thereagainst, as well as the related interest accrued and paid factors. The corporation in question also has a taxable profit, which provides an opportunity for comparison — return-wise — with a partnership or nontaxable trust type of entity (the latter of which may perhaps be more prevalent now as a result of the recently enacted real estate trust legislation).

The following explanatory comments on these statements may be helpful in highlighting the points stressed previously:

Operating Statement

(1) The Operating Expense total includes all expenses other than Depreciation (the non-cash item) and Interest on Stockholder's Notes (which, in reality, is an *after*-profit item). It is assumed that any other non-cash expenses, such as amortization of improvements, prepayments, etc., are relatively nominal as a total or net figure. Therefore, the Operating Expense total may be considered the total of all *cash* expenses attributable to the income.

(2) The total of Amortization (of Mortgage) payments (which ties in with the Balance Sheet) is shown as an expenditure. While, technically, this is not the case, the lay investor does realistically so consider it.

(3) The Cash Profit remaining after Amortization is what is left for the investor and the government. At this point, the percentage Return on Investment is first shown. And this percentage figure should mean even more to the proportionate investor than the total dollar amount of cash flow.

(4) The payments to the government and investors are clearly set forth, as is any under- or over-distribution of available profits. And these amounts are easily traceable to the Balance Sheet, either as part of the statement itself or the accompanying cash-flow analysis. Note particularly the tie-in of Insufficiency of Cash Profit as between both statements.

(5) Finally, the tax return or "book" adjustments result in a net amount which is the easily recognizable Earned Surplus increase or decrease.

Balance Sheets

(1) The stockholders' Notes Payable and related interest accruals are placed just above the Capital Stock, enabling one to see the composite investment status more easily.

(2) Similarly, the accumulated Depreciation is placed just below the accumulated Surplus, allowing for a clearer picture of the Cash Profit total as a whole.

(3) The Cash-Flow analysis begins with these two latter figures, and follows through, with each item therein traceable to and from the Statement of Operations.

While the foregoing illustration involves a corporation, the same procedure can just as easily be applied to a partnership. In such instance, the Drawings would be either the equivalent of the Notes and Interest thereon, or an addition thereto — which (latter) effect would be similar to a corporation also paying Dividends.

Reprinted by special permission of author and the publisher of *TAXES, The Tax Magazine,* Vol. 41 (May, 1963).

REAL ESTATE TRUSTS—
A Different Breed

**Enjoying a better record in this market, than the
corporations, trusts offer investors an opportunity
for sound income and long range growth**

The performance of the real estate investment trusts will
help restore investors' faith in real estate, if anything will.
The black eye given this area of investment by the real estate
corporations last year has had a profound effect on equities
associated with land and improvements.

Although the corporate issues — with only a few exceptions — declined far and fast, the shares in the newly created
real estate trusts have held up very well. The issues listed in
the accompanying table are all relatively new and their
present quotations are not far below (and in some instances
slightly above) their offering prices.

Set-up Created in '61

All of these situations are newcomers to the market because they represent trusts set up under a federal statute that
went into effect January 1, 1961. It allows a closed-end trust
invested in real estate to escape the double taxation of the
corporate structure, provided the trust pays out at least 90%
of its net income to its shareholders.

This new set-up was created to give small investors the
opportunity to pool their funds to take advantage of the higher
returns usually available from improved land, i.e. office buildings, apartment houses, hotels, shopping centers and industrial plants. The trusts must comply with rather rigid
requirements to be eligible for the tax exclusion. They cannot
deal in real estate as operators — buying and selling properties
or instruments in rapid succession. They cannot manage the
properties they own, although as owners, they can set
management policy. Moreover, not more than 15% of income
can come from non-realty sources.

In other words, the very basis on which the trusts are set up avoids the great pitfall into which so many of the real estate corporations tumbled. That is, the trusts are not supposed to acquire property in anticipation of rapid depreciation for tax-free return of capital and then sell it for capital gain. The trusts are just what the word usually implies: a vehicle for the long-term holding of property primarily for income. Of course, capital gains will not be ignored.

In this respect real estate often has a distinct advantage over some other forms of investment. Well maintained properties usually retain their original values over the years and obsolescence of improvements is usually slower than in any other field. At the same time, land values in populated areas continue to increase as people multiply. Hence depreciation allowed on real estate has been considered as income that can be used to retire debt, make new investments or spend, even though it is theoretically a return of capital.

Because of this advantage given to realty investors, the Internal Revenue Service looks on the field with a jaundiced eye. There is some indication that it would like to reverse the 1960 legislation. But as there is little likelihood of Congress taking such a tack, the IRS will apply the law as strictly as possible.

This was indicated not long ago by an IRS ruling that First Mortgage Investors would not qualify for the tax exemption because more than a quarter of its income is from construction loans and so-called mortgage warehousing. First Mortgage's problem lies largely in its reliance on "deals" to boost its return over the cost of its bank borrowing. Both First Mortgage and Continental Mortgage Investors — another trust with a similar operation — are appealing the ruling.

Real estate investment trusts that are largely invested in land and improvements, rather than their paper representations, have less to fear from such official hostility.

How Trusts Work

Flato Realty Investments is an example of how one of these trusts is put together to provide investment for the long pull with geographical diversification and at the same time throw off income. Franklin Flato, a realtor of Dallas, Tex., and his associates put together a portfolio by swapping trust shares for ten properties: A Woolworth building in Corpus Christi, Tex., an apartment development in a Pennsylvania suburb, office buildings in Dallas and Big Spring, Tex., and shopping centers in Houston and San Antonio, Tex., Pompano Beach and Hollywood, Fla., Casper, Wyo., and Denver, Col.

In addition, Mr. Flato describes his diversification policy as embodying safeguards beyond those provided in the statute. As a trust Flato will not acquire new holdings which will result in more than 40% of its investments to be located in any single metropolitan area; it will place no more than 25% of its assets in any single property, and it will limit investment in any one type of property to 50% or $10 million, whichever is greater.

Another trust, Greenfield — which is now fully invested, has also gone in for geographical diversification. It owns property in the District of Columbia, New Jersey, Pennsylvania, Delaware and Maryland. The Washington trust is largely concentrated in the area of the nation's capital. In addition to holdings in Bethesda, Md., it has property occupied by a Veterans Administration center in Arlington, Va., and a half interest in an apartment development in Fairfax County, Va. First Union Realty has two large office buildings in Cleveland.

Real estate values benefit from rising population. In recent years they have also been boosted by the declining purchasing power of the dollar. The likelihood is that these two factors will go on operating for some time. A study supported by the Ford Foundation asserts that by the year 2000 there will be more than 330 million people in this country — a rise of better than 80% over the present population. Households will approach 100 million — a boost of about 85%, and new dwelling units will multiply more than twice as fast as population. Building activity — in terms of today's dollars — is expected to increase some 400%.

Although the present market for real estate investment trust certificates is somewhat limited, they do provide a means for investors to participate in this form of investment on

a moderate scale. Before making such a commitment, however, the investor should learn all he can about the management of the trust, its policies and all pertinent details of its
investments.

REAL ESTATE INVESTMENT TRUSTS

These are a number of representative trusts.
They are not offered as recommendations for purchase.

	Statement Date	Equity per Share	Dividends Pd. in '62	Recent Bid
American Realty	Sept. 30, '62	$ 8.93	$ 0.47	10¼
First Mortgage Investors	Jan. 31, '63	13.65	0.39	9⅝
First Union Realty	Apr. 30, '62	11.02	0.70	13
Flato Realty Inv.	Apr. 30, '62	9.43	———	7
Greenfield R. E. Inv.	Aug. 31, '62	18.27	0.45	15⅜
U.S. Realty Inv.	May 31, '62	9.10	0.70	9⅝
Washington R. E. Inv.	Mar. 31, '62	4.44	0.25	6

Reprinted by permission of *Financial World*, Vol. 119 (May 29,
1963).

PERSONAL INVESTING:
The Rise of the R.E.I.T.'s
A New Road into Real Estate

Editor: *Daniel Seligman*
Associate Editors: *T. A. Wise*
Carol J. Loomis

Speaking recently to a somewhat startled audience of real-estate men, Lawrence A. Wien, New York's best-known promoter of public real-estate syndicates, announced that he now saw no justification for the formation of the syndicates. In the future, Wien said, the most popular way to invest in real estate would be through the real-estate investment trust.

The trusts have been a little-known investment medium. There are some fifty of them in existence, with perhaps $500 million in assets, but most have names that are unfamiliar to investors. Most were organized in 1961 and early 1962, and have still not recovered the losses they took in the 1962 market crash. Just recently, however, a number of new trusts have been organized, and it appears that a fresh wave of expansion is on its way. Some people think Wien himself may be entering the field.

Technically, a real-estate investment trust is an unincorporated business association. (There are some legal ambiguities, but it appears that trust stockholders do not enjoy completely limited liability, as corporate stockholders do.) There have been real-estate trusts in existence since the nineteenth century, principally in Massachusetts, but the current crop was inspired by a 1960 federal tax law. The thinking behind this law was that the small investor should be given an opportunity to invest in a diversified real-estate portfolio without being subject to taxation on income at both the corporate and the individual levels — in other words, that he deserved to have the tax benefits that are enjoyed by investors in mutual funds and other regulated investment companies. The 1960 law provided that any trust that met certain strict standards as to structure and investment policy, and that paid out to its stockholders at least 90 percent of its net income, exclusive of capital gains (as regulated investment companies must also do), would be free from any corporate tax on those distributed earnings.

This tax treatment led many people to equate the trusts with mutual funds. Actually, they are more comparable to closed-end funds. Like these, they are traded through stock brokers, principally in the over-the-counter market (although one of the old Massachusetts trusts, Real Estate Investment Trust of America, is listed on the American Stock Exchange). And like the closed-end funds, the trusts may sell well above or below their net-asset values.

From most standpoints, however, the trusts are different from any investment companies. Because they are investing in real estate, not securities, they are geared to provide a high, steady rate of return to their shareholders, and they are enthusiastic users of borrowed capital to obtain leverage. In these respects they are like the syndicates and like the publicly owned real-estate investment companies that were formed a few years ago to house groups of syndicates under one corporate roof. However, these syndicate organizations set out to provide investors with higher rates of return than the trusts have in mind. This is what got many of the syndicates in trouble: their cash flow from operations failed to cover the distributions they had virtually promised investors, and many were forced to cut their distributions. Unlike the syndicates, the trusts have not committed themselves to pay any specified return. In practice, investors seem to have been expecting 6 to 7 percent (the syndicates generally offered 9 to 12), and most of the larger trusts are now selling at prices that afford some such yield.

Filling the Paper Bag

There are several different kinds of trusts. The largest number began as *"blank-check" trusts*. These sold their shares to the public and *then* went out to find properties. In effect, one real-estate man commented, investors were buying "a paper bag with nothing in it." The bag might remain empty for some time: at the end of its first fiscal year, in February,

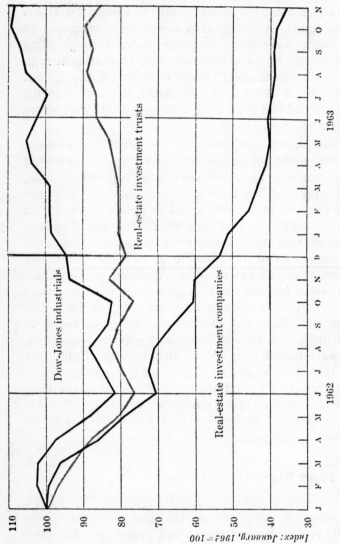

Real-estate investment trusts were hard hit in the 1962 market break but, unlike the better-known real-estate investment companies (most of these are corporations built around syndicates), they have done well since the break. (The stocks used in the trust index are listed on page 161; the company index is one compiled by the Wall Street firm of Eisele & King, Libaire, Stout; and the prices charted are those for the last Friday of each month.)

1962, Greenfield Real Estate Investment Trust, of Philadelphia, had still not found any property it was willing to buy; the $9,400,000 it had raised from investors was sitting in treasury bills, producing earnings of about 2.5 percent — earnings, incidentally, that were subject to the corporate tax, since a trust does not qualify for the special tax treatment unless it has got at least 75 percent of its gross income from real-estate sources. As of last month, Greenfield had succeeded in putting about $7 million of equity capital in real estate, and was still looking hard for properties.

The *"purchase"* trusts, on the other hand, go to the public seeking funds to buy specified properties. Since the SEC requires that the offering prospectus include a full description of these properties, investors have a chance to size up what they are being asked to buy before committing their money. Sometimes what they are being asked to buy are properties in which the promoters of the trust hold interests. This was true of twelve out of the fifteen properties bought by U.S. Realty Investments, of Cleveland, from the proceeds of a 1961 offering. In 1962, First Real Estate Investment Trust of New Jersey raised money through a "blank-check" offering, then invested the proceeds in properties in which the promoters held interests. The State of New York "induced" the trust to offer the shareholders a refund.

The *"exchange"* trusts came into being by offering their shares in exchange for properties. This kind of swap appeals to property owners because it enables them to diversify their holdings and, at the same time, postpone any capital-gains taxes until they sell the shares of the trust. The biggest of the exchange trusts, Liberty Real Estate Trust, whose assets of $17 million are mostly invested in Florida properties, has had rough going. The cash flow generated by the properties it took in has not covered the 70-odd-cents-per-share annual distribution the trust was expecting to pay. To maintain the distribution it has resorted to short-term borrowings — one of the practices that got the syndicates into trouble. The stock, which was originally offered at $10, is now selling at $6.

The *"mortgage"* trusts do not buy properties, but invest instead in mortgages and construction loans. In effect, then, they are in the finance business, competing with all the other financial institutions trying to place mortgage money. The two largest mortgage trusts, Continental Mortgage Investors and First Mortgage Investors, were set up as blank-check trusts and have been investing their money gradually. They are now earning and paying out upwards of 6 percent on the original price of their shares.

Some Choices to Make

The trusts, with only a few exceptions, appear to have been put together by real-estate men of high caliber. These "promoters" are now connected with the trusts in various capacities — as trustees, property managers, investment advisers, or legal counsel — but ordinarily receive a relatively modest compensation, unlike many of the syndicate promoters.

The promoters have differed considerably among themselves in their policies on debt, depreciation, and growth. All the trusts are, of course, users of borrowed capital. The trusts that qualified to sell their original offerings under "the Midwest rules," a set of guidelines used by eighteen states, are permitted to mortgage only up to two-thirds of their total properties' market value. But some trusts appear to have set much lower limits for themselves: e.g., Real Estate Investment Trust of America has held its debt around the 30 percent level. One highly leveraged trust is Washington (D.C.) Real Estate Investment Trust, whose assets of some $13 million are encumbered by better than $9 million of mortgages and other debt. With the help of this borrowed capital, the trust has got its cash flow up to a point at which it is paying out 7.6 percent on the original cost of its shares ($5) and still retaining some of its cash flow. The stock now sells for $6.50.

The trust managers also differ in the choices they have made between straight-line and accelerated depreciation. Many of them use accelerated depreciation, but not for the same reason corporations do — i.e., to defer taxes. The trusts, which are not taxed on distributed earnings, do it to protect their shareholders from taxation. Because any distribution paid out of depreciation instead of net income is a return of capital, the shareholder owes no tax on it until he recovers the full cost of his shares or sells them; and then he pays capital-gains taxes instead of straight income taxes.

Some trusts have been leery of accelerated depreciation, however. Practically all trusts must make regular principal payments on their mortgages, and these are normally made out of funds provided by depreciation. Usually the principal payments get bigger as the years go by, while the depreciation allowances, under an accelerated schedule, get smaller and

Trust	Assets ($000)	Debt ($000)	Net cash flow*	Net income	payout	Nov. 20 Price $	Indi-cated yield (%)
			$ per sh., latest qtr.				
Continental Mortgage Inv.	54,870	30,329	.273	.273	.25	14¾	6.8
First Mortgage Investors	51,800	36,450	.254	.242	.24	15⅝	6.1
First Union Realty	46,042	24,486	.206	.069	.195	13½	5.8
R.E.I.T. of America	37,922	10,963	.344	.310	.30	21⅜	5.6
U.S. Realty Investments	33,951	23,691	.195	.020	.175	9¼	7.6
1st Natl. Real Estate Trust	28,929	14,477	.184	.061	.175	9¼	7.6
National Realty Investors	22,694	10,068	.212	.122	.15	10	6.0
Pennsylvania R.E.I.T.	22,567	15,980	.233	.140	.20	10⅜	7.7
Greenfield R.E.I.T.	20,392	10,661	.225	.112	.225	14⅝	6.2
Franklin Realty	20,258	13,271	.109	.087	.075	9⅝	3.1

* After deducting principal payments on mortgages.

The ten largest trusts operate with dissimilar financial strategies. Some, like Pennsylvania R.E.I.T., have heavy debt burdens and a lot of leverage; some others, notably R.E.I.T. of America, have low debt ratios. The trusts that use straight-line depreciation, such as R.E.I.T. of America and Franklin Realty, show high net incomes in proportion to cash flow. Their payouts to stockholders are usually made out of net income and are thus fully taxable, while the distributions of the trusts that use accelerated depreciation are, in varying degrees, tax-sheltered returns of capital. (The two mortgage trusts have no properties and thus no depreciation allowances.) To figure yields, FORTUNE multiplied the latest quarterly payout by four; however, the payouts of some trusts are likely to be higher because their distributions are still in a rising trend—e.g., Franklin's announced dividend for the December quarter is 12 cents, compared to the 7½ cents shown here for the September quarter.

eventually no longer cover the mortgage amortization. At that point the trust can very easily find itself in a cash bind. The trust managers that are using accelerated depreciation believe that these problems can be handled — e.g., by refinancing mortgages to cut down the payments due on them, or by selling properties and buying different ones in order to acquire new depreciation bases.

Though the trusts are basically income securities, all have a capacity for some growth if real-estate values continue to climb. Some trust managers feel strongly that payouts to stockholders should be made only from net income and that the rest of cash flow should be retained for improving present properties and buying new ones. Their argument against paying stockholders a return of capital is summed up by Harold H. Gebert, president of Franklin Realty: "We feel that if the shareholder wants his money back, he will sell his stock."

FRESH APPRAISAL
The Rewards and Risks in
Real Estate Investment Trusts

By J. Richard Elliott, Jr.

"Real estate investment trusts are the most conservative investment vehicle in the history of real estate, but the stock market isn't exactly beating a path to their door. I admit that it's not a simple industry to understand. It takes a sharp pencil and considerable effort. I suppose that as long as financial fiascos continue to crop up in the real estate business at large, most people will just continue to wince and shrug and decide it's not worth the effort."

Robert M. Burr, Exec. Director,
National Association of
Real Estate Investment Funds

The latest shingle to go up in the world of property investment bears the name of Prudential Real Estate Trust. A New York concern holding title to 17 office, apartment and commercial buildings in 10 states, worth an estimated $26 million, it's one of more than three score real estate investment trusts, or "REITs," to go public in the past four years. What is unique about Prudential is its history. While the other trusts were established for the purpose, Prudential a few months ago was doing business as a concern called Leader-Durst Corp. A few years earlier, prior to going public, it was a collection of separately owned realty partnerships (or, more accurately, two such groups) put together respectively by Manhattan syndicators I. Theodore Leader and Joseph Durst. In short, Prudential became the first of the surviving real estate syndicate companies to seek shelter behind the shiny new facade of the investment trust.

Patience and Prudence

Though safe and sound in what some security analysts are calling the "haven" of the realty business, investors in Prudential, like most syndicate veterans, have been shaken up along the way. Their new managing trustee, Mr. Leader, sought for over a year to bring off the move, only to be balked by a reluctant Mr. Durst. During the protracted clash, the latter "resigned" as president (he says he was fired), sold nearly all his stock and launched a running battle in the courts. He filed — and lost — a suit designed to block the reorganization. A Leader action suing Durst for slander was thrown out. Among issues still unresolved is a Durst counter-action against his former partner, charging libel. Another, of course, is where Mr. Lealer and Prudential go from here. As shares of the trust began trading over-the-counter the other day, he announced ambitious plans to steer Prudential into some higher-yielding realty in order to "enhance" the value of the shareholders' equity.

Far from typical though it may be, Prudential — past, present and future — points up a curious fact about those little-known relative newcomers to the stock market, the REITs: there is really nothing typical about them at all. To be sure, they have several essential things in common. As a class, they are a more conservative, lower-yielding, generally better-grade investment medium than is traditional in publicly owned real estate. The reason is simply that they operate within a rigid code prescribed by Congress and implemented by federal and state regulatory agencies.

Upon this basic blueprint, however, an almost infinite variety of complex financial houses has been built. Some real estate investment trusts, for example, distribute only actual income to their investors; some pay out a combination of earnings and depreciation; some make dividend payments which are (both taxwise and realistically) nothing more than a return of investors' capital. Again, some strive to retire debt and build equity; others employ the highest possible leverage allowed them under the law. Finally, some seek a diversified portfolio of properties; some are content to remain in a single area or even a single building; some elect to take a flyer on real estate that can only be described as speculative.

With all these variables, no two trusts are very much alike in background, condition or outlook. Accordingly, the

stock market scarcely seems to know what to make of them —
and in general has chosen to make as little of the subject as
possible: it is said that the REITs, are, at best, too complicated. More, however, can be said. For what already has
been amply demonstrated about the real estate trusts is that,
in the vital matters of risk and reward, they vary all over
the lot.

A Look at the Lot

They are, of course, all in the same business: owners (or
mortgagees) of real property. Collectively, they are a large
landlord indeed. Best estimates place the holdings of the 65
trusts now in existence at over $1 billion in gross assets (real
estate properties at cost, mortgages owned, cash and securities). They own perhaps 500 properties — from a filling
station on Long Island to the tallest building in Cleveland —
and draw interest on at least $200 million in mortgage paper.
Their own equity in real property (again based on cost) comes
to some $380 million, and at the same time, they are mortgage
debtors to the tune of around $700 million.

All share in common the qualities which enable a trust
to qualify under certain amendments to the Internal Revenue
Code (as finally adopted in 1963, to implement a bill passed
by Congress and signed by President Eisenhower in 1960).
Thus, broadly speaking, they must have at least 75% of their
assets invested in real estate — either in properties or in liens.
They also must be "passive" landlords; that is, the job of
maintaining and servicing properties, and collecting rents,
must be let to independent parties. Moreover, they are
limited as to leverage and effectively prevented from wheel-
ing-and-dealing; they can't derive more than 30% of income
from gains on the sale of properties held less than four years.
Most important, they are intended to be conduits of income
to investors: at least 90% of net income, as defined in the tax
code, must be distributed to shareholders each year. Trusts
which meet these requirements — and this is what the whole
plan is all about — are exempted from paying corporate income taxes.

Only a Few Woes

Three years' experience seems to indicate that the law-makers and regulators knew what they were doing in setting up the trust concept and form. That's not to say the industry is fully satisfied with its lot. In fact, one of the purposes behind its organization of a trade association, the National Association of Real Estate Investment Funds, was to be in a position to do some lobbying when and if the need arises.

There are no plans to ask Uncle for anything more at the moment. "They've got a lot on their minds in Washington," says a prominent trust official, "and we needn't make more problems for them. We feel we've been pretty fairly treated so far." So far, only a few difficulties have cropped up, which the trusts affected have handled on an individual basis. Thus, in 1963 (after the regulations finally came out), Albert M. Greenfield resigned from the board of a trust bearing his name when it seemed likely that his affiliations with "active" real estate operations might involve him in a conflict of interest that would jeopardize the trust's tax-exempt status. Assured at last that it would not, he rejoined the board last year.

A closer call involved the two big "mortgage trusts," First Mortgage and Continental. IRS administrators decided that the income received by First Mortgage from short-term construction loans did not qualify as "passive," and for one quarter the trust was not officially a trust. (Its shares plummeted 30%.) Because this ruling struck directly at the basic operating technique evolved by mortgage trusts — high-yielding construction and development liens enable them to borrow at bank rates and still pay investors 6-8% (since their 5% FHA/VA mortgages would hardly permit such a return), both First and Continental reacted with understandable alarm. Former IRS Commissioner Caplan himself interceded to clarify the code and reexempt the trust.

While other aspects of federal and state rules tend to worry trusts, they feel that more experience is necessary as a prelude to an effective campaign for regulatory relaxation. For example, the principle of sudden disqualification by IRS — and even retroactive rescission of their favored status —

is disquieting, when so many complex problems of accounting, subject to honest differences of interpretation, are involved. Some trust spokesmen feel there ought to be a "fair warning" clause. In addition, the absolute separation of trust management from actual property operation is regarded as an unnecessary hardship by trusts which were formed by veteran realty operators accustomed to making their profit out of building services, particularly in apartments.

At the state level, too, there's a rub. California's regulations require that a trust not only limit mortgage debt to two-thirds of appraised value (as in the 20 states belonging to the powerful Midwest alliance of securities commissions) but also that this ratio must be observed on each individual property — not just averaged out for the portfolio as a whole. All the trusts regard this as unrealistic and harsh. A number of them have simply stayed out of the Golden State.

Guilt by Association?

Finally, the trusts have another thing in common. They all tend to suffer a kind of guilt-by-association mistrust by investors grown wary of realty promoters. "Real estate ought to be considered a public utility," said New York's Mayor Wagner years ago, in another context, and the REITs appear to be acting the part, at least in the stock market, when compared to industrials. With one difference. New offerings have been all but nonexistent since the market break of May 1962. Well over $300 million (of the estimated $380 million of equity they boast) came to market in the big parade of newly formed trusts (Barron's, February 12 and 19, 1962) that started the year after the 1960 legislation was enacted and ended on Blue Monday a year later.

The crash slammed the door on speculative offerings of every sort, but its effects lasted far longer for the real estate industry and were particularly depressing for the trusts. Many an underwriting then in registration was withdrawn, never to see the light again. For example, a $7.5 million offering filed for a trust with important New York backing, North American RET, became effective May 21, 1962; it was withdrawn a year later. Now it may try to go public again (some of the original promoters lately have been acquiring properties with their unregistered shares, by special dispensation of the SEC) but the decision when to seek a new registration still is pending. In Philadelphia, meanwhile, a trust called Prudent Realty Investment, which registered 100,000 shares with the SEC two years ago, has sold only 20,000.

The market, it should be noted, has been more responsive to the capital needs of the mortgage trusts — a group which, among other things, is inherently unable to confuse earnings with depreciation, since it does not hold title to property. Several new ones have come along, styled in the pattern of Continental and First Mortgage; a few are in registration right now. (Indeed, one such was filed with the SEC just last week by — of all people — George Meany, president of the AFL-CIO; Big Labor intends to sell subscriptions to its affiliated unions and invest the proceeds in FHA/VA paper.)

Cool Market

With one or two notable exceptions, though, the market has been cool to the offerings of the equity trusts, old and new alike. Since early 1962, according to an index of price quotations compiled by the Wall Street firm of Eisele & King, Libaire, Stout & Co., REITs have gone nowhere; the index plunged by 20% in the crash and has hovered between 80 and 90 ever since. (A similar index of other realty stock has plunged by two-thirds over a three-year span.) Moreover, shares of the trusts — even the two listed on the American Stock Exchange (Real Estate Investment Trust of America and National Realty Investors) — hardly generate enough trading volume in a good week to be worth reporting (or perhaps to be reasonably evaluated).

Much alike in legal concept and investor regard, then, REITs vary strikingly in practice, portfolio and problems. One area of bewildering variance is in their cost of doing business. Management charges range from the nominal fees exacted by the trustees of Park Avenue Realty Trust (a one-property REIT spun off from the holdings of Tishman Realty & Construction Co. and managed for Park Ave. shareholders

168

by Tishman), to the relatively high expenses for Washington REIT and the brokerage and management fees and commissions taken off the top by firms closely allied with the Greenfield (and City Stores) organization in Philadelphia.

They also differ sharply in their accounting policies — the area where a sharp pencil can make or break any realty deal. For example, a few REITs — notably the oldest, Boston's Real Estate Investment Trust of America, as well as newer ones like Denver Real Estate Investment Assn. and Philadelphia's Franklin Realty — operate strictly by the book. They pay out dividends solely from earnings, retaining any excess of cash flow over amortization for the repair and replacement of depleted properties.

"Syndicator's Guide"

Others, to some degree, follow another set of rules, which might be called "The Syndicator's Guide." Here the idea is to supplement distributions from income with payments out of excess depreciation. (That part of the dividend not actually earned is viewed as a return of capital and is tax-free to the investor.) Among these concerns is the biggest of the property-holding trusts, Cleveland's U.S. Realty Investments, which "shelters" all its distributions (except those from capital gains, on which the investor pays taxes at the lower capital gains rate); most other prominent trusts, including Washington's American Realty Trust; New York's First General REIT and First National RET; and Philadelphia's Greenfield RET and Pennsylvania REIT follow similar policies.

Sometimes as in the case of Greenfield and Pennsylvania, depreciation is accelerated to further enhance cash flow "yields" in the early years. Of course, this technique also brings nearer the day when the write-off (since it declines annually) will fail to cover rising amortization payments on the mortgage principal, and thus will fail to create any excess cash flow, or tax shelter, at all.

Equally at variance is the approach individual REITs take to the structuring of their balance sheets. Certain trusts, like most homeowners, believe in minimizing mortgages and maximizing equity. This policy has the added advantage of maximizing profits (though not necessarily cash flow), since a big cost factor in any deal, amortization, is held down. REITs which think in terms of earnings rather than cash flow when paying dividends, tend to be conservative when it comes to debt as well; those with particularly high equity ratios include REITA, Bradley, Denver and Franklin.

Others, however, go frankly for leverage. For them, the higher the mortgage, the lower the equity investment and accordingly, the higher the percentage return of generated cash. Masters of this concept are most of the New York-Philadelphia-Washington trusts, notably American, Washington, Pennsylvania and Schenectady's Nation-Wide REIT.

Holds the Prize

Parke Avenue, with a $7 million mortgage on a $7.2 million property (at cost) holds the prize: its equity ratio is just 3%. (In order to qualify their securities in most Midwestern and Western states, the trusts must maintain an equity position of at least one-third — but based on appraised value rather than cost.) Park Avenue complies with "bluesky" laws because an "independent" appraisal of its single property, Manhattan's Olin Building, set its value at somewhere over $11 million. Of course as Park Avenue's managing trustee, William F. Purcell (formerly a law partner of Lawrence A. Wien, the No. 1 all-time syndicator) points out, appraisals are notoriously meaningless figures, based on intuition as well as hard values, and sometimes "merely what the owner paying for it wants to hear."

Still other trusts have gone beyond mortgage debt to borrow at unsecured rates, both short-and long-term. The mortgage trusts, insatiable for new capital to invest these days, find this the best way to finance their own loans to builders and developers — which carry interest rates as high as five to seven points above those on FHA- or VA-insured mortgages. Now some equity trusts are going to the banks as well — where their cost of money is below that of the "yields" on their stock.

Heaviest borrower by far is U.S. Realty, more than one-fifth of its total debt having been drawn from a $9 million line of credit available to it. Indeed, a few trusts even have gone the convertible-debenture route. Washington REIT and Pennsylvania REIT in particular have extended their positions through recent offerings of convertibles; several other trusts now are mulling over such a step.

In any case, of course, debt leverage equals risk. How safe the equity remains only time will tell. Unlike builders and syndicate companies, which are geared to profit from property turnover, the REITs are long-term investors by law: to remain qualified, as noted, they must limit the portion of "revenues" attributable to capital gains on property held less than four years to 30% in any given year. In a rising realty market, leverage enhances equity; but in a falling one, the exaggerated effect on a small equity position will work in reverse.

Not surprisingly, some of the most fundamental differences between REITs lie in their portfolios. For example, trusts like First Mortgage and Continental Mortgage specialize in holding mortgages; insofar as these are federally guaranteed, the shares of such a trust probably resemble bonds more nearly than stocks. The equity trusts, contrariwise, own fees (or leaseholds) and the quality, location and diversification of their holdings can vary all over the lot. Thus, Denver's portfolio is located entirely in that city, Washington's in and around the District of Columbia, First Union's in Cleveland. By contrast, First National, U.S. Realty and National Realty each have holdings in eight different states, Pennsylvania and Prudential in 10 apiece, REITA in 15.

Encountering Headaches

Nor is geographical dispersal everything. Boston's Bradley RET, though saddled with some of the Hub City's older buildings, found trouble in the hustings — the result of a preponderant commitment in retailing outlets, particularly in Seattle (since the fair closed) and Minneapolis (where its tenant went into bankruptcy). Not a few of the trusts heavily committed to apartment buildings — such as American, Pennsylvania and Washington — are encountering the headaches resulting from a glut in residential housing. Commonwealth Realty Trust, in turn, came a cropper when it strayed from suburban Philadelphia into the Caribbean: some 20% of its assets at one time were tied up in a mortgage loan to a Jamaica hotel and on some of the island's undeveloped acreage; the mortgagor defaulted, and the trust, working to bail itself out, still carries the properties on its books at $1 million.

Even a portfolio fairly well balanced both by geography and by building type is no guarantee of safety. Two cases in point: Flato Realty, in Corpus Christi and Liberty Real Estate Trust, in Oklahoma City. Both trusts came into being through a tax-free exchange of shares with property owners, but a handicap of this organizational method is that such a trust is not legally a "new" owner and hence cannot begin depreciating the properties at full value.

No Takers

Troublesome buildings only make such matters worse. Thus Flato's 10 properties in five states happen to include a Casper, Wyo. shopping center financed through the Small Business Administration (and hence lacking any big-name stores which it wants to dispose of. But so far, no takers. Liberty, which has over 30 properties today, simply hasn't been able to get to pay off "the way their history said they should," a trustee says. The source of trouble has been a disproportionate number of motels, apartments and bowling alleys in Florida — where, ironically, trustees thought their strength lay.

Nor, finally, do the differences end with the books and the buildings. In their brief history to date, the REITs have demonstrated some remarkable variations in that ultimate test of realty performance — the investor's return. So far most, on balance, have done about as well as shareholders could have hoped, but as has been suggested, some have been more rewarding than others. Certain of the most leveraged ones, for instance, boast dynamic records — particularly the mortgage trusts and the highly geared U.S. Realty Investors, which have overcome the effects of an apathetic stock market by obtaining credit lines elsewhere and putting them to good use.

Penny by Penny

Both Continental and First Mortgage, as a result, have been able to raise distributions to shareholders penny by penny almost since the day they hung out their shingles. U.S. Realty, for its part, upped its quarterly distributions this month to 20 cents a share (all tax-sheltered) from the previous 17½-cent rate. (It then distributed four cents a share in capital gains as a year-end extra.)

Among the equity trusts distributing only earnings, both Franklin and REITA also have brought good cheer to investors' mailboxes in recent months. The Philadelphia trust raised its dividend to 15 cents from 14-cents quarterly, after becoming fully invested at the end of the last fiscal year. REITA, maintaining its fully earned 30-cent quarterly rate, added a 17-cent capital gains distribution at the year-end. First National, which mixes earnings and depreciation in its payout, says it soon will boost the 19-cent quarterly rate to 20 cents.

On the other hand, a few trusts have been less successful. First General, for example, distributed a total of 59 cents a share in a 12-month period through October 31, but established a 12-cent quarterly rate as of the first quarter of fiscal 1965. (Through a quirk in the payment dates that could be misleading to new shareholders, the trust actually paid 47 cents during its fiscal year, ended September. The March and June 1964 quarterlies, however, were 16½ cents each.)

More noticeably, Bradley, which started off fully invested and paying eight cents a share quarterly (plus a four-cent extra the first year, 1961), whittled the distribution to seven cents a quarter last year and, early this year, to six cents. Liberty, after paying out a total of 72 cents a share in 1963, distributed just 15 cents a share in last year's first quarter before abandoning the dividend altogether. "We won't resume distributions," the trust's president told Barron's "until we get our house in order."

No Distributions

Unhappiest is the record of Flato Realty, which has made no distributions at all. Flato is not simply losing money

THUMBNAIL APPRAISAL

Company (yr. org.)	Total Assts (a) (Mils)	States	O	A	R	I	H	M	P	Latest Qtrly Distr.	Indic. Yield (e)
EQUITY TRUSTS											
American (61)	$30.3	6	3	5	1	1	3			$.18	7.9%
B. C. Morton (63)	4.1	4		1	3				X	.15	6.0%
Bradley (61)	16.3	3	4		16	2			X	.06	6.0%
Commonwealth (62)	9.7	3	2		2				X	.15	8.6%
Denver (61)	15.4	1	3	6	3	1			X	.12½	5.6%
First General (62)	11.3	5	3	4						.12	6.7%
First National (62)	38.6	8	9	1	3	1				.19	7.7%
First Union (61)	47.9	1	2							.20	5.8%
Flato (62)	12.1	5	2	1	7					None	Nil
Franklin (62)	24.9	7	6	5			1			.15	6.2%
Greenfield (61)	20.6	4	3		4					.25	6.6%
Liberty (61)	18.0	4	6	7	10	5	4	1	X	(d)	Nil
National Realty (62)	28.1	8	5	3	2	1	1	1		.18	6.6%
Nation–Wide (61)	4.7	2	1		1					.16½	6.6%
Park Avenue (64)	7.5	1	1							.20	7.7%
Pennsylvania (62)	33.1	10	1	5	6	6			X	.20	7.2%
Prudential (64)	26.5	10	3	7	4	2	1		X	.22½	9.6%
REITA (61)	47.1	15	5		31	8			X	.30	5.6%
U.S. Realty (61)	54.2	8	10	2	8	2	5	4		.20	6.0%
Washington (61)	12.9	2	1	4	1	1		1		.10	6.1%

PORTFOLIO DIVERSIFICATION — No. of Properties owned (b)

	Total Assets	No. of States	FHA-VA Prem.	Const. Dev.	Other	Latest Qtrly Div.	Indic yld (on asked)
MORTGAGE TRUSTS							
Continental (62)	$72.3	35	$20.0	$44.0	$1.8	$.33	5.9%
First Mortgage (61)	69.0	41	30.2	31.3		.26	7.0%
Southeastern (64)	(e)19.1	4	11.7	5.8	1.2	.18	6.7%

MORTGAGES OWNED

(a) At cost (before depr. on RE props.). (b) Code: O-office buildings; A-apartment buildings; R-retail outlets; I-industrial buildings; H-hotels-motels; M-miscellaneous (garages, recreational, undeveloped land, etc.); P-"paper" (owned mortgages, other RE notes, securities, etc.). (c) On "Asked" quotation; may include portion representing return of capital. (d) Last distr., 15c per shr., pd. Jan. 61. (e) At end of 7 mos., July 31.

conveniently for tax purposes. It is running a deficit operation in the real sense. Last year, its amortization requirements — for paying down the principal on its mortgages — actually exceeded cash flow by almost 2-to-1. "We aren't thinking about distributions," sighs Franklin Flato, a former appliance salesman, "until we can sell some properties."

Dividendless or not, quite a few trusts are beginning to think about selling properties — sooner or later, they all have to do so — and about the market in which they will be selling them. It's not a thought that trustees go passively to sleep upon. As they know well, the great realty boom ended about the time they came along in the first place — to fill up their portfolios at what in many cases were top prices. By the same token, the deals awaiting them as they replace old assets with new have become lower-yielding — or, alternately, more speculative — than ever. Whatever happens to the rewards in REITs, it's becoming increasingly apparent that the risks can readily multiply.

Reprinted by courtesy of *Barron's National Business and Financial Weekly,* Vol. 45 (March 15, 1965).

FRESH APPRAISAL
The Rewards and Risks in
Real Estate Investment Trusts

By J. Richard Elliott, Jr.

"We have always felt that this is an income fund with overtones of long-term growth. But the growth must be sound and gradual, because our investors are interested first in basic values."

John H. Gardiner
President-Trustee
Real Estate Inv. Trust of America

American Realty Trust, which went public in 1961, a few weeks ago fired off a cheery letter to stockholders. It noted first the successful completion of a further 300,000-share offering of stock late last year — no mean achievement for a real estate investment trust these days. The money, investors were told, quickly was put to good use, as the trust paid off a $1 million bank loan and acquired a 75% interest in a St. Louis office building. The big surprise was where the rest of the funds went: into a 1,300-room, luxury apartment hotel in Palm Beach. From now on, the letter concluded, American should generate enough cash flow from operations not only to cover its current dividends after amortization, but also "to more than make up the distribution accounting deficiency that was said to exist at the end of our last fiscal year."

Between the Lines

Shareholders may have received the report with some reservations. Most of them recall that the registration statement for last year's underwriting stated flatly that past distributions were "in excess of funds generated," and that future dividends, therefore, could be cut. It also is no secret that the new shares sold for less ($9.50) than the original investors paid ($10.00). After underwriting costs, net proceeds came to $8.60 per share, substantially diluting the equity.

All these, of course, could be considered growing pains, if growth seemed to be around the corner. The report to shareholders, however, omitted a number of other pertinent details. For one thing, the most notable growth in American Realty's revised portfolio has been in debt, rather than equity. A shining example is the $7 million deal for Palm Beach Towers. Over a $4.5 million first mortgage, equity of $2.5 million in the property is scaled to earn 10½% annually on a long-term lease. But trustees gilded the lily by borrowing another $1.5 million, at 6% interest. On the $1 million of American's own funds involved, the net return, after amortization and interest, works out to 15%.

Beyond that, to secure the new note, trustees had to pledge American's equity not just in Palm Beach Towers but also in a second major holding. In 18 months, when the note falls due, American plans to repay it "through another stock offer or the sale of a property." The trust's future, it seems, is still as much a question as ever.

American Realty illustrates well the complex interplay of risk and reward which has made Wall Street skeptical of the REITs (see Table 1). For most of the past three years, the nation's financial capital, as previously noted, has given them the cold shoulder. Security analysts who study realty stocks are few, and those willing to make recommendations far between. Says a top researcher at Merrill Lynch, Pierce, Fenner & Smith: "You've got to go out around the country and look at every deal they've got in their portfolio. Even if I could make such a trip for each realty trust, I really wouldn't know how to appraise the properties once I had all the data. When an investor asks me for advice on a real estate security, I simply pass."

Outside New York, to be sure, certain real estate markets are continuing to boom, and realty securities in places like Washington seem to retain a limited appeal. Then, too, REITs which hold only mortgages are able to raise capital when and where they please. Since "mortgage trusts" operate much like savings-and-loan associations, in fact, they boast some of the glamor that once attached to S&Ls themselves.

Attracts Certain Breed

The mutual fund industry, too, attracts a certain breed of investor, and fund veterans who double as REIT sponsors have had recent success in raising money. Thus, the B.C. Morton Group launched its own realty trust in 1963 and sold 150,000 shares to investors. Offering of the rest of an original 1,000,000-share registration awaits the pleasure of the SEC. (Unlike open-end mutual funds, Morton's REIT must stop selling and amend its prospectus almost every time it adds a property to its portfolio.)

Merger Route?

Still another trend that could circumvent Wall Street's indifference is growth by merger, in share-for-share swaps between trusts. Most realty trusts these days find that their inability to obtain regular infusions of fresh equity capital, while not necessarily a detriment to profits, is a serious obstacle to growth. Mergers which may involve little dilution, provide one answer.

To date, however, very few have been brought off. Liberty Real Estate Trust, which started out as a "swap fund" heavily based in Florida, merged with a two-property Minneapolis REIT called Science Industry Real Estate Trust two years ago. Liberty gained diversification, but last year had to stop paying dividends anyway. For the rest, the trouble is that any REIT is so unlike any other that trustees usually find it impossible to come to terms. "We know where the bodies are buried here," a trustee says. "But we don't know where another fellow may have buried his."

The truth is that starting from the common blueprint imposed by regulations, the REITs have taken their $1 billion in assets and built up a bewildering variety of capital structures (see Table II). Virtually all by now are fully invested — that is, have at least 90% of their portfolios in real estate. Today, seeking growth in income as well as in equity, they are adding to or replacing their bricks and mortar in ways that range from the discreetly conservative to the astonishingly risky.

Let's look more closely at a few of each type. By all odds the most conservative is Real Estate Investment Trust of America, the oldest, and until recently, the biggest. The Boston concern can trace its origins back to the 19th century, when the trust concept evolved as one means of channeling Eastern capital into the nation's Westward expansion. More recently, REITA, after years of lobbying, helped bring about 1960 legislation that created a shelter for realty trusts similar to that available to mutual funds. REITA then became the first to make a public offering of stock.

Since most of its properties had been in the portfolio for some time, many fully depreciated and amortized, REITA also was the first to enter the real estate market as a seller. Last year, it acquired no new properties, while disposing of four. Two resulted in losses, two in gains; overall, the trust realized a net capital gain of $247,000 (19 cents a share) and distributed 17 cents per share as an extra. So far this year, two more have been sold.

The Equity Builder

REITA boasts another important distinction. It's the least leveraged of all the trusts, by a wide margin. At year-end, its equity ratio stood at an enviable 74%. Thus just one-fourth of the pre-depreciation value of its properties is mortgaged. REITA's trustees concede that an equity-debt balance of 50-50 probably would be safe enough. "But that's positively the limit," one of the managing trustees says, "and we're not setting out to achieve that much debt."

The big Boston trust has overhauled its portfolio drastically since 1961. Less than a quarter of book value now represents properties 20 years old or more, as against 45% four years ago. The mix also has changed in other ways. Since 1961, shopping centers have grown from half to four-fifths of the total portfolio, supplanting smaller retail outlets. Finally, New England has been displaced by California as REITA's prime location.

Trustees emphasize that their first duty is to enhance the underlying worth of their shareholders' investment. Thus, last year REITA reduced mortgage debt by $613,000, to some

$10.8 million, while committing the balance of its $712,000 in depreciation to improvements and additions on existing property. As a result, book value rose above the $20 per share offering price of 1961, the first time such a feat had been accomplished by any REIT. What's more, investors' equity in real estate (probably a better indication of break-up values) shot up to $34.37 per share, some 60% above both the initial and the current market price of the stock. Again, no other trust comes close.

Other Conservatives

REITA's brilliant record provides a handy yardstick with which to measure other REITs. One that is philosophically akin to the Old Tory of Boston is Denver Realty Trust. Another and faster growing one is Franklin Realty, of Philadelphia. Though it suffers from vacancies in some of its apartment houses, Franklin has built a portfolio of solid assets in such places as Baltimore, Boston, Tulsa and Coral Gables. One of the most promising is the Blue Cross Building in Baltimore, next to two new hospitals; adjacent is an undeveloped tract owned by the trust, on which it intends to construct an office building for doctors.

On the policy of distributing earnings instead of depreciation, Franklin's trustees see eye to eye with REITA. Last year, President Harold Gebert was embarrassed to find himself being quoted for an off-hand remark: "If the shareholder wants his money back, he will sell his stock." But that's just what he meant. "It makes me mad," he says, "when somebody tells investors they're going to get a 12% yield on their money, when 8% of it is going to be a return of capital."

Interest in Debt

Where Franklin differs from REITA is in its approach to debt. Although it is building up equity by amortizing its mortgages and reinvesting excess depreciation, Franklin has obtained bank credit totaling $2.5 million, and borrowed $500,000 to date. It intends eventually to use the entire amount to supplement internally generated funds.

"As soon as it makes sense to do so, we'll go back to the stock market for equity capital and pay down the loans with the proceeds," Mr. Gebert explains. "But I believe it's better to invest when you can than to sell stock, only to put the money into government bonds while you hunt for properties."

A third relative newcomer, National Realty Investors, has maintained a fairly high equity ratio (46%) and paid out dividends almost wholly from earnings. It also is following REITA into shopping centers. Last year it acquired a big plaza in Pompano Beach, Fla., and expanded one in Flint, Mich. But in both cases, National went for greater leverage than in the past, in an effort to boost returns above 10%. It also appears headed for a less conservative future in other respects. Just last week, it hired a new contracting firm, which has been specifically directed to seek properties in exchange for stock, even though National's shares now are selling below book value.

The Liberal View

Again, among those trusts which make liberal distributions from cash flow — and they are in the majority today — some are more conservative than others. First Union Realty, for example, which owns two of Cleveland's skyscraper office buildings (each 100% occupied), has as an independent adviser a management firm 40% owned by Wall Street's Harriman, Ripley. Moreover, First Union has its debt and equity split down the middle. The trust, however, has elected to accelerate depreciation on its second building, acquired in 1963, in order to pay distributions which are more than half accounted for by cash flow rather than earnings.

Mounting Risks

On this score, other trusts go much further. Take the case of U.S. Realty Investments, biggest of the "equity trusts." (The shares, yielding 6%, have been bid up to $13 apiece over-the-counter; they were offered in 1961 at $10, by Hornblower & Weeks, and in 1962 at $10.75.) The trustees, however, don't regard their policies as risky. "If we aren't sound," says trustee Sheldon B. Guren, secretary and fiscal agent, "then there's nothing 'sound' in real estate."

In its portfolio, U.S. Realty does rank as something of a blue chip. Its 35 properties include office and commercial buildings in eight states. The latest acquisition, Cleveland's Terminal Tower was a sale-and-lease-back deal. The trust put up $4.5 million over an $8 million first mortgage; net guaranteed rental will afford a 9% return on the equity. Mainly because of this addition to the portfolio, trustees upped the quarterly dividend to 20 cents a share in this year's first quarter, from 17½ cents.

Conservatism ends right here, however. For U.S. Realty's "dividend" is wholly a tax-sheltered return of capital: It's covered by no earnings at all. Aside from a $46,000 capital gain last year, the trust generated a cash flow of $1.7 million. But it wrote off an even greater amount, winding up the year with a net loss of $3,366. "That," Mr. Guren exults, "is what I call beautiful, precision accounting."

U.S. Realty, as it happens, is one of the most highly leveraged REITs. Actually, real estate costing $53.4 million secures first mortgages totaling just $31.3 million. But the trust doesn't stop with mortgages. It has taken down $8.5 million on an unsecured credit line potentially good for $10 million.

In sum, U.S. Realty's equity ratio boils down to just 25%. And on the $13.6 million of unencumbered real estate (before depreciation), which investors, as of the moment, can call their own, the cash yield is only 12.3%. That's rewarding, to be sure, but by no means exceptional for so small an equity position. After amortization payments, it works out to only 7.2%.

An investor can, if he chooses, climb even farther out on a limb. For example, Pennsylvania Real Estate Investment Trust, which has an interest in 18 properties and is lending on the development of several more, commands an equity ratio of less than 20%. Besides $20.7 million in mortgages, Pennsylvania Trust owes $200,000 on a long-term note and last year sold $4.5 million of 6¼% convertible debentures.

Last year, while Pennsylvania was getting fully invested, net income declined to $375,000 (50 cents a share) from

182

$438,000 (59 cents), but distributions remained constant at 80 cents per share. The reason was that cash flow soared to $1.27 million, from $975,000 ($1.70 vs. $1.30 per share) and, after amortization payments, came to $786,000 against $664,000, or $1.05 vs. 84 cents a share. Since straight-line depreciation only partially offset reportable income, trustees decided to continue using accelerated depreciation on all the properties for tax purposes. The effect was to provide a "shelter" for all but 17 cents of the per-share distribution.

Shareholders receiving 80 cents a share for all practical purposes got 63 cents of their own money back. Ironically, the shares, issued in 1962 at $10, have risen to a recent bid of $10.75, even as book value was declining from $8.35 per share, at the 1963 year-end, to $7.19.

While Pennsylvania has made no acquisitions in over a year, its posture is far from passive. It has some $1 million of its $31 million real estate portfolio tied up in development loans, which will convert eventually to equity positions earning roughly 10%. Moreover, it has its eye on a far bigger deal than any in the business to date: a $25 million package of three California office buildings (to be leased back to the sellers), which would require $10 million in cash over a new first mortgage. Where to get the capital? Trustees concede that $10 million is probably out of reach, but think they can locate a 50% partner. Then they'd only have to worry about raising $5 million. "More convertible debentures, of course, says a spokesman.

Capital at the Capitol

Even more heavily mortgaged is Columbia Realty of Washington. Owner of a dozen properties in the capital area, Columbia has shown remarkable growth in the past year. Shareholders' net equity climbed to $2.3 million from $1.6 million. Cash generated before amortization hit $412,720, compared with $242,875 the year before. Distributions — wholly a return of capital, since depreciation gave Columbia net losses in both years — rose to 60 cents a share in '64, from 45 cents in '63. The stock is quoted at $15 bid, $17.50 asked —

compared to a 1962 offering price of $10, and a value established for several property deals last year of $12.50.

To finance this "growth," however, Columbia gave the art of trust capitalization some new twists. For one thing, it has, like the realty syndicates of old, both an "A" and a "B" stock. For another, it acquired four properties last year on which the equity investment, over mortgages, totaled $1.5 million, but on which not a nickel's worth of cash changed hands.

Notes on Growing

In the first deal, Columbia purchased $427,000 worth of equity with 38,821 shares of its Class A stock. In the second, it put up $249,000 worth of 10-year promissory notes (convertible to 20,747 "A" shares at maturity). Next time, it issued another $700,000 in 10-year notes (convertible to 58,333 shares.) And on the last occasion, it offered $163,000 more of the same (convertible to 13,583 shares).

Trustees also have been recapitalizing mortgages wherever they can. To be sure, Columbia first puts money into a property, so that lenders, after appraising the upgraded assets, are willing to tear up the old lien and talk about a new one. Two such deals came off spectacularly last year. In one, the trust invested $153,000 to rehabilitate its Castle Manor Apartments, which originally had cost $840,000. Against the total cost of $993,000, the property now was worth $1.25 million, according to a mortgage banker who promptly loaned Columbia $830,000 on a new first mortgage. In the second, Columbia spent $300,000 to refurbish the $1.5 million Center Cathedral Mansions (apartments), got a new outside appraisal of $2.6 million and a new first mortgage of $1.7 million. Together, the two deals netted the trust $1.4 million in refinancing proceeds (after paying off the old liens); even allowing for the rehabilitation expenses, it was still $1 million ahead.

Hail Columbia?

Imaginative as all this is, however, where it leaves shareholders' equity is hard to say. The trust's president, Norman

Bernstein, understandably likes to talk about the "market value" of his trust's assets. At year-end, according to an exultant annual report, that value worked out to $6.6 million at net, or some $17.21 per share. Book worth, of course, is something else. By Columbia's accounting, it comes to $6.21 per share. Even when calculated before depreciation — taking real estate at cost — equity per share is $6.45. In the latter terms, Columbia's equity ratio works out to 18%.

A neighbor, Washington Real Estate Investment Trust, is raising an even more impressive monument to debt. Owner of seven buildings in and around the capital, the trust (which calls itself "WRIT") boasts more advisers than properties. Washington has not gone overboard in the uses of cash flow. Last year's distribution of 40 cents a share was mostly from earnings; only 16 cents a share appears to have been a return of capital. Investors, possibly for this reason, have bid up the stock to a premium over the initial offering price of $5, capitalizing the dividend at 6.1% — close to the yield of REITA itself.

Lowest Ratio

But Washington is far from conservative in debt policy. Its equity ratio is about the lowest in the business: 13%. Against real estate valued (at cost) at $11.3 million, the trust has mortgages totaling $7.8 million. Last September it added $2 million in convertible debentures. The decision to float an issue of 6¾% convertibles is particularly notable in that such money costs more than WRIT currently is paying on its equity capital.

Indeed, leverage is a way of life at Washington. Under the heading "Special Risk Factors" in last fall's prospectus, the REIT was required to point out that "it would be advantageous to the trustees and the advisory board to acquire properties with small equity investments and large mortgages, since this would result in greater income being payable to them, with greater risks to the trust."

The reason is that WRIT bases its management fee not on net assets, as other trusts do, but on gross assets. Specifically, compensation to trustees, advisory board members and the investment adviser (a firm wholly owned by trustees and advisory board members) "is allowable . . . at the rate of ⅜ths of 1% of the gross value of the trust assets without regard to existing mortgages and other trust obligations or to accumulated depreciation of trust assets." The same percentage, again, covers other administrative costs, making the total allowed to trustees and advisors ¾ of 1%.

In 1963, the latest year reported, general and administrative expenses totaled $70,000. Fees and salaries added $58,850 — some $12,000 less than the allowable limit in '63 for that category, but still 17.5% of the trust's net cash flow. Trustees thus accounted for $2 of every $6 the business generated. Moreover, such compensation and costs actually amounted to 4½% when figured on net assets — compared to the usual ½ to 1½% allowed by other trusts. Since 1963, the gulf has been widened by the debenture issue, and as the proceeds are used to acquire equity in mortgaged property, it will widen still more. In short, WRIT's management fees will rise proportionately with debt.

Newest of the REITs, finally, is Prudential. As reported three weeks ago, it came into being last year as successor to the syndicate company, Leader-Durst Corp. Before the 3-for-1 stock swap, Leader-Durst was paying a 40-cent annual dividend per share, or 13% on the last, depressed prices. After the swap, the same company, now a trust, set the annual rate at 90 cents per share of Prudential, making the tax-sheltered "yield" just 10%. Moreover, management expects the shares to rise to a level at which the yield would compare favorably with the 6-7% common for seasoned REITs. Indeed, the managing trustee, I. Theodore Leader, believes Prudential merits such a rating more than most.

Leader of the Pack?

Why? For one thing, Prudential has a unique dividend policy. According to its Trust Declaration: " . . . It shall be the policy of the trust to make regular, periodic distributions to its shareholders of at least 90% of the trust's 'excess funds generated from operation' . . . defined as net income generated from the operation of the trust's real estate assets, adjusted by adding back depreciation . . " So far as can be determined, while many realty trusts pay investors such returns of capital from depreciation, Prudential is the only one bound to such a practice by its own charter. "My investors," says Mr. Leader — a one-time New York law professor who got into real estate as an aide to the late syndicator, Robert Futterman — "are people who invested for safety."

Compared to the syndicate business, to be sure, the regulated REIT may appear a safe haven. But when it comes to equity, Prudential doesn't seem to be thinking of safety first. Instead, it is concentrating on "growth." The company had barely hung up its shingle when it announced acquisition of a cluster of garden apartments in Maryland, complete with two swimming pools and, at present, no vacancies. Costing $3.8 million, including a $2.5 million first mortgage, the deal is scaled to return a cash flow of $110,000, or 8½% on the $1.3 million equity. But to spice it up a bit, Prudential gave back a 12-year second mortgage to the sellers, of $450,000, reducing its own equity investment to $850,000 (a 22% ratio for the property), but raising the yield (before interest on the second lien) to 13%.

Transactions to come may be even fancier. Mr. Leader has at least two variations in mind. In one, the trust would split both equity and profit with a second investor, hopefully one with modest income needs. He envisions it working out this way. Taking a shopping-center deal, set up to yield 10% on an equity investment of $2.1 million, Prudential's senior partner (perhaps a pension fund) would put up 48%, or $1 million, capitalized at just 7%. Virtually a preferred stockholder in the property, the partner would have first call on $70,000 of the net cash flow. Since the property theoretically would throw off $140,000 more than that, Prudential assuming all went well, would be in line for a 13% return (plus any overages) on its $1.1 million investment.

In the other variation, Prudential would underwrite builders without spending any money. Instead of risking cash, it would give stock. The recipient, Mr. Leader says, would be issued $10 worth of shares (at then current market value) for each $1 of projected income (after builder's profit)

Table I: SELECTED FINANCIAL DATA

PER SHARE

EQUITY TRUSTS	Orig. Issue Price(a)	Current Book Value	Equity in RE (b)	Recent O.T.C. "Bid"	1964 Performance(e) Cash Flow fr. Ops.	Amort. Pmts.	Net Inc.	1964 Distributions(d) From Earns.	Return of Cap.	Cash Total
American	$10.00	$ 8.02	$ 8.44	$ 9.00	$ .91	$ .37	$ .23	$ .23	$ .49	$ .72
B. C. Morton	10.00	8.53	7.53	N.T.	e.46	.03	D.03		e.56	.56
Bradley	7.50	5.15	8.12	3.50	.61	.23	.28	.28		.28
Columbia	10.00	6.21	6.45	15.00	1.06	.60	d.02		.60	.60
Commonwealth	10.00	8.35	9.30	6.00	.77	.28	.28	(f)	.60	.60
Denver	10.00	8.51	10.25	8.63	.87	.38	.45	.50		.50
First Gen.	10.00	8.51	8.10	6.75	.66	.13	.17	.17	.42	.59
First Natl.	10.00	8.19	9.26	9.50	.98	.20	.25	.25	.47½	.72½
First Union	12.50	10.38	11.85	13.50	1.04	.20	.31	.31	.47	.78
Flato	10.00	9.22	12.25	2.88	.59	1.02	D.10			None
Franklin	12.50	11.18	12.13	9.25	1.23	.67	.47	46½		46½
Greenfield	20.00	17.62	15.40	14.75	1.84	.62	.76	f.38	.57	.95
Liberty	10.00	7.37	7.90	2.75	g.10	N.A.	.04	.04	.11	.15
Natl. Realty	15.00	13.39	13.77	h10.88	1.52	.29	.65	.65	.05	.70
Nation-Wide	10.00	9.60	10.00	N.Q.	N.A.	N.A.	.26	.26	.40	.66
Park Avenue	11.00	.30	.40	9.63	11.04	i21	i.56	i.56	i.24	i.80
Pennsylvania	10.00	7.19	8.00	10.75	1.70	.65	.50	f.17	.63	.80
Prudential	9.00	7.94	13.14	9.00	1.64	.54	D.30		i.90	i.90
REITA	20.00	20.09	34.37	h21.38	1.85	.48	j1.24	1.20		j1.20
U.S. Realty	10.00	7.36	11.06	13.00	1.36	.56	k.00		.70	k.70
Washington	5.00	4.16	2.35	5.75	.72	.22	.24	.24	.16	.40

MORTGAGE TRUSTS	Orig. Issue Price	Current Book Value	"Equity" in Mtgs.	Recent O.T.C. Bid	Earnings History 1962	1963	1964	Divs. Pd Last 12 Mos.
Continental	$15.00	$13.89	$11.92	$21.38	$ .76	$1.13	g$1.05	$1.27
First Mortgage	15.00	13.48	7.41	14.50	.61	.85	1.03	1.04
Southeastern	10.00	n8.73	n8.90	10.38			n.27	.72

on his structure, when 90% rented. He then would use the stock as collateral in getting a construction loan. The trust, for its part, would acquire equity in a hole in the ground (as soon as that stage was reached) and temporarily would see its per-share return diluted. Sooner or later, of course, the property should begin paying off, though its profitability and the value of the trust's equity would depend on the terms of the refinancing.

So much, then, for the rewards, and some of the risks, in realty trusts today. How great actually is the danger? As reported three weeks ago, difficulties already have beset some members of the young industry. In the wake of great expectations (or debt, or excessive depreciation), disillusionment has come to investors in such trusts as Bradley, Liberty and Flato, while bad news also is no novelty for holders of First General, Commonwealth and others.

In real estate, as elsewhere, leverage can work both ways. Yet despite all the lessons of history, only a handful of REITs accord equity the respect that would seem its due — particularly from a tax-exempt fiduciary. "During the 'thirties,'" a trustee of REITA recalled the other day, "we saw values plunge 50, 60, even 70%. If we hadn't been as conservative then as we are today, we'd have been wiped out."

TABLE 1 (a) Or equivalent market value, if exchanged for stock or properties.   (b) Before depreciation, at cost, less debt.   (c) Cash flow is income generated by operations (less expenses, including interest on debt) before depreciation and debt amortization payments for principle). Amortization payments reduce cash flow available for distributions but are not deducted from net income, since such payments represent a gain of shareholder's equity. (If amortization plus distributions exceed cash flow, trust is paying part of distributions from retained earnings or uninvested capital.)   Net income is cash flow less depreciation: if depreciation exceeds net income, trust reports a loss (D), (d) Trust must distribute at least 90% of net income (including capital gains). Distributions which exceed earnings are paid from "excess" depreciation (cash flow less amortization) and constitute a return of investor's capital. Hence, distributions from earnings are taxable to investor as income; those constituting return of capital are tax free to investor (but reduce his cost basis by like amount). Capital gains distributions taxed at capital gains rate (e) Net cash flow equalled total distributions of approximately $65,000. Difference in per share figures is due to increasing number shares outstanding during year. (Shares still are being offered.) Shares outstanding at beginning of year received full $.56 in total monthly distributions; those issued later received less (f) Earnings reduced or eliminated (for tax purposes) through accelerated depreciation. Tax "shelled" the abc being used up at accelerated rate. (Trusts cannot carry losses forward) (g) 9 months only. (b) Recent close. American Stock Exchange (i) Annualized, based on 1st quarter results. (j) Excluding $39 non-recurring capital gains; $.17 distributed per share. (k) Excluding $.01 non-recurring capital gain, distributed per share, (n) 7 months only.

189

Table II: SELECTED FINANCIAL DATA

MILLIONS

EQUITY TRUSTS	RE at Cost(a)	Mortg Debt.	Unsec. Debt.	Net Assets	Equity % Ratio(b)	1965 Indic. % Yield(e)	Net Cash Flow(d) as % RE Equity	Earnings as % of RE Equity	Price(c) Times Earns
American	$29.8	$20.2	$ 1.5	$ 7.7	27	7.9	6.4	2.7	41.3
B. C. Morton	3.8	2.6	——	1.3	32	6.0	5.7	—	—
Bradley	14.2	5.5	.5	5.2	58	6.0	4.7	3.4	14.3
Columbia	13.1	10.7	——	2.3	18	3.4	7.1	—	—
Commonwealth	9.6	5.1	.5	3.6	42	8.6	5.3	3.0	25.0
Denver	15.2	6.5	.5	6.8	54	5.6	4.8	4.4	19.7
First Gen.	10.5	5.8	——	4.9	44	6.7	6.5	2.1	44.1
First Natl.	37.7	22.6	——	13.3	40	7.7	8.4	2.7	39.5
First Union	47.0	24.0	——	20.1	49	5.8	7.1	2.6	44.8
Flato	11.7	6.8	——	3.7	42	Nil	—	—	—
Franklin	24.5	16.6	.5	6.8	30	6.2	4.6	3.9	20.5
Greenfield	17.7	10.0	——	8.8	44	6.6	8.0	4.9	20.1
Liberty	17.5	10.0	——	7.0	44	Nil	N.A.	0.5	81.2
Natl. Realty	26.7	14.3	——	12.0	46	6.6	8.9	4.7	16.7
Nation-Wide	4.6	3.3	.35	.96	25	6.6	N.A.	2.6	38.5
Park Avenue	7.2	7.0	——	.14	3	7.7	217.5	140.0	18.5
Pennsylvania	31.4	20.7	4.7	5.4	19	7.2	7.4	3.5	22.3
Prudential	25.5	15.7	.58	5.6	36	9.6	8.4	—	—
REITA	45.7	11.4	.3	25.4	74	5.6	4.0	3.6	17.2
U.S. Realty	53.4	31.3	8.5	9.1	25	6.0	7.2	—	—
Washington	11.3	7.8	2.0	2.7	13	6.1	9.1	4.4	27.1

MILLIONS

MORTGAGE TRUSTS	Mtgs. at Cost (e)	Long-Term Debt.	Short-Term Debt.	Net Assets	Equity % Ratio(f)	1965 Indic. % Yield (c)	Earnings as % of "Equity" in Mtgs.	Price(c) Times Earns
Continental	$65.8	$11.0	$34.1	$25.3	35	5.9	g11.8	g15.8
First Mortg.	61.5	14.6	38.6	15.1	22	7.0	13.9	14.4
Southeastern	18.7	——	9.8	8.7	46	6.7	N.A.	N.A.

TABLE II—(a) Before depreciation, at cost. (b) Portion of real estate value (at cost) unencumbered; 27% equity ratio also may be expressed as 73% debt ratio. (c) Price used is recent "asked" quotation. Yield may include return of capital (see Table I), (d) After amortization payments. (e) Permanent hold mortgages reflect amortization; short-term mortgages at cost. (f) Portion of mortgages owned (at amortized cost) representing shareholders' equity, after debt (g) Based on estimated full-year earnings of $1.40 per share.

Reprinted by courtesy of *Barron's National Business and Financial Weekly*, Vol. 45 (April 5, 1965).

MORTGAGE INVESTMENT TRUSTS

Leverage provided by borrowing has enabled these vehicles to show earnings growth, but the road may get bumpy before climbing higher

The unusual combination of high yield and long-term growth prospects are the attributes of a little-known investment vehicle — the mortgage investment trust.

These uncommon common shares came into being as a result of a piece of Lame Duck law signed by President Eisenhower in late 1960. It enabled real estate investors to hold either real property or mortgages in much the same way a mutual fund holds and manages a diversified portfolio. Later, amendments to the Internal Revenue Code permitted these real estate investment trusts to avoid double taxation of income (peculiar to corporations) by paying out at least 90% of their net to shareowners.

Only One Listed

The three trusts shown in the table are the largest such organizations specializing in mortgage investment rather than owning properties. Continental Mortgage Investors has the distinction of being the only outfit of this genre to be traded on the New York Stock Exchange. It was listed early last year and the price of its shares has about doubled in the interim.

Because it is the largest and appears to have originated a procedure that has received the flattery of imitation, Continental's approach is worthy of examination:

Step One: An amount roughly equivalent to the trust's $32 million equity (represented by slightly more than two million shares) is invested in long-term first mortgages insured by the Federal Housing Administration or guaranteed by the Veterans Administration.

Step Two: Originally on the basis of this equity and now on the strength of successful operation, CMI has a line of commercial credit with leading banks, permitting the trust to borrow at the prime rate. Also, it has sold its own commercial paper in the market.

Step Three: The borrowed funds are invested in first mortgage construction and development (C & D) loans (of up to 36-month maturity but averaging between 18 to 24 months) for the improvement of vacant land into dwelling sites and the building of houses. On a few occasions CMI has financed motel construction.

Thus income is obtained and capital periodically returned from the amortized government-insured mortgages and additional earnings are obtained from the spread between the cost of borrowed funds and the interest and fees received on C & D lending.

Frequent inspection and control of projects under construction are necessary safety precautions. This involves an organization capable of traveling to all parts of the country fairly regularly. This Continental is able to do.

First Mortgage Investors began its operations by concentrating on first mortgages, but soon found the cost of money and operations left too small a margin. Consequently, it has begun to follow the Continental system. At present, both First Mortgage and Southeastern Mortgage Investment Trust follow a policy of splitting their assets roughly 50-50 between government-insured mortgages and C & D loans. The latter trust concentrates its investments in the Southeastern area of the country.

Latest figures offer the following comparison of the three trusts:

	CMI	FMI	SMI
Gross Assets (millions)	$95.9	$74.1	$24.3
Debt (millions)	63.5	58.3	15.4
Portfolio:			
Cash & equivalent	11%	10%	7%
FHA/VA mortgages	22%	39%	46%
Conventional mortgages	—	—	10%
C. & D. loans	67%	49%	37%

192

In recent market experience, the mortgage REIT's have been able to compete satisfactorily with commercial banks in advancing C & D credit. Continental explains this as the result of its highly developed knowledge of the field, the assistance it is able to give a developer as a consequence, and its ability to take on an entire project which may be beyond the reach of a local institution.

The recent advent of a tighter money market naturally affects these operations. For one thing it has its advantage. Capital being returned through the amortization of first mortgages can be re-invested at a higher rate of return. For another, it presents the disadvantage of more costly short-term borrowing. So far, the trusts not only seem to be able to pass the higher costs along to developers and builders, but are receiving more applications than they did when the commercial banks were in an easier position.

There is the danger, of course, that the trusts could be caught between their short-term borrowing and their longer-term lending. Continental's experience is pertinent here. The compensating balances it must keep with the banks from which it borrows affords a cushion. In addition, the $5 milllon a month it receives in cash collections of principal amortization on its government-insured mortgages could always be used to meet its bank obligations should roll-over become difficult.

So far the leverage provided by the return on borrowed funds, as compared to what could be earned on net worth alone, has enabled the trusts to show significant growth. Continental, for example, reported 77 cents a trust share in fiscal 1962 and will have about doubled that in the year ending this month.

Leaning heavily on the demographers' projections that show large family formations as the World War II baby crop matures, beginning in late 1967, the trust managers see further expansion in their future. Money market conditions in the months ahead may provide some bumps in the road, however, before it turns sharply upward. The investor must be aware that — as with any investment trust shares — he is buying management and the results of his commitment will depend largely on its ability.

MAJOR MORTGAGE REITs

	Years Ended	Earned Per Share Nine Months 1965	1964	Annual 1965	1964	*Equity Per Share	†Divi- dends	Recent Price	Yield
Continental Mortg. Investors	Mar. 31	$1.16	$1.04	$1.44	$1.14	$15.76	$1.75	b31	5.6%
First Mortg. Investors	Jan. 31	0.92	0.76	1.03	0.85	13.31	1.20	16	7.0
Southeastern Mortg. Investors	Dec. 31	a0.78	——	c0.52	——	8.73	0.78	10	7.8

*Latest available. †Indicated rate. a-Full year. b-N.Y. Stock Exchange. c-Preceding year.

Reprinted by permission of *Financial World*, Vol. 125 (March 30, 1966).

FRESH APPRAISAL

Real Estate Investment Trusts
Regain Favor on Wall Street

By Dana L. Thomas

"The understanding and acceptance of (REITs) is a 'grain-of-sand-at-a-time' undertaking. We must make speeches, write articles, present illuminating shareholder reports and cooperate with our investment bankers and security analysts . . . to get our story across to the financial community and to the public."

John R. Courshon
Trustee-Secretary,
First Mortgage Investors

Earlier this month, 200 real estate brokers, investment bankers and institutional money-managers showed up in Boston for the eighth annual conference of the National Association of Real Estate Investment Funds (NAREIF) — essentially a dead-serious, and usually rather deadly, get-together of and for the nation's real estate investment trusts. This year's conclave, on the surface at least, promised to be no livelier than any other. The program of events at the staid Sheraton Plaza included, for example, set speeches by a mutual savings banker, a professor from M.I.T. and a vice president of the Morgan Guaranty. As it happens, however, attendance set a new record for a NAREIF function — twice that of last year's conference — and when the savings banker spoke of economic forces affecting the realty market, the professor outlined the "future of American cities" and the Morgan man described how pension and profit-sharing trusts are hedging against inflation by putting funds into land and other real property, enthusiasm in the Plaza's jam-packed Venetian Room was no less real.

Back From Oblivion

Some such response was clearly in order. For in autumn 1968, with inflation running rampant once more — and almost nothing else certain for the months ahead except, presumably, death, taxes and a new Administration — real estate and its "hidden values" suddenly have caught the eye of a large segment of the investment community. Inevitably, Wall Street is turning at last to a searching scrutiny of those ready-made but complex commodities call real estate investment trusts, or REITs.

It's hardly surprising. Diversified, well-regulated, usually well-managed and highly rewarding (they must distribute 90% of their income to shareholders), REITs nonetheless had been neglected in the stock market since 1962. That year's precipitous break, along with the earth-shattering collapse of most realty values and a few scandal-ridden realty investment companies, left the whole bloc of REIT stocks looking like a burned-out neighborhood in the slums. But a good many years have elapsed. Phoenix-like, the best of the trusts have risen from the ashes, more firmly established than ever; together with newer models, they offer an array of under-valued assets, recapitalized potentials and income-tax shelters. Against the background of today's jerry-built market, some of the REITS stand out as stately mansions indeed.

Equity or Debt

At the moment, 61 REITs have made at least one public offering with SEC registration — a number of others operate intrastate or are atherwise exempt from federal filling — and they boast assets totaling more than $1 billion. The majority are so-called "equity trusts," a type which invests directly in real properties and derives its income chiefly from rentals. About a dozen other are "mortgage trusts," organized specifically to deal in debt paper rather than equity positions; in other words, they make loans for construction, development and long-term real estate financing, deriving their income from interest. Some enterprising REITs, finally, represent a blend of both types.

While figures on the growth of all SEC-registered trusts are unavailable, NAREIF recently analyzed the statistics of 24 leaders from 1964 through 1967, finding that gross assets had increased 30% from $474.9 to $621.9 million; gross income was up 59%, from $44 to $70 million; and net income rose 62% from $9.4 million to $15.3 million. Responsible for much of that record are the top mortgage trusts: Continental Mortgage Investors, the industry leader; First Mortgage Investors; B. F. Saul, and Federated Mortgage Investors (both of which own properties as well) ; and others named Selected, Western, Southeastern and Sutro. Three new trusts recently filed offerings with the SEC: Associated Mortgage Investors, General Mortgage Investors and Republic Mortgage Investors. Furthermore, a realty investment company, Basic Properties, Inc., announced its intention this month to reorganize as a REIT specializing in mortgages.

The equity trusts are a far more varied group, with portfolios and policies markedly different from one to the next. Biggest (or most distinctive) include Real Estate Investment Trust of America (REITA), the industry's oldest; U.S. Realty Investments; Bradley R. E. Trust; Pennsylvania REIT: Prudent Resources (formerly Prudential REIT) ; Greenfield REIT; Franklin Realty; Denver R. E. Investment Association; Massachusetts REIT; Mutual REIT, Kavanau R. E. Trust; American Realty; First General; Nation-Wide, and National Realty Investors.

Property Accounts

So much for A, B and C. How well are they doing in the P&L? Depending upon payout policy and the treatment of earnings, depreciation and cash flow, almost any REIT's report is likely to differ from any other's. Equity trusts have the option of either paying out all (or part) of cash flow as shareholder distributions, or making such payments only from earnings, after depreciation. Mortgage trusts own no real property as a rule (hence, can claim no depreciation), and so pay their dividends only from earnings.

In the latter group, Continental Mortgage plainly knows prosperity; over the last five years it has tripled earnings. In the latest reported 12 months, mortgage portfolio value jumped 36% to $132 million. For fiscal '68 (ending March 31) net soared to $2.25 a share (prior to this year's 3-for-1 split) from 1967's $1.92. Net for the first half of the current fiscal year, after the split, reached a record 44 cents a share, up from 35 cents a year earlier. Last month, Continental declared a quarterly dividend of 21 cents per share, the twenty-third straight quarterly increase.

First Mortgage, equally representative, has been enjoying brisk business, too. Assets on July 31 were 39% higher than a year before, at $88.6 million, while over the last six months, dollar growth of assets was the greatest in First Mortgage's history. Earnings, naturally, are up strongly: for the first half, net climbed to 68 cents a share from 60 cents. In the last fiscal year, ended January 31, net per share reached $1.23, compared with $1.20 the previous year. In August, FMI declared a 33-cent quarterly dividend, the fourth consecutive increase, and, like Continental, FMI now has split the stock — 8-for-5.

Where the Options Are

The equity trusts, as noted, have options available in reporting to (and rewarding) investors. Thus REITA, with a conservative policy of paying from earnings only after depreciation, reported for the nine months through August 31 a rise in net to 93 cents a share from 91 cents in the year-earlier period. Accordingly, REITA is expected to maintain its regular annual dividend rate of $1.20. Another conservative trust, Denver Real Estate Investment, in the first quarter of 1968 earned 12 cents a share, against year-ago's 10 cents. For the first half, net is reported up 10% from last year's. For all of 1967, Denver earned 58 cents a share (vs. 1966's 50 cents); the trust is paying a 60-cent annual dividend.

Greenfield, contrariwise, makes distributions from cash flow. For the first half of fiscal '68, net income rose to 28 cents a share from year-ago's 27 cents, but cash flow (before depreciation) hit 85 cents a share (including 14 cents of non-recurring income), compared with the 1967 period's 62 cents. Hence the trust paid 60 cents a share in both periods. Similarly, Prudent Resources is committed by its charter to distributing 90% of annual cash flow to shareholders, as a return of capital. For the nine months ended August 31, actual earnings were 40 cents a share (exclusive of four cents in extraordinary costs), against 24 cents (excluding 38 cents in extraordinary income from property sales). However, cash flow for the same period hit 65 cents a share, up from year-ago's 43 cents, enabling Prudent to pay distributions at a 72-cent annual rate. Other leading REITs, for the most part, have been posting comparable gains.

Eye on Wall Street

Prudent or spendthrift, though, the REITs go about their business in different ways. Indeed, those of the so-called equity type vary all over the lot. One, for example, has added to its portfolio of ordinary real estate a plunge into oil and gas wells. Another has been buying up apartments and intentionally converting them to integrated housing. Others, as noted, have become moth "equity" and "mortgage" trusts in an effort to capitalize on the best of both worlds. All have a common purpose, of course. They want to make money for their investors, to be sure, and increasingly they want to whet the interest of Wall Street.

If professional money men at last are making a fresh appraisal of the REITs, it's been a long time in coming — and for good reason. Throughout the history of realty trusts, and particularly in recent years, the industry has shown a less-than-inviting facade. Until the 'Sixties, actually, the REIT concept was confined to Massachusetts, where corporations were not allowed to invest in real estate (other than that considered integral to their business), and the trust device evolved as an alternative. At first, such groups had limited participants, but before long the general public was invited in. By 1912, trusts owned $250 million worth of real property in Boston alone — capital which enabled the Hub City, and many another town (as trusts followed the railroads westward in quest of investments) to grow toward the sky.

The Great Depression put a stop to REIT expansion; in 1935, the Supreme Court withdrew their exemption from corporate taxes. A number of trusts were liquidated, their assets sold to tax-exempt institutions. Eventually, investors turned to real estate syndicates, as well as to mutual funds, for tax-sheltered income. Meanwhile, though, lobbyists for the REITs were busy behind the scenes, seeking equitable treatment.

New Exemption

In 1960, Congress decided their argument was fair. The Internal Revenue Code was amended, making an REIT — if unincorporated, managed by trustees and offering transferable shares of beneficial interest — exempt from the corporate income tax, subject to certain stipulations. Specifically, it had to have at least 100 beneficial owners, with no combination of five controlling 50% of the shares; it had to be a "passive" investor, turning over the operation of its properties to independent managers; it had to derive 75% of gross income from holdings in real estate, with at least 90% from real-estate dividends, interest or capital gains on the sale of properties held less than four years.

Beyond all else, the revised law said, to qualify an REIT must pay out 90% or more of its net income each year to shareholders. The amount actually paid out is then exempt from corporate taxes. What's more, a trust's income and dividends enjoy the same tax-shelter as those of other realty investments. Accelerated depreciation can be taken on newly acquired properties (writing off, say, 150% of the straight-line charge in the first year), to generate greater cash flow. By doing so, a trust may show no net earnings at all, yet pay any amount of cash dividends. To the extent depreciation exceeds debt-amortization, of course, that portion of the dividend is a tax-free return of capital for the investor.

No Wheeling-Dealing

What made the REIT a different animal for would-be real estate shareholders — particularly those grown twice-shy of the wheeler-dealer syndicates of the late 'Fifties — were the restraints imposed by Congress on property management and turnover. Smacking of conservative values, the "new" REIT concept was an instant hit with investors, and promoters rushed in during the market hey-day of 1960-'61 with a variety of offerings.

Some went public as owners of a single property; others offered shares in a ready-made portfolio of properties (or simply converted an existing real estate investment company to the trust form); still others came on the scene much like "swap funds," with tax-free exchanges of shares for the equity positions in specific real estate; not least, a few debuted as "blank-check" trusts, soliciting investors' capital before even acquiring any properties at all. (Mortgage REITs, of course, were akin to the latter variety of equity trust: shareholder capital was converted to loans almost as fast as it came in.)

Now, some eight years later, nearly all these REITs have found a permanent place on the investment map — but somehow, until recently, the industry had failed to set the world on fire. Despite averaging anywhere from a 5% to 8% return on investors' money, the trusts excited little interest in Wall Street: both offerings and trading volume of REIT shares sagged well below industry expectations. Congress had expected the trust concept to perform at least two useful public functions — providing an opportunity for the nation's small savers to invest in land, and, in turn, providing a new source of capital for large-scale real estate development (including metropolitan-area renewal). The results were less than earth-shattering.

Indeed, today's investor or trader — keyed on "earnings" and "multiples" — understandably may find the real-estate equity an investment beyond his ken. Cash flow, after all, may be rising while the P&L records a loss. The odd terminology of REITs, moreover, remains a puzzlement. Thus, trust shares are not "stock" but "certificates of beneficial interest." Trusts that pay out of cash flow do not talk of "dividends" but of a "return of capital through the tax shelter of depreciation." Then there's the upside-down world of the debt-equity ratio, endemic to real estate. Cash-flow-conscious trusts, seeking maximum leverage, may have $3 or even $9 of debt for every dollar of equity — debt ratios of, respectively, 75% on up to 90%; a "conservative" REIT, interested in building equity, may hold the ratio down to 50%. By contrast, an industrial company with debt off-setting more than 30% of assets would be rated as out-of-joint by almost anyone.

Finally, some REITs have made trouble for themselves. Several of the more highly leveraged trusts, paying out too high a proportion of cash flow, actually were forced out of business when income dribbled away. Several other trusts, after finding the restrictions too severe for their taste, converted back into the corporate form, leaving the market to wonder how attractive the REIT set-up really could be. Recent examples of this sort of thing are First National Real Estate Trust of New York, now merged into United Investors Corp.; and Furman-Wolfson, the principal shareholders of which are negotiating to sell out to a couple of New York real estate investors (the latter planning to acquire the remaining shares and liquidate the trust).

Still No Easy Street

In trying to win over Wall Street, the REIT industry clearly is still having its problems. Some, however, are nearing solution at last. For example, several states still burden the trusts with restrictions beyond even those demanded by the federal code. In particular, they have refused exemptions on state taxes. Recently, California (one of the worst offenders) had a change of personnel administering the code, and the official attitude has begun to mellow. Other states have been undergoing a similar change of heart.

On the federal level, too, a major burden has been eased. Under the Treasury Department's original interpretation, a trust, to maintain its "passive" status, wasn't permitted to elect to its board any officer or employee connected with a contractor who managed property in the portfolio or provided related services. Hence, the trust couldn't make better use of some of its best available operating experience. Last year, Treasury amended the rules: while a REIT cannot actively manage its own properties, it now is permitted to have such "affiliated" persons on the board.

202

One big regulatory snag does remain. The rules covering qualifications for tax exemption are so intricate it's possible for a trust suddenly to be disqualified without the trustees knowing — until too late. If it fails to meet IRS requirements in any given year, a REIT becomes liable for tax payments at the corporate rate for that year, even though all (or nearly all) of its taxable income may have been distributed, in good faith, to shareholders. If a disqualification is found to have existed for a longer period, the trust could be faced with a serious tax backlog and, conceivably, could be forced to liquidate. Industry spokesmen are pushing to have the code modified in such a way as to lighten the penalty in such extreme cases.

The troubles that plague realty trusts — both real and, as it were, imagined (but no less deleterious to the REIT image among investors) — have had the potential for serious impact. Even more than mutual funds, the real estate investment trusts need dependable sources of fresh capital. That need, indeed, can become urgent for a highly leveraged REIT, since when accelerated depreciation begins to wane (and cash flow is reduced), the ability to refinance properties or sell them (and, through new acquisitions, create new tax shelters) depends on a healthy real estate market. Lacking it, the only recourse is to a stock market ready and eager to supply funds. In the best of times, of course, easy access to the equity marts — something the straightforward "mortgage trusts" have enjoyed from the outset — would be a boon to growth for "equity trusts" of conservative and free-wheeling bent alike.

Years of frustration, since those short-lived good times of 1960-'61, have led some industry leaders to rather radical thoughts on how to improve the trading climate — and with it, market favor — for REIT securities. They acknowledge that real estate is a tough subject for most Street analysts to grasp (to say nothing of brokers and salesmen), and that almost any type of industrial stock is easier to sell the ordinary investor. Accordingly, it's been suggested that REIT shares be bought and sold through real estate brokers. Even further, the idea has been seriously advanced of a "real estate stock exchange," where REIT certificates (among other things) could be traded via specialists, in an atmosphere as remote from the hurly-burly of "earnings" and "multiples" as, say, the commodity marts.

That New Look

Such exotic departures, however, may not be necessary. For the signs abound that Wall Street — ever sensitive to where the hidden values are — now has begun to take a new look at the trusts. The reason is almost painfully self-evident: bookkeeping complexities aside, REITs are, after all, essentially real estate equities, and in a day when attention is turning to the inflationary hedge of land-ownership, a well-managed REIT could be made to order. Since 1945, U.S. land values have nearly trebled; meanwhile, values in office, commercial and apartment buildings (the typical REIT's stock in trade) have more than trebled.

Nor does that tell the whole story, even to an unsophisticated investor. For while real property has obvious worth as a source of income, the retirement of mortgages against it serves to increase the owner's stake in its inflation-spiraling equity. Accordingly, a conservative REIT, which has been paying down debt (and at the same time reducing its reported book value through depreciation) almost certainly has a substantial hidden asset in the actual market worth of that rising equity. For the latter can be recapitalized with new mortgage financing, based on the higher underlying value of the property.

As a leading REITs consultant puts it: "The books usually do not take into account the higher value of recaptured property, when, in a period of inflation, leases on apartment houses and buildings owned by the trust are matured and renegotiated at a higher figure." Far from least (to a Wall Streeter), if the REIT should sell its "depreciated" (actually, appreciated) assets, or be taken over by another trust or realty corporation — or even by an industrial firm (many are increasingly alert to such tax-shelter possibilities) — the gains stand to be substantial.

One-Stop Lenders

Let's dig deeper into the assets underlying a few representative REITs. Take first the mortgage trusts, which play a unique role in the real estate industry. Unlike other lending institutions that specialize in certain types of paper, a mortgage REIT offers one-stop, first-mortgage financing. It stands ready to finance every stage from the acquisition of raw land through development and construction all the way to completed buildings. The biggest such REITs, operating nationwide, developed a stock market following from the very outset. The reason: steadily rising, uncomplicated earnings. And the main factor behind that: an emphasis on interim construction loans (pulled in by the "one-stop" feature), which not only earn higher interest rates but also run for only a year or two, enabling relatively fast turnover of the REIT's investment portfolio — faster, in fact, than those of most commercial finance companies.

The mortgage trusts have thrived particularly in tight-money times. Their flexibility has allowed them to concentrate proportionately more of available resources on short-term construction-development paper (where the spread between borrowing and lending costs can be better maintained), even as commercial banks and other lenders were reducing their traditionally dominant stake in the same market. Accordingly, in recent years First Mortgage Investors has upped the construction-development portion of its portfolio at the expense of lower-rate FHA and VA mortgages.

Continental has done the same, and the industry leader has gone a step further in search of profit. Its charter permits a limited amount of real estate equity investment, so a few years ago Continental (in process of negotiating a loan) took back $80,000 of common stock in U.S. Land Co. Last year, when Boise Cascade took over U.S. Land, Continental swapped its holdings for some $2 million of Boise stock. Enthusiastic Continental shareholders responded by amending their charter, raising the limitation on equity investments from 3% to 6% of the REIT's portfolio.

All Out for Equity

The out-and-out equity trusts, of course, wouldn't mind making that kind of a killing now and then either. Not being geared to the quick turnover of capital, however — and, anyway, limited in the gains they can take on short-term property sales — they tend to seek good-quality real estate in which equity can be enhanced over the longer term. Thus, the better-managed REITs concentrate their holdings in properties bearing leases with prime tenants, and carrying built-in escalation guarantees (increasing lease payments as tenant revenues rise). Top-rated at present are shopping centers in growth markets; next in favor come apartment houses with prime leases, then modern office buildings and prime-tenant buildings in well-developed industrial parks. General location can be Anywhere, U.S.A., but the particular site in a given urban-suburban area is carefully scrutinized for population and transportation trends, and the related socio-economic forces.

In practice — in one of the most competitive businesses in the world — this means the better-managed REITs must go for conservative, rather than spectacular and highly leveraged deals. Appropriately enough, REITA, the most venerable trust of all, is the most conservative. In 1960, when it reorganized into its present form, REITA started anew by recapitalizing properties that had been in the portfolio for years, and hence were fully depreciated and amortized.

Ever since, the trust has been reinvesting its cash flow in equity, to increase book value. Its ratio of long-term debt to the net book value of real estate assets currently is a mere 29% — astonishingly low in this business. Only 12 of the 47 properties owned at the close of fiscal 1967 still were subject to mortgages. Accordingly, the book value, if anything, is substantially understated — and represents huge potential borrowing capability, should the need ever arise. Significantly, although REITA's dividends at present are fully taxable to the shareholder, the stock enjoys a premium over the more highly leveraged trusts, which pay their tax-free distributions out of capital.

The old trust hasn't been resting on its laurels, however. In recent years, REITA has gone through a profound portfolio transformation, unloading much of the old downtown property (while distributing some of the capital gains), and replacing it with suburban stuff: 72% of latest reported assets now consists of shopping centers and other retail outlets, and nearly half the Boston fund's overall portfolio now is located in California.

At the same time, REITA has not abandoned the Bay State, and in fact has had much to do with the re-flowering of New England. For example, it recently bought a research and office building (under lease to Polaroid) in Waltham, for $787,500, of which $325,000 included an existing institutional first mortgage. Last January, it acquired (from other trusts, in exchange for stock) an industrial site in the Harvard-M.I.T. campus town of Cambridge, on which current prime lessees include DuPont, General Electric, Parke-Davis, Squibb and Bio-Dynamics; ironically REITA thinks the site is under-developed, and plans a major high-rise project for it when present leases expire.

If REITA nonetheless remains unchallenged as the Old Tory of realty trusts, it's not the only conservatively run operation; most other REITs, however, tend to be a bit more radical, in one respect or another. Take Mutual Real Estate Investment Trust, for a rather extreme example. Organized just three years ago by a group of 22 investors — they included the inventor of xerography, Chester Carlson, and the head of the nation's largest Negro-controlled bank (Durham's Mechanics & Farmers Bank), John Wheeler — its stated purpose ("not a philanthropy") was and is "investments from people who believe that housing, open to all . . . is sound business and a sound investment."

Mutual has sold some $6.2 million in shares to the public, including $1 million subscribed to by the Ford Foundation, and, distributing from cash flow, has returned an average 3% per year (equal to nearly 5% for upper-bracket taxpayers) on invested capital. What it does is to buy all-white apartment buildings, far from ghetto neighborhoods, usually at prices below independently appraised value. The typical deal involves one-third cash (for equity) and two-thirds debt (first mortgage).

Finances, obviously, are only Phase One of each project. Mutual's trustees work, in cooperation with local Negro community leaders, to integrate each building — without setting up any "quota system." Nine such buildings currently make up the portfolio — in New York, New Jersey, Illinois and Virginia — and four more are under contract for purchase. Mutual claims nearly 100% occupancy (it says former vacancy rates actually have been reduced), with both whites and blacks said to be on all the waiting lists.

Virtues of Prudence

Even less conservative, in its fashion, is the highly leveraged Prudent Resources Trust — a REIT once known as Prudential, and before that as a realty investment company made up from syndications of the former Leader-Durst organization. Prudent's trustees boast openly that they've unearthed "angles" unknown to rival REITs. As noted earlier, it's the only one legally committed, by charter, to paying investors a return of capital from cash flow.

Moreover, Prudent has been quick to exploit the IRS rule allowing a trust to earn 25% of its income from non-realty sources. It has been buying, of all things, oil and gas wells, in an effort to tack depletion-allowance benefits onto the tax shelter provided by its 22 income-producing real estate properties. (Prudent is not unique; at least one other prominent trust, First General, is attempting the same ploy, via oil and gas holdings in Canada.)

The modus operandi is to offer a tax-free exchange of shares for oil and gas rights. Prudent's program began with acquisition of the rights to 100 such leaseholds in the East Canton, Ohio, field. Schlumberger Well Services was retained to estimate productivity of the find by scientific testing, and already, more than 30 wells have been completed. Wall Street, not surprisingly, has paid Prudent more heed than most REITs of late, even though most observers agree it's still too early to tell just how big a gusher the adventurous trust can become.

Kavanau's Capers

Not so unconventional, but no less venturesome, is Kavanau Real Estate Trust. A Johnny-come-lately to the REIT concept, Kavanau was a syndicate operation prior to going public as a realty investment company in 1960, switching to trust status only in 1967. But Ira Kavanau, the imaginative founder (now managing trustee), apparently has suffered no clipping of wings; he still looks for the kind of leveraged deals on which the minimum return on equity runs to 11% (far higher than most REITs today are willing to settle for). The Kavanau technique is unchanged: Sale-and-leaseback, a type of realty deal in which Mr. Kavanau pioneered. Operating a trust, Mr. Kavanau now can offer a kicker to prospective sellers: the tax-free exchange of property for shares in the REIT. His trust reportedly has more offers than it can handle.

The typical Kavanau deal involves a shopping center — although the portfolio has included garden apartments and bowling alleys as well — since the promoters of such suburban plazas usually are anxious to recoup their capital and move on to something else. Kavanau waits until enough prime tenants have signed up to carry the fixed costs, and until the trust has commitments for interim and long-term mortgage financing. Then the transaction is made for Kavanau Reit "stock" (giving the seller a continuing, prorata interest in the venture) — Kavanau also may supply developmental cash, via the mortgages, where necessary — with the leaseback operator agreeing to pay such expenses as realty taxes, maintenance and insurance, leaving Kavanau to assume only the debt charges. In that kind of arrangement(the REIT's equity position usually winds up thin enough to assure a cash-flow return at or above its 11% target.

Several recent acquisitions (of a number which, in the last eight or nine months, are said to have doubled the trust's rental income) seem especially promising to Mr. Kavanau: as it happens, they're also somewhat more than typical. One is the acquisition (for stock) of Bel-Dor Building Co., a St. Louis construction concern; another is a joint venture to build an industrial park in Durham. The biggest is Kavanau's purchase (for $3.5 million in stock) of Durham's Consolidated Properties Inc., which added to the trust's portfolio in a lump some 20 parcels of improved realty valued at $8 million. In the same deal, Kavanau acquired unimproved parcels on which 589 apartments and a 100-room motel will be built and then leased to a third party. The trust estimates that these projects will generate nearly $1.5 million in new (cash-flow) income.

Saul's Hedge

Perhaps the most unorthodox of all, finally, is B. F. Saul Real Estate Investment Trust. A Washington-based REIT, which registered a public offering of 400,000 shares last summer, it has elected to pay distributions only from net income, after depreciation, and by and large is an investor in relatively conservative properties. But there orthodoxy ends. For against any danger of running out of depreciation in a tight-money market, Saul has come up with a novel hedge: its charter calls for investments in both real property and mortgages, making it by choice a combination "equity" and "mortgage" trust. (There are, of course, other examples; Continental was cited earlier and Federated Mortgage Investors, for its part, owns several properties.) Saul's logic seems sound. If for any reason the cash-flow income from properties should drop to a point at which mortgage payments are squeezed, income from the trust's own lending operations would more than make up the difference.

Portfolio aside, B. F. Saul is radically different in its approach to the stock market. When going public, the trust shunned experienced underwriters (and the conventional underwriting fee), preferring instead to sell its shares through an affiliated firm — one that specializes in the sale of mortgage paper to private investors — for a commission of 1%. Further, since no market in Saul certificates has been established by any brokerage house, Saul makes the market itself. The trust maintains a revolving fund for the purpose, buying back its shares at 99% of par value (recently reduced from $100 to $10 via a 10-for-1 split). Since this makes Saul, in effect, an unlimited (open-end) trust, much like any mutual fund, it is required to maintain a "live" prospectus, not to mention a fairly lively investmenet policy. Investors seem happy with the set-up; last year, according to trustees, over 50% of new capital came in on repeat sales to satisfied shareholders.

To sum up, then, whatever their idiosyncracies — and it's clear from the foregoing sample that no two REITs are very much alike — the realty trusts, as far as most of Wall Street is concerned, all live on the same block. Now, for reasons that apply generally to the industry, and because of the dynamics a number of individual REITs have added to the picture, institutional and private investors alike seem to be taking a new look at the group. Given the alternatives today, that makes sense. A little piece of tax-sheltered real estate — of one sort or another — probably isn't the riskiest investment around. After all, 60-odd real estate investment trusts add up to quite a lot of land, bricks and mortar.

Reprinted by courtesy of *Barron's National Business and Financial Weekly,* Vol. 48 (October 28, 1968).

MISPLACED TRUST?

Tight Money, Footloose Expansion
Plague the Mortgage Funds
By Dana L. Thomas

"We are not here to sell a parcel of boilers and vats,
but the potentiality of growing rich beyond the dreams
of avarice."

Samuel Johnson,
at the sale of Thrale's Brewery
(Boswell, 1781)

June 27 may not have been Black Friday, but for one of
Wall Street's few recent red-hot groups it was more than
a little blue. On that fateful date, a new real estate trust
called Larwin Mortgage Investors came to market. Of late,
such an event had been not only fairly common (over a
dozen "mortgage trusts" have gone public in less than a year
and twice as many more have filed offerings) but also festive:
as though these money-lending outfits dealt in nursing homes
or chicken franchises, the stock of almost any new mortgage
trust was snapped up — and often a cinch to run up 100% or
so with scarcely a pause.

This one, moreover, had plenty else going for it. The
Larwin offering of $40 million (two million shares) was one of
the biggest ever; the underwriting syndicate included such
blue-chip names as Bache & Co., Dreyfus, Oppenheimer and
Drexel, Harriman, Ripley; the trust's management co-starred
housing expert Lawrence Weinberg and mutual fund im-
presario Gerald Tsai. Investors, however, were unimpressed.
In a lackluster first day of trading, bids for Larwin Mortgage
sank below 20 and the syndicate was hard pressed to sustain
the offering price.

Rise and Fall

As it turned out, Larwin was merely one of three new
mortgage trusts — if the most widely heralded — to have its

high hopes dashed last month. Other more "seasoned" issues also buckled. To be sure, the stock market plays few favorites these days, but the rise and fall of the mortgage trusts has been breathtakingly sudden. According to one battered trader: "Rarely has a boom got off so quickly and so quickly become a bust." The evidence on both counts is striking. Only a year ago, almost nobody in the Street knew or seemed to care much about mortgage trusts. Unincorporated but complex entities, they function somewhat like a mutual fund (though they aren't open-ended), allowing the public to participate in a diversified portfolio of real estate mortgages rather than securities — meanwhile enjoying the same tax exemption on distributed earnings as do the funds (Barron's, October 28, 1968).

Nevertheless, the two oldest trusts had been building impressive records of performance for a number of years with scant notice. Continental Mortgage Investors, the largest in the business (it began operations in 1962) can boast a compound earnings growth of 25% annually, and has seen its shares move up ninefold since the original offering. First Mortgage Investors, in business for a slightly longer period, after a slow start has managed to boost its earnings over the last five years at a 12% compounded annual rate, with its stock soaring some 200% over the initial price.

Not until last fall did all this begin to attract widespread attention. With the advent of tight money, commercial banks switched out of the high-risk construction and development loans and the trusts moved in. Not only did they know the field — Continental and First Mortgage had become specialists — but they seemed ideally suited to the conditions of a money squeeze as well, for they offered investors built-in leverage of unusual potency. As such yields rose to 12%-14% on every dollar lent out, it was clear that so long as a trust could attract cheap equity capital (based on the high multiples of a growth stock), it could leverage above its book value and thereby boost the price of its shares still more. As borrowing rates rose further, moreover, profits would continue to widen and stock prices skyrocket in a kind of "self-reinforcing" cycle that could go on indefinitely.

213

The bright idea, in any case, captivated Wall Street. One leading business publication reported that the "smart money" viewed mortgage trusts as the No. 1 glamor stocks of 1969, possessing "the stuff that fireworks are made of." Scores of promoters in real estate (and outside it) rushed headlong to set up their own. "People with no background whatsoever in the business came to me and demanded that I raise $40 million to start a trust," a well-known underwriter noted. "I asked them what they knew about the field. They replied that they didn't need to know anything; they could always hire a mortgage man from a bank." Many an underwriter needed no convincing; some actively recruited new trust promoters.

Tulip Time?

The results today recall the euphoria which marked that Dutch tulip craze centuries ago (see table). Of the 40 (or more) mortgages trusts currently in being or in registration, only a few, as noted, were around just a year ago: besides First Mortgage and Continental, they included the relatively small Southwestern, Western, Sutro, B.F. Saul and realty income (the latter two in equities as well as mortgages). The newcomers already have come to market for well over $300 million in equity capital; those still to come — assuming the well does not (or has not) run dry — plan to offer stock, convertibles and warrants worth considerably more even than that.

Despite all the glamor attending these new issues, however, few had anything much on which to evaluate them. Take Associated Mortgage Investors, for example. Just one year ago, it was launched (by portfolio managers formerly under contract as advisors to Continental) with an offering of stock and debentures worth $25 million. Management says it now has $23 million invested in loans, of which some $20 million has been "rolled over" into originating higher-yielding paper than the 6¾%-7½% notes it took down at the outset. The shares, which got up over 40, by late last month were back down to around 23 bid.

New and "Old"

Similarly, General Mortgage Investors debuted last November with a $15 million offering (at $15 a share). Management hopes to boost its return, from the 6%-6¾% FHA-VA mortgages (purchased at from 93% to 96% of par) with which it was quite heavily invested at the start, by accelerating the velocity of turnover. In the first quarter of 1969, the trust earned 16 cents (and paid a dividend of 15 cents); after hitting 25, the stock was back by the end of June to around 17. Another, which went public in December — Republic Mortgage — raised $30 million, selling 1.5 million shares (with warrants) at 20. (The recent bid was just above that.) At the time of the offering, the trust had committed itself to $10.5 million worth of loans bearing effective interest rates of from 7% to 8¼%. In its first quarter (ended March), Republic netted 26 cents a share.

Of the more recent offerings, finally, one was made by Sutro, a trust started in 1962. Last April, it sold $25.6 million worth of stock to the public at 16. (The bid on June 27 was just under that.) In this rare case, investors had a performance record to study. Hitherto entirely in FHA and VA paper, Sutro said it would use the new capital for construction and development loans, thereby increasing its leverage. In the three fiscal years ended March 1968, Sutro's revenues climbed from $27,653 to $185,727, and its distributions per share rose from 28 cents to 96 cents. (Another recent offering, it might be added, is not wholly new to investors: North American Mortgage, reorganized as a trust from a realty investment firm called Basic Properties, by Sonnenblick-Goldman, the nation's leading conventional-mortgage brokers.)

Sound Footing

The concept behind mortgage trusts, as originally written into the 1960 law establishing tax-free real estate investment trusts, is — for all the recent sound and fury — both sound and useful. Congress wanted a vehicle which would allow the nation's small shareholders to invest in a diversified portfolio of real estate ventures, while at the same time providing a substantial new source of capital for large-scale developments (including urban renewal).

Under the IRS code, a trust is exempt from corporate income taxes if it is unincorporated and managed by trustees representing transferable shares of beneficial interest. There must be at least 100 beneficial owners, with no combination controlling 50% of the shares, and the trust must be a "passive" investor, turning over active operations to independent managers. Further, it must derive at least 75% of gross income from real estate and at least 75% of its assets have to be in real estate, cash and government securities. Finally, the trust has to pay out at least 90% of its net income each year to shareholders, with the amount distributed exempted from taxes.

Since the trust is nothing more than an income conduit, prohibited from actively engaging in the real estate business, the day-to-day operations of investing its funds, originating and servicing its loan portfolio must be carried on by a management company. The trust enters into a contractual relationship similar to that of the mutual fund business. Usually, the management fee is a fixed percentage of the value of the trust's assets, or the value of its assets invested in mortgages. (In addition, some contracts provide for an incentive fee based on performance.) The typical tab runs between 1% and 1½%.

When Pressure's On

So much for structure. What makes interesting those trusts specializing in mortgage investment (as opposed to those which take equity positions in real property) is the role they seem designed to play in a period of tight money. When pressure is on the commercial banks to curtail loans, the first borrowers typically to feel the pinch are builders, on which banks of despair of having to keep a day-to-day check. That gives the mortgage trust an opportunity to expand its portfolio of construction and development loans (currently yielding 12% and 13%-14%, respectively).

Development loans are made by trusts for the acquisition of land, and the installation of utilities, sewerage and road systems. The funds are provided for an average of 18 months, usually limited to 60%-65% of the appraised value. Construction loans, made for all types of income-producing properties, also usually run 18 months: they tend to be limited to 75% of the value of the improved property, or that of the site plus cost of improvements.

Unlike the banks — essentially local operations pressed with many other demands — mortgage trusts are organized, at least theoretically, to act on a nationwide basis. Moreover, they are geared to servicing the building industry. "We serve as portable banks going wherever the need arises," explains one trustee. "We offer one-stop mortgage financing all the way from the acquisition of raw land through completion of the project and placing of the permanent mortgage."

Ideally, as analysts lately had been pointing out, here is how the leveraged mortgage trusts ("money machines," as some called them) were supposed to operate when money tightened. Say a trust is earning $1.50 a share and selling at $20. To get new capital cheaply for expansion of lending activities, it might sell 100,000 shares for $2 million. Then it would put these funds right to work in construction and development loans yielding 14%, generating new earnings of $280,000. In other words that last 100,000 shares' worth of new capital would return $2.80 "per share," boosting overall earnings as well as book value. Thus, the trust could make another equity offering at an even higher price — and so on, and on.

Even before the stock market turned sour, however, there were risks aplenty attached to the scheme. Hardly least, almost everything rides on the brains, business acumen and financial reputation of management. "That would-be investor had better take a hard look at the background of people rushing in to form trusts," warns one veteran operator. Says another: "I would ask each newcomer registering for a public offering whether he has sufficient credit lines and if not, how he is going to get his leverage. Where will his loan business come from? Does he have experienced personnel to inspect and appraise the properties he intends to advance loans on? What experience do his trustees have in the interim mortgage field?"

Booby Traps

The big risk, as noted, lies in the fact that such a leveraged operation — if it's to work — must concentrate in the highly speculative construction-development mortgages. The experienced First Mortgage and Continental, to be sure, have suffered virtually no losses on such loans in eight years of doing business. Nevertheless, according to a veteran real estate man: "The field is loaded with booby traps. There's often a great variance between "appraised" value and actual value. A builder can get virtually any appraisal he wants, and it's up to the trust manager to verify it."

Usually, the trusts won't make such a loan unless a permanent lender is willing to take over the long-term mortgage on the property — from which construction advances can be repaid. But if the builder defaults, the "permanent" lender can withdraw, leaving the trust holding the bag. Indeed, a builder may default for any number of reasons — adverse economic conditions, suddenly reduced demand for real estate, poor cost-management, missed schedules owing to bad weather or strikes. If it happens, the trust at best faces increased operating and interest charges; at worst, it may be forced to take a loss on the loan.

Even less certain, ironically, is a new trust's ability to attain that 12% average yield it needs to make leverage work — and to keep the "point spread" over rising costs of borrowed funds to which all of them must resort. Unlike some of the older, established trusts, the newcomers are paying 1% or more over today's 8½% prime bank rate — effectively 10%-11% when compensating balances are added.

Tightening the spread are several factors. For one thing, trusts are subject to usury laws in several key states; California, to illustrate, sets a maximum rate for lenders at 10% simple interest per annum. For another, even where no such ceilings are imposed, a new trust often is tied down to lower yields before it can go public. New York State requires that the stock-offering prospectus show prior commitments for 60% of the proceeds. Thus, a trust wishing to raise $30 million from a new issue must show nearly $20 million in loans already committed.

The way a newcomer usually obtains such initial loans for its portfolio, in fact, is with hat in hand. Banks will offer "participations" in their own portfolios, but at sharp discounts. Accordingly, many wind up with unprofitable paper simply to meet the qualifications for going public — not infrequently, mortgages yielding as low as 7%, as noted in earlier examples. The hope, of course, is to raise the average return by rolling over the portfolio, once equity capital is obtained. Participating loans, however, ordinarily cannot be sold but must be held to maturity.

Maintaining its qualification for tax-exemption, finally, is a serious problem confronting every trust, every step of the way. The rules are highly technical and few if any of the newer trusts have had a federal return examined by IRS. Should a trust fail to meet its requirements in any given year, as interpreted by IRS, it could, retroactively, become liable for income taxes even though it may have distributed virtually all of its taxable income to shareholders in good faith. If disqualification is ruled over a longer period, indeed, the backlog of tax liabilities could force liquidation. What's more, since a trust is unincorporated, shareholders technically can be held personally liable for certain damages — if the trust is inadequately insured — such as those resulting from operations in areas where the trust is not recognized as a valid organization with respect to tort, contract or tax claims.

Veteran's Day

To be sure, most of these problems beset brand-new trusts more than the older, wiser ones. Nevertheless, underscoring the point is the fact that both First Mortgage and Continental have made their share of mistakes along the way, profiting by them at some cost. FMI, as the very first mortgage trust, began quite conservatively, with a heavy 50% of its investments in low-interest FHA-VA loans and government securities. Meanwhile, it was borrowing short-term (when this kind of money was more readily available). By mid-1965, it was apparent that both volume and yields in FHA-VA loans were declining steadily, relative to the total mortgage market, even as short-term borrowing costs were climbing. In the credit squeeze of '66 some of FMI's bank loans were called in, and the trust had to cut back its operations. Earnings suffered.

For several years now, therefore, FMI has clamped a 30% ceiling on that part of its portfolio in low-yielding FHA-VA loans; the bulk of its money goes into construction development mortgages. (By last year-end, 77% of all investments were in such loans.) Meanwhile, it has switched to longer-term financing. Last year, FMI sold $15 million of senior debt at 6¾% (with warrants) and then placed privately $20 million in convertible 5¾% notes. In addition, two offerings now are in the works — one involving 600,000 shares (plus 600,000 more offered by shareholders), the other a $10.3 million issue of 5% senior debentures (with warrants). Cheap money helped FMI boost net for fiscal '69 (ended January) to a record 92 cents per share, up from 77 cents in '68. This year, first-quarter earnings rose to 30 cents from 20 cents (adjusted for an 8-for-5 split).

Continental Mortgage, for its part, learned the same lesson sooner and at less expense to a large degree, indeed, from FMI's experience. (Continental, now the larger, was launched several months after FMI.) Thus, in a three-year period through 1967, FMI built its senior debt to $52.3 million (through sales of debenture-equity packages), bearing just 4½% to 5½% interest. Last February, the trust beat bank rates again, placing another $80 million of 5% subordinated convertible notes. Hence, CMI currently has over $130 million costing a fraction over 5% annually at work. Of total investments at year-end, $131.8 million was in construction-development paper. Earnings for the fiscal year ended March 31 jumped to a record $1 per share, against 1968's 75 cents (adjusted for a 3-for-1 split).

What Now?

Whether either of the two leading trusts can long sustain that kind of record, in the face of an ever-tightening money market and a less-than-cordial stock market, is a matter for some conjecture; regarding the newer trusts, however, matters are up in the air. Investors clearly have grown dubious. Last

220

MORTGAGE TRUST NEW OFFERINGS

Name	Offerings Date	Amount (Equity)
Associated Mtg. Investrs.	6/21/68	$25 million
Fraser Mtg. Inv.	6/ 3/69	$18 million
Galbreath First Mtg. Inv.	2/27/69	$17.5 million
General Mtg. Inv.	11/26/68	$15 million
Guardian Mtg. Invstrs.	3/ 4/69	$12.5 million
Larwin Mtg. Invstrs.	6/26/69	$40 million
Midland Mtg. Invstrs.	6/17/69	$20 million
Mortgage Inv. Group	4/ 2/69	$45 million
North American Mtg. Invstrs.	6/24/69	$ 9.2 million
National Mtg. Fund	2/28/69	$ 4 million
Realty Income Trust (a)	6/26/69	$10.7 million
Republic Mtg. Invstrs.	12/20/68	$30 million
Security Mtg. Invstrs.	3/ 6/69	$16.5 million
Sutro Mtg. Inv. (a)	4/24/69	$25.6 million

a-Went public in 1962

IN REGISTRATION

Name	SEC Filing Date	Est. Amount (Equity)
Alison Mtg. Inv. Tr.	6/19/69	$30 million
American Century Mtg. Invstrs.	5/29/69	$50 million
Atico Mtg. Invstrs.	5/29/69	$40 million
Burnham Mtg. Tr.	6/ 5/69	$45 million
Capital Mtg. Inv.	6/20/69	$20 million
Cavanaugh Mtg. Tr.	6/ 6/69	$30 million
City Investing Mtg. Tr.	5/20/69	$70 million
Colwell Mtg. Tr.	6/25/69	$30 million
Empire Mtg. Tr.	6/20/69	$30 million
Fidelity Bond & Mtg. Invstrs.	6/20/69	$25 million
Fidelity Mtg. Invstrs.	6/ 3/69	$25 million
First Lincoln Mtg. Invstrs.	6/ 2/69	$34.5 million
First Mtg. Invstrs.	6/25/69	$30 million
GBS Mtg. Invstrs.	6/17/69	$25 million
Great American Mtg. Invstrs.	4/22/69	$25.4 million
IRI Mtg. Invstrs.	6/10/69	$45 million
Mortgage & Equity Invstrs.	6/ 5/69	$45 million
Mortgage Invstrs. of Wash.	6/25/69	$25.5 million
Mortgage Tr. of America	5/28/69	$60 million
National Mtg. Fund	6/19/69	$ 7.2 million
Nooney Mtg. Invstrs.	6/ 5/69	$33 million
Realty Mtg. Invstrs.	6/13/69	$10 million
Saul (B.F.) R.E. Inv. Tr.	6/18/69	N.A.
Sibley Mtg. & Realty Tr.	6/26/69	$30 million
United Mtg. Invstrs.	6/13/69	$50 million
U.S. Realty Inv.	4/ 1/69	$20 million

month's prime rate hike by the banks to 8½% sent most of the mortgage-trust followers scurrying for cover. "The big play had been Wall Street's expectation that the trusts would come in quickly for a second and third round of public financing," explains one trader. Now it's a different matter. "Why," he asks, "should anyone pay a premium over book value for a new offering when others are waiting to be offered at book or below?" Indeed, from early May through late June, against an 8.4% decline in the Dow-Jones Industrials, an index of all the mortgage trust stocks plummeted by more than 35%.

Beyond the current crunch — for those trusts which manage to survive it — the outlook is not much more certain. "What happens," asks an expert "when money eases and the banks and other institutions which now are channeling their funds to other customers, return to the interim-mortgage field?" The trusts hope there will be enough business to go around. In 1968, after all, they accounted for less than half of 1% of the $60 billion construction loan field. "We can grow as an industry to at least 10% of that market before there's any sign of saturation," predicts one managing trustee. Moreover, the residential home market should then perk up (as it did after 1966). Owing to their flexibility, the trusts may be able to shift quickly into it, acting in their role of nationwide "portable banks."

Chances are, those among the new trusts which combine in their managements some savvy in money matters with sound experience in the real estate mortgage market may be able to muddle through. But the trust business, at the moment and from any standpoint, hardly looks like everybody's sure thing, and a thoroughgoing shakeout probably is inevitable. In the process, moreover, a number of the potential newcomers with offerings now on file simply may not be heard from again. "The men," sums up one observer, "are going to be separated from the boys."

Reprinted by courtesy of *Barron's National Business and Financial Weekly*, Vol. 49 (July 7, 1969).

REAL ESTATE INVESTMENT TRUSTS:
A New Financial Intermediary

By Peter A. Schulkin

INTRODUCTION

Within the last 3 years, real estate investment trusts (REIT's) have become an important source of construction and development loans, as well as of long-term mortgage and real estate equity funds. Much of the rapid growth of REIT's can be explained by the recent tight-money conditions and government restrictions on the traditional real estate lenders. These factors combined to bring about a scarcity of mortgage money and high yields, which in turn provided a favorable climate for new REIT formations. It remains to be seen whether REIT's will continue to grow rapidly during the current period of easing monetary policy. It is most likely, however, that the rate of new REIT formations will slow markedly.

REIT's are in effect financial intermediaries which serve to improve the flow of funds from savers to real estate investors. REIT's obtain their operating funds from many sources including individuals, banks, mutual funds, pension funds, and bank trust accounts. They channel the funds into both real estate ownership positions and different types of mortgage loans, including construction loans.

This article describes the brief history and current state of REIT's. Among the topics included are: types of REIT's and advisers, reasons for their rapid growth, prospects for the future, and questions concerning conflicts of interest and regulation.

WHAT ARE REIT's?

REIT's were made possible by 1960 tax legislation which exempts them from Federal corporate income taxes provided that they meet certain requirements. This tax advantage was extended to enable individuals to invest in real estate and mortgages through REIT's in the same way they can buy common stocks through mutual funds. Consequently, the requirements to qualify as a REIT are designed to insure that the REIT is essentially a real estate and mortgage mutual fund.

To qualify for tax exemption, a REIT must meet the following principal requirements:

1. The REIT must be a passive investor rather than an active participant in the operations of its properties. But the active manager of a REIT's properties can own up to 35 percent of the REIT's stock.

2. At the end of each quarter 75 percent of the value of the REIT's total assets must consist of real estate (including mortgages), cash, cash items, and government securities.

3. At least 100 persons must own shares, and five or fewer persons cannot own more than 50 percent of the shares during the last half of any tax year.

4. At least 75 percent of the gross income of the REIT must be derived from rents, mortgage interest, and gains from the sale of real estate.

5. At least 90 percent of the REIT's ordinary income must be distributed to the shareholders within 1 year after the close of the taxable year.

Although the law allows either the open-end or closed-end form of REIT, all existing REIT's have chosen the closed-end option. That is, they do not redeem shares on request; rather, the owner must sell his shares in the stock market in order to liquidate his investment. Consequently, the market price of a REIT's shares can deviate substantially from the net asset value per share. By being closed-end, REIT's do not have to be greatly concerned with liquidity of their assets.[1] While

---

[1] The potential shortcomings of the open-end REIT were recently highlighted by the problems of a foreign mutual fund that invested heavily in American real estate. This mutual fund, U.S. Investment Fund-Real Estate, was overwhelmed by redemption requests in 1970 and is now in the process of liquidating its operations.

most REIT's have started business with a public offering, a few have chosen the private placement route.

TYPES OF REIT's

Within the limits imposed by requirements for tax exemption, the investment powers of REIT's are quite broad. Moreover, where a REIT's declaration of trust (equivalent to articles of incorporation) is specific with regard to investment policies, no permanence is implied because changes can be (and in some instances have been) made with shareholder approval. And there have been on occasion changes in legal status from REIT to taxable corporation and vice versa. Nevertheless, REIT's may be classified by their investment policy into one of three categories — construction and development loan, long-term investment, and miscellaneous.

Construction and Development Loan REIT's (C & D REIT's)

At the present, the most important category of REIT's in terms of total assets consists of those investing mainly in construction and development loans. Construction loans are secured by a first mortgage and are used primarily to finance the construction of single-family homes, apartment houses, and commercial structures.[2] Development loans are used to finance site improvements such as clearing and leveling land and constructing roads.

Construction and development loans have typically earned very attractive yields; in the first half of 1970 they averaged 12 to 14 percent per annum for REIT's. These high yields made existing C & D REIT's very profitable, and encouraged the formation of new ones. During the last half of 1970, however, yields fell sharply.

---

[2] For a description of the construction-loan market by the author, see *Commercial-Bank Construction Lending,* Research Report to the Federal Reserve Bank of Boston, No. 47, and "Construction Lending at Large Commercial Banks, *New England Economic Review,* July/August, 1970, pp. 2-11. Both are available on request from the Research Department of this Bank.

Some older C & D REIT's have included comparatively low-yielding FHA- and VA-insured permanent mortgages in their portfolios in order to present a less risky balance sheet to banks extending them loans. However, most of the recently-formed C & D REIT's have found that they can make satisfactory credit arrangements without having FHA- and VA-insured permanent mortgages in their portfolios.

Of the 114 REIT's which are included in the compilation in Table 1, 45 are C & D REIT's. Their total assets currently exceed $2 billion, and they are making 7 to 10 percent of the dollar volume of all construction loans.[3]

LONG-TERM INVESTMENT REIT's

The second major type of REIT invests primarily in long-term assets. Some are *equity* REIT's specializing in direct ownership of income property (principally office buildings, shopping centers, and apartments); some are *long-term mortgage* REIT's specializing in mortgages secured by such property; and some are a hybrid of these two types.

From 1961 through 1968, the investments of these REIT's were largely in direct ownership. But since the beginning of 1969, when mortgage credit became difficult to obtain and yields rose sharply, newly-formed long-term REIT's have generally concentrated their investments in long-term mortgages.

One of the more unusual long-term REIT's is the Stadium Realty Trust, which provided the $5 million equity financing for the new stadium for the Boston Patriots Football Club. Another unique long-term REIT is the Mutual Real Estate Investment Trust. This REIT, committed to open housing, specializes in the ownership of apartment buildings in mixed

---

[3] The 7 to 10 percent estimate is based on figures extrapolated from those in the Appendix to "Construction Lending at Large Commercial Banks," *op. cit.*

[4] The following is a quotation from Mutual's 1969 Annual Report: "We the Trustees and the staff are greatly indebted to all the 9,000 M-REIT shareholders whose faith in the Trust and whose commitment to open housing opportunity has made possible our progress. We will continue to make every endeavor to achieve the Trust's maximum achievement both as an investment and as a social force."

Table I

CLASSIFICATION OF REIT'S BY TYPE AND ADVISER, 1970 *

(Dollars in millions)

	TOTAL			Commercial Bank			Life Insurance Company			Financial Conglomerate			Mortgage Banker			Other		
	No.	Ass'ts	Eq'ty	No.	Ass'ts	Eq'ty	No.	Ass'ts	Eq'ty	No.	Ass'ts	Eq'ty	No.	Ass'ts	Eq'ty	No.	Ass'ts	Eq'ty
ALL TRUSTS	114	$4310	$3109	22	$847	$750	8	$596	$566	12	$672	$578	13	$415	$290	59	$1780	$920
Construction & Development	45	2181	1539	14	586	500	3	126	98	7	327	238	12	354	253	9	788	449
Mixed Maturity	8	470	386	3	92	86	1	150	150	1	40	40	1	61	37	2	127	72
Long-Term	60	1630	1155	5	169	164	4	320	318	3	276	271	—	—	—	48	865	402
Homeowner's Instalment	1	29	29	—	—	—	—	—	—	1	29	29	—	—	—	—	—	—

*The REIT's were identified with the aid of a list furnished by the National Association of Real Estate Investment Funds and standard sources of financial information. The asset and equity figures are based on the latest financial statements available as of December 31, 1970. In the case of new REIT's which have not yet issued financial statements, the offering amount was used for both assets and equity. Asset and equity figures for those REIT's with an ownership interest in properties may be substantially understated due to accounting practices. Where the type of REIT or adviser did not clearly belong in one of the above categories, its designation was arbitrarily determined. The number column includes the small construction and development trust and, one small long-term trust, both affiliated with "other" advisers, for which asset and equity figures could not be obtained. Convertible bonds are considered to be a component of equity. Totals may not equal sums due to rounding.

racial areas.[4] To support Mutual's social goals, the Ford Foundation has purchased over $1 million of its shares.

MISCELLANEOUS TYPES

Of the other types of REIT, only the *mixed maturity* type has an appreciable total of assets, currently almost $0.5 billion. Mixed maturity REIT's split their investments between short-term constructions loans and long-term real estate assets.

Finally, there is one *homeowners' installment loan* REIT. Security Mortgage Investors, which buys consumer paper secured by a first or second mortgage on a single-family residence. This REIT deserves special mention for two reasons. First, it is the only REIT with an adviser which owns nearly the maximum permissible amount (50 percent) of total shares. Second, it is the only REIT whose adviser guarantees to buy back any notes that are in default.

REIT ADVISERS

A REIT is almost always organized by the management group that will serve as its investment adviser, the primary incentive being to obtain the fee that the adviser charges the REIT. In addition, the adviser may wish to use the REIT to generate business for its allied activities, or to finance some of its real estate ventures. The adviser is an entity which is completely distinct from the REIT in order to comply with the Internal Revenue Code requirement that the REIT itself (but not the adviser) must be a passive investor.

All REIT's have trustees who are elected by, and responsible to, the shareholders of the REIT in the same way that corporation — the adviser runs the REIT's day-to-day oper-poration shareholders. Carrying the analogy further, the REIT's adviser plays much the same role as the officers of a corporation-—1the adviser runs the REIT's day-to-day operations and presents investment opportunities to the trustees. As in the election of corporate directors, REIT shareholders are given only one slate of trustees to vote on. Moreover, for most REIT's some of the adviser's officers also sit as trustees.

And as in the case of corporate directors, outside trustees are obviously sympathetic to management.

While there are no restrictions on who may act as a REIT adviser, in general the adviser has been a commercial bank, financial conglomerate, mortgage banker, or life insurance company. Moreover, some REIT's are able to operate without an adviser. These are small equity REIT's organized by trustees who may be affiliated with companies which collect fees for servicing their REIT's properties.

Commercial Bank Advisers

Besides wishing to earn the advisory fees, commercial banks may have many other motives for forming a REIT and acting as its adviser.[5] For example, a bank may want to form a C & D REIT in part to avoid the existing bank restrictions on land and development loans. Similarly, a bank might want to form an equity REIT to provide its customers with real estate financing which is prohibited for a bank, such as a joint venture or a sale and leaseback. Moreover, since banks have predominantly short-term liabilities, they are generally reluctant to commit funds to either long-term or illiquid assets. As a result they may find REIT management the most satisfactory way to participate in long-term real estate investments.

During a period of tight money, when a bank would like to use its funds to service its regular commercial and industrial customers, it may form a C & D REIT in part to keep its construction-loan staff fully utilized and to avoid having to turn away its construction-loan customers. Moreover, by selling a portion of its C & D loan portfolio to its REIT, a bank can obtain funds to lend to other customers or to rebuild its liquidity.

A bank may also want to form a REIT in part because the REIT and its customers would be a source of deposits as

---

[5] The adviser is in some instances the bank itself, but usually it is a subsidiary of a bank holding company.

well as potential purchasers of other services offered by the bank and its affiliates.

Forming a REIT also allows the bank to capitalize on its reputation. A REIT run by a bank, particularly a large one with a good reputation, undoubtedly creates a favorable image in the mind of investors, thus helping the REIT to attract funds. Justified or not, the feeling may also exist that if the REIT runs into difficulties, the bank will stand behind it, rather than jeopardize the bank's name.

The principal advantage that bank REIT's have vis-a-vis those managed by others, is their easy access to bank lines of credit. Such access is important both for direct borrowing and as a back-up credit line to insure that any commercial paper issued by the REIT can be redeemed if necessary. Furthermore, a bank may also buy its REIT's commercial paper.

Financial Conglomerates

The desire to obtain advisory fees is the primary motivation for financial conglomerates to form and advise REIT's. In addition, the companies can sometimes use their REIT's to promote their other business activities by such methods as tie-in sales to REIT customers, and by using their REIT to finance some of their own real estate ventures.

Insurance Companies

In 1969 and 1970 monetary restraint forced insurance companies to turn down some of the attractive real estate proposals which were offered to them. Moreover, many insurance companies believed that the shortage of long-term real estate funds would persist for years. Thus, in order to increase their own income and to more fully utilize their real estate staff, several insurance companies have formed long-term REIT's during the past year.

Mortgage Bankers

Mortgage bankers, who have always done a limited amount of construction lending, have found C & D REIT's to be a perfect adjunct to their regular business of arranging real estate financing packages.

Other

This catchall category consists principally of individual enterpreneurs and small companies which form REIT's solely for the advisery fees. In the case of some of the small equity REIT's which do not have an adviser, a motivation for founding was the servicing income generated by the REIT's real estate holdings.

THE RECENT GROWTH OF REIT's

From the time of the 1960 legislation permitting tax exemption through March 1962, only five new REIT's were formed involving public offerings of $10 million or more. And in the more than 6 years from March 1962 to June 1968 there were three.[6] By contrast, in 1969 and 1970 there was a steady procession of 53 new REIT's with initial public offerings in excess of $10 million. In all a total of more than $2 billion of new shares were sold since the start of 1969.

What happened to make the REIT's more attractive to investors since 1968? The answer is in part that it was not until then that investors began to recognize REIT's as very profitable and relatively safe. This recognition was closely followed by a long tight-money period which created new opportunities for REIT's and at the same time constrained their competitors.

Impact of Tight Money on Thrift Institutions

During the recent tight-money period, lending activities of savings and loan associations and mutual savings banks were severely restricted. Thrift institutions were locked into low-rate mortgage assets and could not afford to compete for

---

[6] The figures through 1968 were obtained from William B. Smith and Benjamin R. Jacobson, "Real Estate Investment Trusts: In the Money and Here to Stay," *Real Estate Forum* (October, 1970), pp. 26 ff.

savers' dollars as interest rates rose. Fearing for the safety of these institutions, Federal regulatory authorities placed ceilings on the rates that they could pay for savings money and on the rates that could be paid by their competitors, commercial banks. The rate ceilings protected the thrift institutions from serious financial difficulties but also limited their deposit inflows and lending.

Since REIT's were not restricted by rate ceilings, they were able to compete with high yields for the savings dollar.[7] And since the thrift institutions did not have enough funds to accommodate all of their builders, some became REIT customers.

Commercial Banks

Deposit rate ceilings seriously hindered the commercial banks' ability to raise funds which were needed to satisfy a strong loan demand. Banks, therefore, increased loan rates and rationed loans among existing customers. Under these circumstances, banks were very willing to sell some of their C & D loans to REIT's, both to their own REIT (if they formed one) or to REIT's sponsored by others. As in the case of thrift institutions, rate ceilings placed banks at a competitive disadvantage with respect to REIT's.

Life Insurance Companies

During the 1969-70 period of monetary restraint insurance companies found their real estate lending restricted by a heavy policy loan demand and by a slowdown in mortgage prepayments. Since virtually all new real estate financing by insurance companies is for income properties, the insurance company cutbacks provided many profitable investment opportunities for new long-term REIT's.

---

[7] REIT shares with their high dividend rates and low prices (generally less than $30 per share) have been considered somewhat competitive with savings deposits. C f. "The Boom in Real Estate Investment Trusts: Good News or Bad?" *Savings and Loan News* October, 1970, pp. 34-40. One very successful REIT pays dividends monthly, thereby heightening the competition with thrift institutions.

Tight money and growing investor acceptance have bene-fited REIT's substantially in the recent past. Over the longer run their continued growth will depend on the relative im-pacts of their inherent advantages and disadvantages. These are discussed below.

Tax Exemption

REIT's have an advantage over competing taxable cor-porations, in that REIT's do not have to share their net operating incomes or capital gains with the Federal Govern-ment.[8] However, this advantage is partly offset by the requirement that a minimum of 90 percent of net earnings must be paid out in dividends, thus eliminating the possible conversion of retained earnings into shareholder capital gains.

Possible Shareholder Capital Gains

Although virtually all the earnings of long-term mortgage and C & D REIT's are paid out in dividends,[9] the prices of the shares of these REIT's can and in some instances have, ap-preciated substantially. Price appreciation can result from three factors. First, the legally required dividend payout may be high enough to cause the price of a REIT's shares to increase. Second, if a REIT can profitably leverage, i.e., ex-ploit the difference between its lending and borrowing rates,

---

[8] In the case of long-term capital gains, REIT's may either pay them to the shareholders or retain them and pay the capital gains tax.

[9] Equity REIT's can in effect retain earnings since depreciation allowed by tax laws usually exceeds actual depreciation. In fact, in many instances property appreciates. However, because equity REIT's cannot assign a value other than book value to a property until it is sold, the stock market often does not translate increases in the actual value of assets into increases in share prices. While a small number of equity REIT's and real estate corporations have published appraised value figures for their real estate holdings, the SEC strongly frowns on such disclosures due to the uncertainties associated with appraised values. Moreover, reputable accounting firms will not permit appraised values to appear on balance sheets.

a REIT can increase its earnings (and dividends) per share and cause its share price to rise. Third, if a REIT is able to sell new shares at a price such that the dividend yield on its shares is lower than the yield it can obtain on invested funds, it can increase its earnings per share and share price, i.e., the REIT can "leverage" by exploiting the difference between its cost of equity capital and the rate it obtains on invested funds. This phenomenon has been called "negative dilution."[10]

Lack of Regulation

As noted earlier, REIT's are subject to very few restrictions. Their investment flexibility gives them an advantage in areas where the traditional real estate lenders have their hands tied, such as in land, development, and equity financing. Moreover, unlike the institutional lenders, REIT's can work with whatever debt and equity structure they deem appropriate and are subject to no restrictions on the rates that they can pay for borrowed funds.

High Cost of Funds

Compared with competing depository institutions, REIT's have a high cost of funds. In 1969 the average cost of funds was about 5½ percent for savings and loan associations and mutual savings banks and about 3½ percent for commercial banks.[11] By contrast the average cost of funds for REIT's was in the area of 10 percent.[12] Thus, if rate competition reduces the return on real estate investments below what REIT's must obtain to attract capital, then the REIT's relatively high aver-

---

[10] Since a rising share price is necessary for negative dilution, REIT advisers generally pursue the same indirect means of support employed by corporations — favorable press releases, meetings with financial analysts, listings of shares on a national stock exchange, etc. A direct means of support that both REIT advisers and corporations can employ is the purchase of shares with funds over which they have discretionary control such as pension funds, or in the case of bank REIT's, trust accounts.

[11] Sources: Federal Home Loan Bank Board, Federal Deposit Insurance Corporation, and Federal Reserve System.

[12] Author's estimate.

age cost of funds will turn out to be an important competitive disadvantage.

REIT's may also suffer from the competition of government or quasi-government institutions such as the Federal National Mortgage Association (FNMA) which have a low cost of funds or which may be subsidized.

COMPETITION AMONG REIT's

REIT's might grow so rapidly that competition among them would result in a general decline in REIT earnings with some possibly showing large losses. An overpopulation of REIT's, however, is unlikely to persist for long periods since REIT's would have difficulty attracting new funds until they were again making satisfactory earnings. Nevertheless a temporary glut may lead to a reassessment of the long-run risks in a REIT investment, and dampen investor enthusiasm.

Bad-Loan Risk

Of all the older REIT's only one small one, a C & D REIT, has experienced substantial problems with bad loans. The two largest REIT's have made over $600 million in C & D loans from their inceptions in 1961 through 1969, and have had losses of principal amounting to less than one-tenth of one percent. Nevertheless, bad loans may prove to be more of a problem in the future.

Loss of Tax Exemption Risk

A REIT always runs the risk of failing to meet all Internal Revenue Code requirements and consequently losing its tax exemption. The penalty is high since a disqualified REIT would have to pay taxes on all income earned during the entire year in which a violation took place, no matter by what margin the Code requirements were violated. This problem is aggravated by the numerous grey areas in the wording of the Code. One requirement, for instance, is that 75 percent of a REIT's income must come from mortgages or real property, but what constitutes such income is sometimes questtionable. For example, does a commitment fee on a construction loan represent income from mortgages? Many such questions remain to be clarified by the Internal Revenue Service. This study, however, has found no instances of REIT disqualification.

Interest Rate Risks

Interest rate movements may have entirely different impacts on the market price of REIT shares depending upon the type of REIT. Moreover, it is obvious that REIT's which employ borrowed funds face certain risks if their borrowing commitments are not synchronized with their lending commitments. For example, if a REIT borrows short and lends long, its earnings will be adversely affected if rates rise.[13] And, if a REIT borrows long and lends short, its earnings will be adversely affected if rates fall.

For purposes of this exposition it will be assumed that all interest rates move in the same direction, and that the differentials between rates do not change. With this simplification it can be said that a *decline* in rates is generally favorable for the shareholders of long-term mortgage REIT's and equity REIT's, but is generally unfavorable for the shareholders of C & D REIT's.

C & D REIT's. Since REIT construction loans average a year or more in duration, a decline in rates is not immediately translated into a decline in earnings.[14] Moreover, if a C & D REIT uses short-term borrowings, its earnings may improve to the extent it is able to fund old fixed-rate commitments with new, lower-rate borrowings. And REIT's may be able to increase their leverage during periods of low rates and monetary ease. However, as long as REIT's have substantial

---

[13] If it cannot arrange new financing, the REIT may not be able to repay its short-term debt.

[14] Floating (tied-to-prime) rates are sometimes employed in construction lending. However, the rate in effect at the start of the loan is often used as a floor rate.

amounts of long-term debt and equity funds, a decline in rates will, with a short lag, lead to a decline in earnings per share.

Long-term Mortgage REIT's. Shareholders in these REIT's will benefit from a rate decline since the market value of fixed-return claims like mortgages and bonds will rise. A rate decline has more of a favorable impact for these REIT's than for C & D REIT's because their portfolios do not turn over as rapidly as those of C & D REIT's.[15]

Equity REIT's. Obviously, interest rate fluctuations do not affect the earnings of equity REIT's as much as mortgage REIT's. If rates decline, however, the position of equity REIT's is improved to the extent that real estate assets are valued upward due to the lower capitalization rates. Their position is further improved if they can refinance their long-term mortgage liabilities at lower rates.

Outlook

It seems likely that the rate of new REIT formations will slow markedly during the current period of monetary ease as the yields on new mortgages decline, and the competitors of REIT's find themselves with large amounts of funds to invest. However, the asset size of *existing* REIT's will be little affected since they are closed-end. In fact, the existing REIT's may be able to grow if they find that monetary ease increases their access to borrowed funds at rates which make leveraging profitable. Whether REIT's will expand rapidly again in the next tight-money period remains to be seen.

CONFLICTS OF INTEREST

In the typical corporation a separation of ownership and management gives rise to potential conflicts of interest. However, the coincidence of the interests of ownership and management may be furthered by management's ownership of shares, or by the employment of various devices which tie

---

[15] Today most long-term mortgages cannot be prepaid for at least 10 years, followed by a period in which there are declining prepayment penalties.

management's compensation to the profitability of the company or to the price of the company's shares. But, unless management has a very substantial ownership interest, opportunities usually exist for management to enrich itself by taking actions which are not in the shareholder's best interest. It should be noted that if management takes such actions, the company need not have a poor showing as a result. All that can be said is that the company would have had a better performance had those actions not been taken.

As mentioned earlier, the Internal Revenue Code states that in order to qualify as a REIT the five largest shareholders may control not more than 50 percent of the shares. Of all the trusts reviewed only in one case did the holdings of a shareholder approach the 50 percent figure. In general, the trustees and advisers owned none or only a token amount of their REIT's shares. It appears, then, that trusts are subject to the same conflict of interest problems that confront most corporations. Following is a discussion of potential conflicts.

Advisory Fees

As a part of organizing and operating a REIT the adviser unilaterally determines its advisory fee.[16] Generally, the advisory fee is set as some percentage of *gross* invested assets with a provision for additional compensation depending upon how much the yield on shareholders' equity exceeds a stated amount. However, provision is usually made for a ceiling amount on the advisory fees paid.[17]

How the adviser sets his initial fee schedule is not clear; in any case, it is by no means permanent — at least three

---

[16] It should be noted that the advisory fees of different REIT's are not strictly comparable since different advisers absorb different proportions of their REIT's operating expenses. See the box on page 242-243.

[17] The Midwest Securities Commissioners Association *recommends* that its members (the securities commissioners of 24 states) require that all REIT's wishing to sell new securities in their states pay an advisory fee of no more than the greater of 1½ percent of net assets or 25 percent of the net income of the REIT before deducting advisory and servicing fees but not exceeding 1½ percent of invested assets.

recent increases have been reported, higher operating costs being given as the reason in each case. Obviously, the more the adviser charges over the minimum rate that would induce it to form a REIT, the worse off the shareholders are.

Financing Adviser Ventures

In a number of cases REIT's have stated that the adviser or its employees have an interest in properties on which the REIT is making a mortgage loan. Still other REIT's have informed the shareholders that such transactions may arise. These transactions can benefit both the adviser and the REIT shareholders. The management can obtain needed financing for its own projects at fair market prices, and the REIT can use the management as a source of investment opportunities. (Obviously, the advantage will be of most value to the REIT shareholders when good investment opportunities are in short supply.) However, the potential for sacrificing some of the shareholders' interests is clearly present as the adviser may give itself financing terms which it could not obtain from other sources. The favorable terms may not be easy for the shareholders to detect, since they can take non-price forms — for example, a mortgage might be given for a larger amount than could be obtained elsewhere.

The Same Type of Loans

Potential conflicts may arise if the adviser or an affiliate makes the same type of loans as the REIT does. The adviser may take the better investment opportunities, leaving the REIT with the inferior ones.

Size of REIT

The adviser of the REIT can sometimes take actions which increase the size of the REIT and consequently, the size of the advisory fee, even though sucs actions may not be in the best interests of the REIT's shareholders. For example, by leveraging its REIT the adviser can increase its management fees (based on invested assets) even though interest rates may be such that leveraging is not profitable for the REIT share-holders. This type of conflict may also arise in connection with the sale of new shares at prices which dilute the interests of the existing shareholders.

Tie-In Business

In some cases, the adviser or its affiliates sell different types of insurance and such services as arranging financing packages to real estate developers. In order to sell these services, the adviser may offer developers unusually favorable financing terms from its REIT which would, of course, be to the detriment of the REIT's shareholders.

Bank REIT's

In addition to being subject to the conflicts cited above, banks are vulnerable to still others.[18] For example, a bank may direct its REIT to borrow from the bank when the REIT may have the less expensive option of issuing commercial paper. And the terms on which the bank extends lines to (or buys paper from) its REIT may not be competitive.

If the REIT keeps its deposits at the sponsoring bank, conflicts may arise because the bank, through the adviser, manages the REIT's cash balances. Moreover, the bank may sell its REIT various banking services, such as being registrar or transfer agent, at higher prices than are available elsewhere.

And in many areas, customers of the bank-affiliated REIT may be offered a tied product. One example, which is unique to banks, is the requirement possibly at the expense of the REIT, that the parties that do business with the REIT must maintain deposits with the bank.[19]

---

[18] Cf. Representative Wright Patman's Remarks in the *Congressional Record* for July 15, 1970, pp. H6799-H6801.

[19] At the time of writing Morgan Guaranty Trust Co. was being sued for damages stemming in part from the allegation that the stock transactions of the Bank's trust accounts were executed with brokers who kept relatively large balances at the Bank (which were of benefit to the Bank, but not the Bank's trust accounts).

Regulations of REIT's

Other than having to meet strict requirements to qualify for tax exemption, REIT's are subject to very limited government regulation. They must satisfy the disclosure requirements of the SEC, both in their initial offerings and in their regular financial reports to their shareholders. And, like corporations, REIT's have to meet the requirements of state securities laws ("blue sky" laws), if they wish to sell new securities in those states.

Given the various conflicts of interest to which REIT's are subject and given that some REIT's may have an "unfair" competitive advantage over others (e.g., the access to credit of bank-sporsored REIT's), the question arises as to whether the regulation of REIT's and their advisers should be increased. The answers to this question should, of course, be set within the context of a consistent regulatory philosophy which could be applied to other organizations as well as REIT's.

The Case for More Regulation

Adviser Compensation. Among factors suggesting the need for greater regulations is the very poor disclosure of adviser earnings, both direct and indirect, which can be attributed to its REIT. For example, the stated advisory fee is not a good measure of how much direct compensation the adviser gets from its REIT because the adviser always absorbs some of its REIT's operating expenses.

Moreover, the shareholders of REIT's can do little if the adviser decides to increase its advisory fee without justification. Coordinated opposition would be difficult because share ownership is usually very widely scattered (in compliance with the Internal Revenue Code requirements). And in at least two recent cases, shareholders were not given the opportunity to vote on increases in the advisory fee.

As pointed out earlier, the REIT tax legislation intended REIT's to be mutual funds for real estate investments. Thus, one can argue that to be consistent Congress ought to pass legislation on REIT advisory fees for the same reasons it passed legislation on mutual fund advisory fees in 1970 allowing the SEC or shareholders in a mutual fund to bring a court

FINANCIAL DATA ON C & D REIT's

Of the different types of REIT's only C & D REIT's had financial data which were amenable to analysis. The data were limited for mixed maturity and long-term REIT's because these types were formed recently, while for equity REIT's the data were of limited use because the true value of the real property they owned was not accurately reflected in their financial statements.

To provide some indication of C & D REIT earnings, advisory fees, expenses, and short-term indebtedness, recent data were compiled for 28 of the 45 C & D REIT's identified in this study. The 17 remaining REIT's were excluded because data could not be obtained or because the only data available were for the first quarter of operations.

The aggregated statistics from four financial ratios are shown in Table I. Although the results are not presented here, the ratios were also analyzed by type of adviser. This factor undoubtedly affected the ratios of individual REIT's; however, it did not show up in any overall pattern, i.e., there was little correlation between the type of adviser and each of the four ratios.

GROSS EARNINGS

The gross earnings that REIT's are able to obtain are the product of many different factors. For example, the risk-taking policies of the REIT are important since higher risk loans and

Table I

Latest Ratios for 28 C & D REIT's*

	Mean for 28 REIT's	Range	Standard Deviation
Gross Earnings to Average Assets (annual rate)	11.9%	9.9—14.2%	1.2%
Total Expenses to Average Assets (annual rate)	1.8	1.0— 2.5	0.4
Advisory Fee to Total Expenses	73.5	25.0—97.6	16.4
Short-term Debt to Average Assets	23.8	0.0—63.4	17.4

*Figures are taken from the most recent REIT financial statements available (July-October, 1970). "Total Expenses" are defined to be total expenses less interest expense and provision for possible loan losses. The means and standard deviations were computed with each REIT receiving the same weight.

investments will pay higher returns than the lower risk ones. Higher earnings may also represent an active pursuit of non-rate income, such as the collection of various commitment fees or the extra income generated by selling loan participations. Moreover, new trusts have often shown relatively low gross earnings because much of their initial funding was invested in relatively low-yield participations.

ADVISORY FEES AND TOTAL EXPENSES

A problem in the interpretation of advisory fee data is that different REIT managers render different services for their advisory fee. When a REIT requires services not covered by the advisory fee, it must pay for them in addition to the advisory fee. Consequently, the best indication of a REIT's cost of operation is not the ratio of the adviser's fee to average assets, but rather the ratio of total expenses (excluding interest expense and provision for possible loan losses) to average assets.

The length of time a REIT has been operating must also be taken into account when evaluating advisory fees. The reason is that most REIT's have an incentive clause in their advisory agreement which makes the advisory fee rate dependent upon the rate of return on shareholders' equity. And the return on shareholders' equity usually increases substantially as a REIT becomes more seasoned. However, the ceiling on adviser compensation may limit the incentive payments after the REIT has been in operation for a year or two.

Still another factor that is sometimes important in evaluating advisory fees and management compensation is the amount of non-advisory fee compensation that accrues to the adviser (and affiliates of the adviser). Such compensation may take the form of profits made on non-advisory services sold to the REIT or the REIT's customers, or it may take the form of the acquisition of its REIT's shares at an attractive price (possibly before the shares were sold to the public). If the non-advisory fee compensation is considerable, the adviser may charge a lower advisory fee than it otherwise would.

SHORT-TERM DEBT

As pointed out earlier, REIT borrowings can make an important contribution to REIT earnings. Consequently, access to credit markets is important for a REIT's profitability. Unfortunately, while the figures in Table I provide an indication of the extent to which C&D REIT's *utilize* short-term borrowings, they give only a vague indication of actual borrowing capacity.

In this analysis only short-term debt was considered because no REIT's have sold straight long-term debt. All long-term debt issues of REIT's have been sold in a package which also offered the buyer a chance to buy shares of the REIT in question. The REIT would either offer the shares directly, make the long-term debt convertible, or attach warrants.

suit to test whether the adviser's management fee is appropriate for a fiduciary.

Other Conflicts of Interest. A case may be made for regulating REIT's in order to eliminate other *possible* conflicts of interest. For example, REIT advisers might be barred from making REIT loans to themselves or to any party with which they have financial ties. Moreover, the adviser might be barred from offering the same type of real estate financing as is offered by its REIT.

There are also possible courses of action which would limit the adviser's ability to take advantage of its economic power (to their REIT's advantage and to the disadvantage of less fortunate REIT's) as well as eliminate some possible conflicts of interest. For example, the adviser (and affiliates of the adviser) might be barred from using discretionary funds to purchase its REIT's shares. Similarly, an argument might be made for barring all business dealings between the adviser (and its affiliates) and the REIT (and its customers) other than the normal advisory services. In the case of a bank Reit, for instance, a bank would not be permitted to lend funds to its REIT or to accept deposits of its REIT or its REIT'S customers.

The Case Against More Regulation

Despite the arguments in favor of more regulation, it is possible to make a case to the contrary based on such factors as REIT competition and the similarity of REIT's to ordinary corporations.

Competition. Judging by the usual corporate standards, REIT's are highly competitive. Moreover, most large REIT's operate on a national basis — there are no restrictions on where they may do business. And, in addition to competing among themselves, REIT's also compete with a formidable array of other financial intermediaries. The high degree of competition might suggest that no additional regulation is needed.

Competition is also furthered by the relative ease with which a new REIT may be organized. As noted earlier, the

SEC and the state securities commissioners must approve the REIT's share offerings, but that amounts to little more than a check to insure honest disclosure. And, as in the case of mutual funds, very little capital is needed to start a REIT. In sum, the major obstacle to REIT formation is the selling of the shares to prospective shareholders.

Similarity to Ordinary Corporations. As pointed out earlier, taxable corporations are subject to the same conflicts of interest as REIT's are. If one makes a case for regulating the income and activities of REIT advisers, one may apply the same arguments to regulating the compensation and activities of corporate executives.

It should also be noted that in the case of both corporations and REIT's, the principals involved are liable for those decisions which they know are not in the shareholders' best interests.

Coincidence of Adviser and Shareholder Interests. The incentive for advisers to have their REIT's show the best possible earnings per share is similar to the desire of mutual fund managers to have their fund outperform the others. In short, the advisory fee of both is largely based on some measure of the dollars of assets that they are managing. And the better the performance, the easier it will be for the adviser to increase the asset base through the sale of new shares. In addition, REIT advisory contracts often contain incentive compensation for good performance. Adviser penalties for poor performance, however, are limited by the REIT's closed-end nature, in sharp contrast to open-end mutual funds where investors, by selling their shares, reduct the total assets of the fund.

SUMMARY

Real estate investment trusts have grown very rapidly in numbers and assets during the past 3 years. Acting as a financial intermediary, REIT's have increased the flow of funds into different types of mortgages, and to a lesser extent into real estate ownership positions. The REIT's growth was largely the result of the recent prolonged period of monetary restraint which handicapped their competitors and pushed interest rates to record levels. However, as monetary policy eases, it seems likely that the rate of new REIT formations will slow markedly. In addition, the possibilities for conflicts of interest between REIT advisers and shareholders may lead to pressure for increased government regulation.

Reprinted by special permission of *New England Economic Review*, a publication of the Federal Reserve Bank of Boston, November/December 1970.